introduction
—— to ——

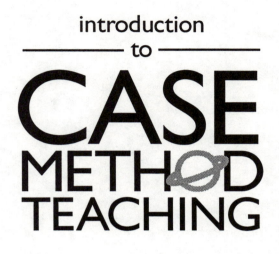

CASE
METHOD
TEACHING

A Guide to the Galaxy

introduction

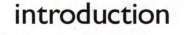 to

CASE
METH🪐D
TEACHING

A Guide to the Galaxy

SELMA WASSERMANN

 TEACHERS COLLEGE PRESS

Teachers College
Columbia University
New York, NY 10027

Published by Teachers College Press, 1234 Amsterdam Avenue
New York, NY 10027

Library of Congress Cataloging-in-Publication Data

Wassermann, Selma.
    Introduction to case method teaching : a guide to the galaxy /
Selma Wassermann.
        p.   cm.
    Includes bibliographical references and index.
    ISBN 0-8077-3368-7 (alk. paper).—ISBN 0-8077-3367-9 (alk. paper
: pbk.)
    1. Case method.   2. Teaching.   I. Title.
    LB1029.C37W37   1994
    371.3'9—dc20   94-12521

ISBN 0-8077-3368-7
ISBN 0-8077-3367-9 (pbk.)

Printed on acid-free paper
Manufactured in the United States of America

98 97 96 95 94   8 7 6 5 4 3 2 1

Contents

Preface

It was a natural sequence of events that led me to teaching with cases. I had spent 20 years immersed in promoting "teaching for thinking," developing programs to help teachers use curriculum materials and instructional strategies that required students to reflect on important issues in the curriculum. My first experience in a case teaching seminar quickly revealed the connections between my own teaching-for-thinking work and case method. I immediately saw how cases were, in fact, "curriculum materials" that engaged students in higher order mental processing, requiring their reflection on the substantive issues in the curriculum. I saw how intimately connected discussion teaching was to my own work in teacher–student interactions. So, for me, case method was a logical extension of my own earlier work, allowing me to take teaching for thinking forward in new and intriguing ways. Ironically, advancing the cause of case method teaching was considerably easier than promoting teaching for thinking, and why that should be so is anybody's guess. But it is exciting to see the extent to which teachers have seen the potential of teaching with cases for their own classrooms and gratifying to see how teachers and students have benefited from and enjoyed the process.

Case method teaching, long associated with the highest quality of instruction at the Harvard Business School, is perhaps most closely connected with business schools, where cases of actual companies are dissected and analyzed by students to better understand the complex factors involved in business management. Cases are also widely used in medical ethics courses, and, in the New Pathway Program at the Harvard Medical School, case method is the primary instructional method in the training of doctors. Harvard Medical School is not alone in this shift to case method. The medical school at McMaster University in Canada has long been renowned for its case method training program for doctors.

The past few years have seen increased attention to teaching with cases in schools of education, and texts containing a wealth of "in-school" cases, in which aspiring teachers must wrestle with the dilemmas of classroom practice, are now readily available. The good news from these teachers and their students is that cases are an exciting and effective way to study teaching.

Where case method teaching has made the most impressive inroads is, I believe, in the arena of the public secondary schools. Spurred by the pioneer work of a small group of teachers at the Centennial School in British Columbia, Canada, teaching with cases has now become a viable modus operandi in virtually every secondary subject area, from mathematics, biology, and general science, to English, government, history, law, and family life, to name a few. Teachers who have adopted this approach talk about renewed enthusiasm for teaching. Students are pressing to get into these class sections. The evidence is mounting that something good is going on.

It is exciting for me to be in the midst of such important educational change, and I am enormously gratified to be associated with a group of professionals who, I believe, are in the vanguard of promoting major and significant change on both the secondary and postsecondary educational scenes. Yet, along with the quiet cheering in my heart, are signals of warning. Educational innovations that have risen to prominence in the past have had notoriously short lives, and new methodologies and highly touted "movements" in educational practice have waxed and waned in the blink of an eye. What's more, the significance of these innovative movements for the intellectual development of students does not appear to be related to a new program's shelf life. An educational record in which new methods are embraced and discarded as if they were disposable diapers does not inspire confidence. On the surface, it must seem that we teachers are always on the quest for *the* educational panacea that will do it all; the magic formula that will right every wrong, deliver every student from apathy to productivity, make every class an unmitigated success. Maybe we have yet to learn that it's not a methodology alone that does the job, but teachers, in the trenches, that make methods work. Methodologies, no matter how full of promise, no matter how effectively implemented, are never one hundred percent perfect.

That is only one part of what worries me about the future of case method teaching. Another has to do with what I perceive to be teachers' lack of enthusiasm for any method that requires long-term professional development. "Come into my class and show me how to do 'teaching for thinking,'" a teacher once asked me, as if I could give her all the skills and understandings necessary to do the job in the twitch of a rat's whisker. We teachers may be intrigued by innovation, but we want to "have it all" learned today or, at the latest, tomorrow. Patience, commitment to serious study of complex interactive classroom processes is not our strong suit. If that seems to be overstating the case, one needs only to look at how professional conferences are organized: The most "long-term" commitment to skill development generally is reduced to a 2-hour workshop session.

Will case method teaching, now an educational buzz word, peak and fade? The optimist's side of me prevails, fed by what I have been observing in the field. Teachers who have understood the need for long-term professional development have committed their time, their energy, and their resources to studying the complex interactive processes of case method. Teachers who have made initial forays using cases in their classrooms quickly see its promise. Students show new interest in school and in the subject being taught with cases. "This is the best science class I ever had," announced a tenth-grade boy whose teacher had just taught his very first case. Students are generally more engaged and more productive. Academic achievement improves. I believe that teachers' enthusiasm for case method teaching is fed largely by the gains they see in their student groups.

Will case method teaching endure? Will it make the kinds of inroads in educational practice that will help turn humdrum, ineffective teaching–learning situations into exciting, stimulating, rich laboratories of in-depth inquiry? Maybe a full-scale movement is too much to ask for, but one thing is clear. Those teachers who have crossed the bridge and have become case method teachers are not likely to retreat. And with each new teacher who dares to try is the promise of an ever-expanding force.

To those teachers who are thinking about embarking on the developmental process of becoming case teachers, I humbly offer the following caveats:

- Consider case method teaching only if you believe it has promise for you and your students. Don't consider it simply because it's the latest fad or something different to do.
- Recognize the need for commitment to developing the essential discussion teaching skills. These are skills that are not learned in a day or week, or even a year. Good discussion teaching means a lifetime of commitment to studying the process. If such a prospect is daunting, think again about case method teaching. If it is challenging, then you are already on the way.
- Remember that any educational innovation, no matter how full of promise, can never be one hundred percent successful all of the time. There will be some students who hate cases ("You're asking us to think,

and that's too hard!") and who would greatly prefer that you lecture. There will be some days when the class does not respond as you hoped. There will be days when you are not at your best in debriefing a case, when you have failed at helping the students make the important connections. This has less to do with the methodology than it has to do with idiosyncratic circumstances. Keep your "reflective practitioner" hat on during these trying times and try to find out what went wrong and why. It is precisely when things go wrong that we have the greatest chance of learning more.

• Remember, too, that case method teaching does not work by itself. You are the one who makes it work. When it is successful, you study what went well and why. When it is less than successful, you study what went wrong and why. When things go wrong, it is not necessary that you abandon ship, but that you learn from the experience and do it differently next time.

• Be kind to yourself in the process of learning. Most teachers are dedicated, caring souls, deeply committed to the growth of their students. When students fail to learn, when strategies misfire, when tactics derail, teachers are full of self-recrimination. Their allowance for misadventure is zero. Such attitudes are not conducive to healthful growth and learning in a case method classroom. Teachers are not perfect, nor should they expect themselves to be. The path to professional development is an arduous one, and missteps along the way are common. Learning to value error is one of the more precious and life-saving attributes of a case teacher—the one that permits us to stay in the game.

Teachers who have already been experimenting with teaching with cases, and who have turned to this book for help, will already know that the methodology, while exciting and full of promise, is neither easy to do nor simple in what it encompasses. It is my sincerest hope that what I have written here will illuminate the journey across the bridge and provide resources and understandings that will ease the way. For teachers who are considering teaching with cases, I hope this book sets the stage for learning as well as provides tools for growth.

There are many people who have, in great and significant ways, informed my thinking and my understanding of teaching with cases, and I would like to acknowledge them individually. I have been enormously privileged to know and to have learned from that master case method teacher, "Chris" Christensen, who set me on the case method pathway and kept me on course. This extraordinary teacher has set the standard against which all who would teach with cases measure themselves. The teachers who worked with me in the Centennial School

Project, those pioneers who advanced the cause of case method in the secondary school, taught me much about courage, commitment, and willingness to risk, as they opened new vistas of understanding of the process—to Maureen Adam, Laura Bickerton, Rich Chambers, George Dart, Steve Fukui, Joe Gluska, Brenda McNeill, and Paul Odermatt, my profound admiration and thanks. Diane Austin picked up the case method teaching ball and carried it into the Cowichan School District, where it has taken hold and caught fire. She is an educational leader nonpareil, and I have learned much from her and from the entire Cowichan teacher cohort. My students at Simon Fraser University have always been my best teachers. They have been generous in allowing me to be less than perfect, and they have been my true partners in learning. They have been the best of the best, and I hold them in the highest esteem. My good editor, Susan Liddicoat, has worked hard to "tame" this (and other) manuscripts for me, from computer-processed pagelet, to bound book. She is a writer's treasure. Dear Jack, with whom I've shared a lifetime of experiences, has always encouraged me to be everything I could. To all, and others too numerous to mention, my deepest thanks and heartfelt appreciation.

introduction

—— to ——

CASE
METHD
TEACHING

A Guide to the Galaxy

1 | Teaching with Cases: A Pedagogy for All Seasons

Professor Ecks teaches Pediatrics in the Faculty of Medicine at a major western university. He is a distinguished scientist, with an international reputation in his field. He is also highly regarded within his department by colleagues and by students. Recently, he chose to offer an elective course for senior students dealing with life, death, and human values in medicine. He ran the course in a lecture format, and there were 50 students enrolled. The course met twice a week, and each session ran for 2 hours.

Professor Ecks is knowledgeable in his field, and his orientation to teaching is that he has a lot to tell his students. In his four-hour-a-week presentations, Professor Ecks is center stage virtually one hundred percent of the time. During these presentations, the professor gives information to his students about the issues in the course. Sometimes, it is data about infant mortality or the incidence of birth defects in newborns. Sometimes, it is personal and anecdotal. At times, main points from the text are reiterated and emphasized. Ecks may read aloud from the text. From time to time, a student may raise a question that Ecks answers by providing more data, or Ecks may raise a question for students to consider (e.g., "Which state do you think has the highest incidence of birth defects in the United States?"). Almost never in these lecture format sessions is there anything that resembles an interactive discourse between students and teacher. Almost never does Ecks work with students' ideas. From what he says, and from what is observed in what he does, it is Ecks's ideas that are presented for students to absorb.

Professor Ecks describes what he does as "teaching with cases." He explains how he injects "cases of real events," for example, extracted from clinical experience about doctors who must make life or death decisions, and presents these to students so that they may understand what doctors face in these situations. In presenting these "cases," Ecks highlights what he considers to be the key issues and what he sees as their implications for medical practice. Ecks is very clear about his own views, and he explicitly interjects his opinions, beliefs, and values into his lectures, so that the students will "get the right ideas." Ecks's course is well attended, and student evaluations give it high marks.

Professor Wye's course is Introduction to Criminology. By way of preparing to teach it, she has spent about a hundred hours collecting materials about crime and punishment: short articles from books and professional journals, examples of state and federal laws, cartoons, newspaper articles, case histories of crimes and punishments, and other primary source materials that shed light on the complex aspects of criminal justice.

Professor Wye uses these materials to write cases—narratives that are rooted in real events and that center on key issues of the course: criminal law, crime detection, penology, prisons, recidivism, justice, the legal system. In her classes, students study the cases, then dialogue in small study groups in response to the study questions that are appended to each case. Following the work in study groups, Wye debriefs each case by asking students to offer their ideas and by promoting teacher–student dialogue in which students' ideas are thoughtfully and critically examined. After Wye has taught a case, she presents students with data sources: journal articles, material from texts, newspaper articles, court transcripts, documentary films—and any other sources that further inform their studies of the issues. While Wye meets with her class of 35 students twice a week, for a total of 4 hours, she is rarely seen presenting information. What is seen is an interactive dialogue between teacher and students, in which the teacher's questions require students' thoughtful examination of the significant issues in the case. Professor Wye calls this teaching with cases.

What Professors Ecks and Wye do in their classes appear to be radically different. May both of these methods appropriately be called case method teaching? Can anything an instructor chooses to call "a case" be acceptable as "case method"? May the name be used only when what is seen is consonant with what happens in the Harvard Business School, the place that spawned and built its reputation on case method teaching? What are those distinguishing characteristics that significantly mark case method as a unique pedagogy? What variations, if any, are allowable?

WHAT IS CASE METHOD TEACHING?

While there is room for variation in case method teaching, certain conditions in form and style must be present, if what is happening in the classroom may be so described (Christensen & Hansen, 1987). There is good reason to believe that if basic principles of case method teaching are ignored, the promised goals will be forfeited.

Cases

One obvious feature of case method is the use of an instructional tool called a case. Cases are complex educational instruments that appear in the form of narratives. A case includes information and data—psychological, sociological, scientific, anthropological, historical, observational, and technical material. While cases are centered in specific subject areas, for example, history, pediatrics, government, law, business, education, psychology, child development, nursing, and so forth, they are, by their nature, interdisciplinary. Good cases are drawn around problems, or "big ideas"—those significant issues in a subject that warrant serious, in-depth examination. The narratives are usually constructed from real-life problems confronting real people.

> A good case is the vehicle by which a chunk of reality is brought into the classroom to be worked over by the class and the instructor. A good case keeps the class discussion grounded upon some of the stubborn facts that must be faced in real life situations. It is the anchor on academic flights of speculation. It is the record of complex situations that must be literally pulled apart and put together again for the expression of attitudes or ways of thinking brought into the classroom. (Lawrence, 1953, p. 215)

Hundreds of cases already exist, offering an extensive library from which teachers may select materials for their classroom use (see Chapter 3). Cases are available for college and university courses in as diverse disciplines as business administration, education, government, history, law, biology, educational administration, human relations, real estate training, psychology, English, counseling, economics, medicine and math—to name a few. Cases written by secondary school teachers are also increasingly available for secondary school use in such areas as history, government, law, business, Western civilization, art, math, biology , general science, and "family life" (Bickerton et al., 1991; Case Studies, 1993).

Study Questions

At the end of each case is a list of study questions—questions that require students to examine ideas of consequence, concepts, issues relevant to the case. The way study questions are framed demands students' intelligent thinking about the issues—a giant step removed from questions that require recall of factual information and coming up with specific answers. The writing of good study questions is an art form equal to that of writing good case narratives. Study questions do not lead students to *know* certain bits and pieces of factual information, but encourage the application of knowledge in the examination of ideas. Study questions are directed at promoting understanding. Rather than merely calling for names, dates, labels, or slogans, study questions call for students to apply what they know in analyzing data and in proposing solutions.

Questions such as "How do you explain that? What hypotheses can you suggest?" replace questions that ask, "Give the three reasons that explain Lady Macbeth's behavior." In the former example, students are asked to generate hypotheses that must come from how they have processed the data, from their reading of the play. In the latter example, students are implicitly instructed to give *the* reasons—that is, to try to come up with those reasons that the teacher has established as "correct." The difference in the quality of thinking required in response to each is sometimes referred to as "higher order" and "lower order."

Small Group Work

Another feature of case method teaching is found in opportunities for students to discuss, in small study groups, their responses to the study questions. Depending on how the instructor organizes his or her instructional period, study group sessions may be arranged as out-of-class assignments or they may take place during class. There are benefits and limitations to each arrangement. In the balance, the arrangement should be made based on how the class time is to be deployed; the primary consideration is that students do, in fact, have opportunities to discuss the cases and questions with each other prior to the whole-class discussions. Small group sessions give students their first chance at examining the issues. Here, ideas are tried out in the safest of contexts. Study groups begin the ball rolling in the court of intelligent thinking about the issues in the case. They prime the students for the more demanding whole-class discussion that follows.

Teachers who arrange for study group sessions to occur during class time will benefit from observing how the groups function. How do individual students function within groups? To what extent are questions and issues discussed intelligently in the group? Which students seem to take the initiative most of the time? Which students feel inhibited about speaking, even in the small group context? Which students tend to dominate the discussion? Which seem too eager to go along with what others have said, reluctant to voice their own views? Which groups seem to race through the questions, touching each only briefly, and with minimum in-depth analysis? Which tend to go off topic, meandering about personal-anecdotal fields?

Data from observing groups at work yield high return for teachers who want to know more about how their students think and how they function interpersonally; teachers are then able to use that knowledge in providing individual student help. Yet, teachers may understandably balk at devoting too much in-class time to small group work. An alternative is to require that small group work be done outside of class. To what extent students take these assignments seriously will soon be clear, from the ways in which whole-class discussion is informed by small group exercises. While outside-of-class study groups do not allow for teacher observation of individual and small group functioning, the additional time available for whole-class discussion may be worth that sacrifice. When study groups occur outside of class, one advantage is that teachers are not tempted to take control of a group. Groups benefit when they are able to solve their own problems. Whichever organization is chosen, what may not be sacrificed is adequate class time for the whole-class discussion: debriefing a case.

Debriefing a Case

If the quality of a case is critical to generating student interest in the issues, the teacher's ability to lead a case discussion, to enable students to bring sharper analysis to bear on the issues and work toward deeper insights, is the *sine qua non* of case method teaching. It is this feature of case method teaching that singularly determines whether the entire pedagogy stands or falls (Christensen & Hansen, 1987). Known at the Harvard Business School as "discussion teaching," the term used here is "debriefing a case."

In many classrooms, "class discussion" implies teacher-dominated discourse injected with information-type questions thrown out at students in rapid-fire assault, with as many as two or three being asked in a minute (Cuban, 1993). While teacher–student interchange occurs, teachers are found to talk 64% of the time; 34% of student talk is made up of brief, one-word responses. The quality, texture, and content of the discussion in debriefing a case are significantly different.

Thirty-five students sit in a large semicircle, with the teacher, Professor Wye, standing in the open part of the arc. The students have just come from their small study group sessions and are now preparing for the whole-class debriefing. Under discussion is "The Case of Donald Marshall" (Wassermann, 1991a), dealing with the issue of equality under the law and a person's rights to a fair and impartial trial before independent judges who apply the laws of the land. Donald Marshall, a Micmac Indian, was, at age 17, tried and convicted of murder and sent to prison for 11 years, in what was one of Canada's most notorious miscarriage of justice trials in the history of criminal justice.

"Tell me," Professor Wye invites, "what you see as the significant issues in the case? Who would like to start?" There is an understandable delay, a shuffling of papers, an air of tension, as students wait to see who will break the silence. The teacher also waits, smiling, until a student's hand signals a volunteer. She acknowledges Sylvie, who will open the case.

"To me," Sylvie puts out her ideas forcefully, "this is a case of a gross miscarriage of justice. The police were ruled by their prejudices, rather than by the evidence, in arresting Donald Marshall in the first place. Evidence was further ignored, and even suppressed in the trial. There was inadequate defense representation for the defendant, and the trial judge did not rule according to the laws of evidence. I think that this case is the worst example of everything that can happen in a police state, to gang up on and punish an innocent person. That it can happen in a democratic country like Canada is, to me, shocking," Sylvie finishes, breathless. She sits back in her chair and looks at her classmates, as if for affirmation. Several nod and smile. A student across the room gives her a "thumbs up" sign.

The teacher leaves the open area of the arc and moves closer to Sylvie. She has listened carefully to what Sylvie has said and is processing the information in her head. As she moves toward Sylvie, her response to the student and the next question she will use are already forming in her mind. "As you see it, Sylvie, the case of Donald Marshall represents a flagrant miscarriage of justice. In Canada, we are supposed to have our rights protected by the law; each person is entitled to a fair and impartial trial. You are suggesting that Donald Marshall did not get such a trial."

Sylvie nods. The teacher has captured the essence of Sylvie's ideas and has played them back to her. Sylvie has a chance of hearing her ideas in a new form, and of examining what she has said from this new angle. With Sylvie's acknowledgment, Professor Wye continues, "I'm wondering, Sylvie, to what extent this case shakes your faith in that principle of 'equality before the law'? If this can happen once, to Donald Marshall, has it happened before? Can it happen again?" In the teacher's follow-up questions, she elevates the issue of equality before the law immediately. This big idea, in which the case is rooted, will be examined again and again in the discussion, as the teacher raises questions that demand examination of the issue from various perspectives.

Sylvie's hand goes up again, as do others. The teacher shifts to another student. In the 90-minute debriefing session, the teacher's responding and questioning skills highlight examination of the issues of a person's rights to a fair and impartial trial, equality before the law, the meting out of justice by those in the criminal justice system according to their own interpretations of the law, how judgments and decisions are made by those in the criminal justice system. The discussion is never less than intense, and the teacher knows how to keep it focused on the significant issues, elevating the complexities and the conflicts, while at the same time extracting students' ideas and challenging them to think more clearly. She works the class like a maestro conducting the symphony—now the violins, not too loud; now the tympani; now all the strings together. Her artistry allows for managing the discussion so that issues of relevance—the big ideas—are in the forefront of the discourse, while personal-anecdotal comments fall away, like wrong notes. At the end of the debriefing time, the issues are far from resolved. Students will leave the class with the knowledge that complex issues do not lend themselves to tidy solutions. These cases are not TV sitcoms with trite and simplistic answers. In real life, people wrestle with issues, have to make their own meanings and find their own resolutions. The process through which this is done is called thinking. The students have not been privy to the teacher's opinion about the case. In promoting students' critical analysis, the teacher refrains from interjecting her own thoughts, lest they influence and impede students' thinking.

Debriefing demands the very best that teachers can give. Teachers do not just appear in class, slip out of their suitjackets and launch into debriefing. Christensen, who has taught with cases at the Harvard Business School for over 40 years, still spends "several hours" preparing—even when he is teaching a case he has taught many times before. Debriefing requires skill in listening to and comprehending students' meanings; encapsulating their ideas in a tightly woven paraphrasing; formulating questions that call for intelligent examination of key issues; orchestrating the discussion so that all students feel safe to volunteer their ideas, so that all students' ideas are respected; keeping the discussion "on track," so that it does not go off course by students' introduction of personal anecdotes and unrelated issues. Teachers are required to suspend their need to tell students what to think. They must refrain from passing judgment on a student's ideas. Even as innocuous a judgment as "That's interesting" could mean death to spirited inquiry.

Debriefing also demands the very best that students can give. No one is spared from doing his or her best thinking about the issues. As the semester unfolds, students learn the seriousness of giving their best. The yield from the rigorous examination of ideas in debriefing is seen in higher level critical analysis in small group work, as well as in the whole-class forum. Before-class preparations are better focused; habits of thinking begin to grow.

Successful debriefings are electric. They keep students' minds buzzing for hours, sometimes days afterward, as students try to find their own resolutions from within the web of dilemmas. Effectively done, debriefing develops students' mental habits so that they are increasingly able to recognize and appreciate complexities, reason from the data, suspend judgment.

The secret of successful debriefing lies in the way teachers interact with students. An effective case discussion reveals the key features of that interactive process. No matter how tough the teacher appears in demanding students' best thinking at all times, he or she always treats students and their ideas respectfully, and that is what makes it safe for students to voice their ideas. Teacher responses and questions give students something more to work with, taking them to new levels of understanding and keeping their attention riveted on the issues under examination. As big ideas are examined in their complexity, as the teacher works to help students extract meaning, students come to a richer appreciation of the complexities and ambiguities of the case and grow in their understanding of the issues. Tolerance for ambiguity is elevated as is increased ability to live with uncertainty. These are no small measures of accomplishment.

Follow-up

If a case drives the students' need to know, debriefing a case escalates that need. Interest is high. How could this have happened? Students want to find more data. Because answers have not been given, because ambiguities have been elevated, tension is increased. The need to know grows more urgent. Motivation is high to read more, to find out. This is an important avenue for knowledge building. Information about the issues is not dispensed by some orderly schedule, but comes as a result of heightened student need. This paves the way for the acquisition of relevant information.

Some cases come with a healthy list of follow-up activities. In some instances, teachers will draw on their own file of references: textbooks, articles from newspapers and magazines, tables and charts with primary data, research reports, editorials and other commentaries, other writ-ten information. Novels are another good source of gathering perspec-tives on issues and are powerful resources. Films, both commercial and documentary, are a vital source of information and offer fresh perspec-tives. Follow-up activities may be carried out by individual students or in groups. They may be incorporated in subsequent classwork as fol-low-up to case discussions. Whatever follow-up activities are used, their value is enhanced by further debriefing-like discussions, in which issues get extended examination and new perspectives are introduced. Through this process, students' thoughtful, critical examination of the significant issues continually evolves.

How long does the cycle take? How long from the introduction of, for example, "The Case of Donald Marshall," through the study groups, debriefing, and follow-up activities? As in many things the teacher does, it depends. This is a matter of teacher judgment about students' need for time in processing data. How much time *should* the issues in this case be given? A teacher may decide to introduce a new case approximately every 2 weeks, giving time for additional discussions on new material introduced from the follow-up activities. Some cases, touching on issues that warrant more extensive examination, may take longer. In some professional schools where students are on a fast learning track, a new case may be discussed at each class session, with study groups and fol-low-up assignments all done outside of class. There are no rules set in stone about the time cycle for case study, group work, debriefing, and follow-up activities. The teacher is always the best judge of how much time is allocated to case, debriefing, and follow-up activities, keeping in mind that there is never enough time to do justice to all the issues; never enough time to debrief all the materials; never enough time to teach *everything*. Time is always the good teacher's enemy, and each teacher learns, in his and her own ways, to resolve the ever-present conflicts between time available and the material we wish to see learned.

CONCLUSION

It is possible to call anything one does, in the act of teaching, by any name one chooses. "I run a *democratic* classroom," announces the seventh-grade teacher whose students may use the bathroom only at 10:15 A.M. "My Grade 11 math program emphasizes *higher order think-ing*," claims Sally Brown, the instructor whose skill and drill math worksheets insist the students use only a single, acceptable procedure in working out the right answers. "My goal is to help every student *understand* these physics concepts," Rob Anderson boasts, in a classroom where all instruction is concentrated on memorizing and following, without deviation, the instructions in the lab manual. Finding newer and nicer words for what we do as teachers emerges from our talent for euphemism—to paint a better picture of ourselves by using descriptors that are intended to win favor.

Labels fall easily from the lips. Should we be more flexible about calling lemon curd, jam? Is it acceptable to describe the whipping of a child as an "act of love"? Why is so much heavy weather being made over the descriptor "case method teaching"? Why not merely accept a teacher's claims that "I do cases all the time" as case method teaching? Is this need for accuracy in definition merely pedantic nit-picking?

Appropriate labeling helps us to define our terms: A rose is a rose is a rose. But some flowers are dandelions. In a given definition, there may be a range of variations, but certain basic characteristics must be in evidence. Definitions and labels give us a means for talking to each other, so that we know what we are talking about. Without some common ground, some agreed upon parameters beyond which the thing or act may not extend, we have little basis for talking to each other with any real meaning. The results are more than confusing. Descriptors that run countercurrent to our perceptions of reality make us crazy.

But that is only one reason for insistence on an appropriate match between the use of the term *case method teaching* and certain classroom practices. Another reason has to do with results. Different methodologies produce different results. For example, lecturing to dispense information to students does not achieve the same results as engaging students actively in activities that challenge their thinking. If teachers could paint the label "case method" onto any form of pedagogy, it would be too easy to say, in the end, that "case method teaching" did not work. It did not deliver on its claims. "You see, I taught with cases and did not get those results!"

Teachers who use case method teaching effectively are proud of the kinds of results that they find in student learning. Students learn to communicate their ideas more effectively. They are able to examine complicated issues in more critical ways. There is dramatic change in students' ability to make good decisions. Students become more curious; their general interest in learning is increased. There is increased respect for the different views, attitudes, and beliefs held by other students. Students are more motivated to read material beyond that presented in class. Discussion of issues that began in class extend beyond the classroom, to the lunchroom, and to the dinner table. Students enjoy classes more and find school more challenging and more interesting

(Adam, 1992). Ewing (1990) writes about what happens in the Harvard Business School.

> You need only to compare what comes in with what goes out. . . . The incoming students, bright, energetic, talented, exhibit a naivete about business and about their own powers that is "colossal." Two years later, these same students possessed a remarkable understanding of profit and nonprofit organizations large and small, had an astonishing ability to put their arms about complex management problems and analyze them, were able to make decisions with imperfect information with great skill, possessed penetrating insights into their own strengths, weaknesses, and aims in life. . . . From dealing with data in an amateurish way, missing significant points, pontificating, applying glib solutions to complex problems, making every other mistake that a group of bright, but wet-behind-the-ears people might be expected to make, and being so sure of themselves that it was frightening, students change profoundly in their ability to undertake critical analysis and discuss issues intelligently, coming to greater understanding of the complexity of doing business. (p. 10)

There are good reasons to believe that, effectively carried out, case method teaching is a methodology for all seasons. Teachers can see that students acquire knowledge and become more intelligent analyzers of data. Teachers can see that students increase their tolerance for ambiguity and grow in their understanding of the complexities of concepts and issues. Teachers can see that case method teaching can be effectively applied in virtually every subject area, at most educational levels, from the elementary school, through graduate and professional programs. But in order to realize the claims made for student learning, the methodology must be faithful to the basic principles of case teaching.

How to do that is what the rest of this book is about.

2 | What, Me? A Case Teacher?

He fixes me with his eye, causing me to take a step back. "Teaching Western Civilization with cases troubles me," he tells me. "Cases are too . . ." he pauses, groping for the appropriate adjective, "slanted," he finally decides. "I worry about how that will influence my students."

"Slanted?" I ask, frankly not understanding what he means, hoping he will explain.

"Yes—you know, like that social studies teacher who was accused of indoctrinating his students with his own racist ideas? I think if we are not careful we may be giving students materials that create and foster certain prejudices."

I am trying hard to comprehend. "Do you mean that you see cases presenting a particular point of view, and are concerned that students will 'buy into' that point of view? And that would be dangerous?" I make an attempt to capture his meaning by saying his ideas back to him.

"Exactly," he tells me. "It's dangerous to use material that goes beyond the facts. The textbook, you see, is neutral. There are no biases in textbook material. Students just get the plain facts."

I am taken aback by the assumptions he has made but do not argue. What he sees as bias in cases, I see as issues that have been highlighted, so that they may receive thoughtful, critical examination. The idea that case method teaching is the equivalent of teaching bigotry I find incomprehensible; the belief that course material as presented in textbooks is nothing more than a collection of "pure" and unquestionable factual material, astonishing. But this teacher is not quite finished with me.

"I see Western Civilization as teaching students certifiable truths. I can't see how cases would fit into the way courses are taught in my department."

I consider it futile to argue. He is so clear in what he believes and appears so irrevocably wedded to his particular teaching orientation that argument, I believe, would drive us further apart. He and I are out of synch. We see teaching from very different perspectives.

"I see what you mean," I tell him. "Given what you have told me, I, too, cannot see how teaching with cases would be a viable methodology for you. In fact, I have a suspicion that teaching with cases would drive you crazy."

I begin to address the other teachers in the "teaching with cases" workshop as he leaves the room without a backward glance.

There are many roads to Rome, and many ways to teach Roman history. Some ways are primarily information-based—the core instructional task centering on information dispensing by the teacher and information receiving on the part of students. This particular style is generally shaped by the teacher's belief that students need to learn the important facts in the program of study. In this style, teachers use classroom lectures, blackboard exercises, and pencil and paper exercises to present the information. In classrooms where information dispensing is the central teaching mission, teachers also use classroom discussions to determine whether students know the answers to important content-related questions. Questions beginning with *who, what, when,* and *why* that lead to single, correct answers dominate the discussion.

In other ways of teaching, the core instructional task is centered on developing students' skills in using information to comprehend issues. These kinds of classrooms usually are characterized by students' active involvement in group work, projects, and other assignments that involve library or field research, experimentation, and other investigations on course-related issues. In classrooms where students' understanding of ideas and issues is the central teaching mission, teachers use classroom discussions to get at how students think about the issues. Questions asking for explanations, for examples, for comparisons, for data to be interpreted, for principles to be applied to new situations, dominate these discussions. Discussions become one means of promoting students' higher order thinking about issues of significance in the curriculum content.

Between these two instructional styles are a variety of others, combinations of methods in which teachers adopt procedures in accordance with perceived learner needs. But even with such a variety of teaching styles and strategies, it is clear that what most teachers do largely tilts toward one or another primary mode, with its central mission of "covering the mandated content and maintaining control" (Cuban, 1993, p. 253) or "extracting" students' meanings. Each style comes from quite a different perspective on the role of a teacher.

From one perspective, a teacher's job is seen as demanding the imparting of *the essential* information that learners need to *know*. Such a perspective is implicitly based on several assumptions about students, *viz.*, that they are largely disinterested; that the only way to get them to learn anything at all is to work hard at "filling the empty vessels"; that they have no ideas of their own of any value; that large doses of information must precede any work in getting them to think, which then occurs after all the information is stored.

From the other perspective, the teacher's job is seen as teaching students how to process information: to *know about*. This perspective is rooted in a different set of assumptions about learners, *viz.*, that learning of significance requires the learner's active involvement in the process; that the responsibility for learning the material lies with students; that information acquisition is more effective when it is incorporated with thinking about the issues. The assumption that students do, in fact, have ideas and that these ideas may be productively mined to strengthen knowledge, has been borne out in teachers' anecdotal reports, as well as in classroom research (Raths, Wassermann, Jonas, & Rothstein, 1986).

An individual teaching style will, of course, incorporate many different strategies. Even teachers whose styles are predominantly information dispensing will ask their students to do projects; while teachers who work in the "extracting meanings" group will also, on occasion, be seen to give information. However, as surely as water seeks its own level, "extractors" and "transmitters" remain largely true to their own styles. How they teach defines not only what they do, but what they implicitly believe about the act of teaching and the assumptions made about learners.

While the *what* of teaching is usually determined outside of the classroom, the *how* is, to a large extent, shaped by teachers' beliefs, by their psychological needs, by how they have been inducted into the profession, and by the cultural ethos of the institution in which they work. All these variables (and others) enter into the equation and create individual teaching styles that are idiosyncratically each teacher's own and are about as resistant to change as the stone faces on Mount Rushmore.

A STYLE OF ONE'S OWN

Milos Fenster teaches economics at Alderwood Junior College. He has recently been voted "Teacher of the Year" by his students. Students say that he is outstanding! His Richard Burton voice is deep and resonant.

His lectures are well prepared and easy to follow. His use of examples adds spice and livens up his presentations. He is able to hold students' attention easily, and his lectures are always packed. Students consistently give his classes the highest ratings on course evaluations.

In an interview for a local newspaper, *Gazeteer*, Fenster described his teaching style. "I believe that my job is to give my students important information about economics. They need this information to understand basic economic theory. I'm concerned that they get that information. Part of my success lies in making that information easy to understand. I do that by preparing my lectures carefully and by using examples and anecdotal material to make the concepts clear."

Fenster believes that his job as a teacher is to give students information; that student learning involves receiving the correct information to build a strong knowledge base. Fenster believes that only when students have the correct information will they be able to think about the economic issues. Thinking occurs later, once the information is in place. Fenster considers that his particular skill as a lecturer makes for more effective information dispensing and knowledge building than is possible through written material, which nevertheless serves as backup to his lectures. In his classes, Fenster maintains tight control of the three important aspects of the teaching–learning situation: *time*—when a task begins and how long it takes; *operations*—sequencing of lectures, monitoring students' mastery of concepts, monitoring mastery of procedures; and *standards*—monitoring control over student performance (Berlak & Berlak, 1981).

"What happens," asks the interviewer, "after the course is over? Do the students remember the information?"

Fenster shrugs and his eyes travel beyond the reporter's notebook, out across the large, green lawn of the school. "Well, we can only hope they do. But I wouldn't want to bet my pension on it."

When asked how he developed his teaching style, Fenster reported that the teacher whom he most admired was also a highly successful lecturer, who could turn a roomful of slightly bored sophomores into an alert, attentive audience. Fenster told how he studied that teacher's style and tried, with some variations, to make it his own. Fenster is a much admired colleague in his faculty, where the teaching ethos is centered in the lecture mode.

At the other end of town, Terry Mayle, who teaches economics at Island Junior College, is also being interviewed by the *Gazeteer*. Terry, like Milos Fenster, is extremely popular with his students, who consider him "the best teacher in the school." His classes are always the first to be filled, and they are always the most crowded. "He teaches economics in a way that I can understand it," one student says. "He really makes us think about what is happening. You begin to see how economics is not just a bunch of vague theories in a book, but how it applies to real life."

"We work very hard in his classes," says another student, "harder than for almost any other teacher. But we come away with more—real understanding of what economics is all about. I don't think a teacher can spoon feed that to you; a teacher has to know how to make you work so you get to figure those things out for yourself."

Mayle, who has been teaching for almost 15 years, abandoned the lecture style 5 years ago, in favor of teaching by the case method. During class time, you will find him conducting class discussion on a case that has been studied outside of class. Almost never does Mayle use class time to dispense information.

In answer to the interviewer's question about how he developed his teaching style, Mayle responded, "I do not see my job as the giver of information."

> Why would I want to take up valuable class time to do that? There are books, articles, films—all manner of ways for students to get information. It's not that I think that information is not important; it's just that I think that class time needs to be spent in my helping students to use that information to further their understanding. Just knowing the information does not guarantee understanding. I see my job as getting students to think about the issues; not just to sit there passively and suck up the information that I dish out. I'm not here to entertain them with dazzling lectures that are easier to listen to than sloughing through the written material. They need to be made responsible for reading the material themselves. I'm here to make them think!

Mayle talks about the beliefs that have reshaped his teaching style. "I used to think that all I needed to do was to make sure that students got the right information and that they would use it to think about the issues. But, you know, I never tested them on how well they understood; I always tested them on what information they had stored. I liked to believe that they *could* understand; but in my heart, I knew that information, not understanding, was what it was all about. I allowed myself to make the assumption that receiving information would automatically result in understanding; but it is an untenable assumption. When I let myself wake up to the reality of what I was doing, and let me tell you, that was not an easy awakening, I had to acknowledge that information dispensing does not make students think. If you want to get students to think about ideas, the teacher has got to provoke that thinking. That is what class time is for!"

Mayle is just getting warmed up. "Understanding ideas, issues, concepts—that's what I consider paramount in students' learning. Remembering information is not enough; it's how students use information to build their understanding. That is now my central mission in teaching."

In Mayle's classes, he has relinquished much of the control of time and operations to students, allowing them wider berth in how they address economic issues, how they develop group work procedures, how they organize their discussion time, how they work toward mastery of concepts. It is in the domain of standards that Mayle maintains control.

"What happens when the students leave your class? What, if anything, do they take away with them?" the interviewer asks.

Well, if you can believe what they tell you, they say that they continue to think about the issues long after the course is over. They say that the habits of thinking built during the class discussions endure, and are used to their advantage in other classes. Some say they still discuss many of the issues we discussed in class, even now. I understand that this has been borne out by classroom research [Adam, 1992]. I think if students are still thinking about issues in your course 3 to 5 years later, and are able to use habits of thinking to their advantage in other courses, well, that can't be too bad a job of teaching, eh?

You know, no one ever taught me how to teach. College teachers do not take teacher training. I just learned what to do from watching what my own teachers did. And that was okay when I taught at Alderwood. But here, at the Island School, lecturing is no longer an acceptable mode. We are encouraged to use class time to engage students actively, to work on promoting understanding. Developing this new style has changed my entire outlook on teaching, on learning, on students. It has truly changed my life, and teaching for me has never been more satisfying.

TEACHING WITH CASES—IT'S NOT FOR EVERY TEACHER

How do teachers develop a particular style? How do teachers determine if certain methodologies are incompatible with their preferred style?

The development of a teaching style appears to have less to do with formal instruction than with the way teachers have internalized the practices of their own teachers (Lortie, 1975). This developmental process is further shaped by a teacher's beliefs and expectations; by psychological needs and feelings; by the ethos of the school or department in which teachers work. Lortie claims that these are more often unconscious influences that rarely have been subject to thoughtful scrutiny. Odd as it may sound, and given the thousands of hours spent by many in learning to teach, the development of a particular teaching style may be more similar to the way weeds grow than the way vegetables are cultivated.

Given certain preconditions and influencing factors that have already shaped a teacher's style, how do teachers determine if case method teaching is compatible with that style? For which teachers is such a methodology the professional equivalent of bungee jumping? The paragraphs that follow are not exhaustive guidelines, but they at least raise some questions that you, as a teacher, might address, with respect to what you have to *be*, and what you have to *believe*, in considering case method teaching a reasonable alternative.

Case Method Classrooms

A glimpse into a case method classroom provides a beginning point for deciding. These classrooms have been described as places in which the tension of uncertainty is elevated. These are places in which no single, correct answers are being sought; where discussions are left, suspended, without closure; where students leave class with unanswered questions; where the frustration of not knowing for sure is allowed to ferment.

This is contrasted with other types of classrooms in which knowing for sure makes learners and teachers feel safe; where problems are resolved; where questions are answered with certainty; where facts provide the absolute ground in which knowledge forms. In these classrooms, not knowing for sure gives rise to intolerable frustration and anxiety.

Which classroom descriptors excite you? Which beckon with promises of a tantalizing learning habitat? Which seem significant attributes of what you hope your classroom would offer? Which repel you? Which raise hackles? Which seem representative of the most unacceptable way in which students could learn? Which seem counterproductive to your classroom ideal?

Teachers who are comfortable with the elevation of uncertainty, who have high tolerance for dissonance, who see productivity in not knowing, and counterproductivity in absolute certainty, are more likely to consider teaching with cases. Those who depend on the safety of absolute ground are likely to find teaching with cases abhorrent.

Beliefs

Teachers' beliefs, whether consciously chosen or unconsciously held, lie at the roots of most classroom decisions and hence actions. What does a teacher need to believe about the act of teaching, in order to consider teaching with cases congruent with those beliefs? What does a teacher need to believe about students? About learning?

What a teacher believes, is what a teacher does. Teaching strategies that are not congruent with beliefs are not likely to be chosen and, if imposed, are not likely to endure for long. For teachers to feel satisfied, they must use methodology that is congruent with their deepest beliefs about teaching, about learning, about students. To know what is believed serves as a means of informing classroom choices.

The Beliefs Checkup (see Figure 2.1) offers an informal, nonstandardized, not altogether empirically valid way of identifying certain educational beliefs that have a relationship to case method teaching. You may use the scale to determine to what extent your beliefs are compatible with the demands and expectations of teaching with cases. Complete the exercise and calculate your total score. If it is between 31 and 62, this teaching methodology is likely incompatible with your beliefs. A score between 62 and 93 points to strong reservations. If you score between 93 and 124, proceed cautiously and gather some more data. If your score is higher than 124, this approach is likely to fit well with your own approach to teaching.

At the very least, the Beliefs Checkup will allow you to become more conscious of preconceptions and internalizations about teaching and learning, as you subject teaching experience, both past and present, to critical scrutiny. At the very least, such an exercise ought to help with your examination of the prospects of teaching with cases as a satisfying teaching methodology. At the very least, you should know if reading the rest of this book is to be a valuable or a wasted exercise.

Psychological Needs

No teacher will use, for very long, a teaching style or methodology that is unsatisfying. No teacher will consciously choose to stay with teaching methods that fail to produce the kinds of results he or she considers valuable and significant in student learning. Teachers who are locked

Figure 2.1. Beliefs Check

Use the scale to determine the extent to which you hold each of the beliefs. Then cal-culate your total score to see if the strength of your beliefs supports your consideration of case method teaching as an instructional mode.

5 = agree strongly   4 = tend to agree   3 = uncertain
2 = tend to disagree   1 = disagree strongly

A. BELIEFS ABOUT STUDENTS

1. Students profit more from active involvement with substantive learning tasks.
2. When students are sitting and listening to the teacher, their involvement is limited.
3. The responsibility for learning the material lies with students.
4. Students have the ability to think deeply and profoundly about important issues in the curriculum.
5. Students have ideas about the topics in the curriculum that are worth thoughtful consideration.
6. When students "wrestle" cognitively with the content, learning is enhanced.
7. When teachers expect students to behave responsibly in unsupervised group work situations, they often rise to the occasion.
8. Students do not have to learn a body of information first, before they can think. Learning information is better accomplished by thinking about the ideas.
9. Cooperation, rather than competition, is a better way of learning in class.

B. BELIEFS ABOUT TEACHING

1. Learning of significance does not mean the memorization and recall of "objective truths."
2. The most important aspect of the teacher's job is not to teach students a fixed body of knowledge, to be covered in a given amount of time.
3. Racing ahead, to ensure that all the course content is covered by the end of the se-mester, is not the teacher's most important job.
4. Standardized examinations do not force a teacher to teach with an emphasis on in-formation acquisition only.
5. Students can learn the important content, and are able to pass standardized tests, when thinking is emphasized over fact acquisition.
6. The systematic presentation of content is not a sure fire way to ensure that stu-dents learn important curriculum concepts.
7. A quiet classroom is not necessarily a classroom where students are learning any-thing of value.
8. Giving students short answer tests, in which they have to remember the correct an-swers, is not a valid way to determine if students have learned anything of value.

into unsatisfying methodologies by bureaucratic mandate will not re-main there long. Either they will find ways to subvert and hide from administrative scrutiny what they are actually doing, or they will trans-fer out of the school or district, or even leave the profession. To be forced to behave (teach) in ways that are dissatisfying is a major cause

Figure 2.1. Continued

C. BELIEFS ABOUT SELF AS TEACHER

1. Dissemination of information is not the only way for me to teach. I know that content can be effectively learned in different ways.
2. I do not have to know all the answers about case method teaching before I begin to try it out.
3. I know I can learn more about case method teaching while I'm using it. My classroom can become my laboratory for studying how I can become more effective.
4. Based on what I know, I think the prospect of teaching with cases is exciting—although the newness of it is a little intimidating.
5. I like being in the vanguard of educational change.
6. Giving up old ways of teaching, and moving to new ways is challenging and exciting.
7. I see my classroom as a learning laboratory where I can learn as much about teaching and learning as my students are learning about the subject.
8. Giving so much control over to students is a little worrisome, but my beliefs that students should have more control over their learning will see me through the initial period of uncertainty.
9. I view myself as a "reflective practitioner"—a teacher who can observe and interpret what is happening in my classroom and respond thoughtfully and appropriately.

D. BELIEFS ABOUT GOALS OF TEACHING

1. One of the most important goals of teaching is to develop informed, intelligent citizens who are able to play socially responsible roles in society.
2. Students who are able to think about, understand, and discuss issues intelligently have been better prepared in school than those who only know the facts.
3. Students who have learned the facts, but have not learned the meanings of the significant issues have been shortchanged in their learning.
4. The curriculum should help students develop more than knowledge and awareness about the issues. They should also have developed some feelings about the issues.
5. A teaching style that results in students' obedience, compliance, and passivity is counterproductive to educational goals.

of teacher stress and burnout. All of us need to find satisfaction in our work.

There are, of course, other needs that teachers have, and these are more individual and often unconscious. What's more, needs are fickle, rather than stable. They are heightened, or diminished, depending on psychological states, occasions, contexts. For example, a person who has experienced traumatic loss in her life is likely to find greater need for safety and reassurance than usual. Some people find their need for belonging elevated during holiday times, like Christmas and Thanksgiving. Some people have strong needs to be appreciated in their work, and easily feel diminished when such appreciation is not continually forthcoming.

Unlike beliefs, which are chosen, we do not choose our needs. Rather, they choose us. Because we have limited control over psychological needs, often the best we can do is to know which needs drive us, to what extent we are driven by them, and how best to manage them when they are in danger of driving us off the edge.

Without getting into the murky waters of psychoanalytic discourse, it may be said that we teachers are entirely human, and are consequently ruled by human needs, which play out in various ways in our lives as well as in our classrooms. To a greater or lesser extent, most of us need to be liked and appreciated. We need to feel secure and safe in what we are doing. We need to feel a sense of belonging to a group. We need to feel respected; to feel that we are adequate. Human needs for safety, for appreciation, for love and security, for belonging are not dirty little secrets to be kept locked in dark closets, unacknowledged, and revealed only with a sense of shame. To have self-awareness of one's needs, and to behave out of that knowledge, is more healthy and satisfying than keeping up a pretense that, unlike the rest of humankind, we are unaffected by those psychological states that motivate and drive all our lives.

When our needs are in the "normal" range (and when they are in that range depends on fluctuating psychological states and changes of occasion and context), we generally feel secure, confident, able to face the challenges of life with equanimity. When, because some life circumstance has conspired to threaten our security, our needs fall outside of that "normal" range, we feel less secure and confident, less able to face our challenges. Teachers who feel thus may be less likely to attempt innovative methods, which may be felt to be too risky. Teachers who have very great needs to excel may also shun the new. In trying new methods, there is bound to be an initiation period of less-than-perfect performance.

Yet, in spite of the established relationship between needs and behaviors, it is impossible for an outsider to predict with accuracy how certain needs, elevated in certain teachers, would steer them toward or away from case method teaching. While it might be tempting to make such predictions, experience has taught that teachers are full of surprises. Teachers, for example, who express great anxiety about trying something new, nonetheless may find within themselves both the courage to try and the determination to succeed. Teachers who express great needs for the security that constancy gives may suddenly venture into the new with passion and persistence.

What, then, is to be made of the connection between personal needs and the risk taking involved in putting an innovative methodology like case method teaching to work in your classroom? Only this: that before you consider embarking on a teaching plan that may be radically different from past experience, it might be worthwhile to make some personal, private assessment, to consider how your own psychological needs may facilitate, or stand in the way of, an effective field trial. This may be done by taking a moment or two to reflect on some of the concerns identified by teachers as potentially threatening to their feelings of security in a case method classroom; for example:

> The diminishing of the teacher's authoritarian role
> The absence of closure in a lesson
> Teaching lessons that heighten uncertainty, operating in the "gray areas" between what is known and not known
> The lack of emphasis on "correct" answers
> Trying something new in the classroom
> Having to create structure as you teach
> Seeing your classroom as a laboratory for learning about teaching
> Students "losing out" as you learn
> Not getting it right the first few times
> Failing
> Lack of expertise that will cause students to mock you
> The curriculum not being covered
> How to give grades
> Students' ability to work responsibly on their own
> What others (administrators, colleagues, parents, etc.) will think

These, of course, are not all the needs-related concerns associated with teaching with cases that might threaten a teacher's security. They are, however, more frequently mentioned and may require some personal resolution. Should some, or many, of these concerns raise alarm bells for you, it is not necessarily a signal to abandon the ship. What you need to ask is to what extent you are going to be able to manage the needs that give rise to the concerns. Such considerations are imperative in making your choice about case method teaching.

Power and Control Needs

There is reason for giving power and control needs a category separate from those discussed above, since these are found to be singular in their relationship to how teachers choose a particular teaching style. Among groups of beginning teachers, the fear most prevalent is that of "losing control." This is the stuff of new teachers' nightmares; dreams of students running amok, with the teacher standing helplessly, unable to bring the class "under control." Such control needs come from deeper fears of inadequacy. To be perceived as adequate, one needs to "feel in charge, on top of things." Loss of control is taken as an indicator that the teacher is unable to function adequately as *teacher*.

The old saw, "Don't smile until Christmas," given as advice to new teachers, is a way of holding onto control. The advice implies that new teachers should "run a tight ship" in the first few months of teaching and let the students know who's boss. Then, when the students are brought "under control," teachers can unbend and relax.

There are teachers who, after long years in the profession, still need to maintain rigorous control over everything students do. They are in charge of all decisions of consequence; what's more, they would not have it any other way. They believe that such control is the right and the prerogative of teachers. When offered alternative methodologies in which control shifts, even slightly, into the students' domain, these teachers balk and worry. To them loss of control means that students will learn less; and their function as teachers will be diminished. Needs for power and control over students—what they do, how they do it, how much time they take to do it, and so forth—are not negotiable. Teachers who are ruled by such needs are less likely to be persuaded that the giving up of those controls is in either their, or their students', best interests. The notion of giving up certain classroom controls is almost life-threatening.

Glasser (1986) writes that the need for control (power) is a basic human need built into our genetic structure. Who, of us, is driven by such needs? Who is able to manage them? Who can safely give over needs for control to students, so that students may develop some power of their own? More than any other emotional need, the need for power and control may be the single most important indicator of a teacher's potential for choosing case method teaching.

Teachers who have strong control needs will find that the classroom seems a natural place to get such needs satisfied, in culturally accepted and acceptable ways. They may be less likely to see any negative consequences of maintaining such power and control over students; they may be unable to recognize that the exercise of such power over students must, by nature of that exercise, diminish student power (Kohn, 1993). Students must then sublimate their own power needs, causing considerable stress for them. When students have to give up their power, they will first be frustrated and angry; later, after considerable experience without power, they will become submissive, compliant, obedient (Wassermann, 1990).

Teachers who can safely relinquish classroom control, giving more power to students, will derive satisfaction from other sources. There is satisfaction in seeing students assume power and control over their own learning. There is satisfaction when students are able to grow toward increased autonomous functioning; when they function more responsibly and thoughtfully. Such growth can occur only when students have had experience in using their own power to achieve these ends. No amount of power-over students will result in students' increased power-to. Submission is not exchanged for autonomy upon graduation.

While all of us have power needs that drive us, as teachers each of us must determine to what extent the need for power-over is going to be played out in our classrooms; to what extent we are able to give power to students; to what extent, if we do, such giving up of power will threaten us and make life in our classrooms intolerable. We need to know if there is satisfaction for us in students' increased power-to; if we are going to feel pride in seeing growing student autonomy; if students' challenging of authority will be taken as a mark of successful teaching. Teachers need to know these things before embracing case method teaching. Teachers who are unable to give up classroom control, who see teaching as carrying out power-over students, will be very unhappy as case teachers. Teaching with cases implies entering into a partnership with students—teachers and students partners in the learning process. Partnership cannot be achieved when power-over is exerted by one partner; it can be achieved only when partners share in the power to become more informed.

Case method teaching feeds students' and teachers' sense of power-to. In case teaching classrooms, students gain in ego strength, in self-confidence, and in heightened personal autonomy. Students learn to be more in charge of what they do and how; and they learn more responsibility in doing so. The power to choose may be the single most important variable in effective and satisfying human development. When we, as teachers, are able to allow students to assume that power-to, we may be giving them the greatest gift that teachers can give. When we take that power from them, we may be denying them the most important condition for effective living and learning.

If you are considering the alternative of case method teaching, you will have to examine all of these variables and others, and make your own choices. But choice is never free choice. There are always trade-offs with every choice. So before choosing, you should be aware of what you are likely to gain and what you are likely to lose in deciding for or against teaching with cases.

3 | Cases as Instructional Tools

Julie Briggs's social studies class is getting ready to begin their study of World War II. She is looking for a case that will introduce students to that period in world history and serve as a departure point for the examination of issues related to that event. She wants her students to examine issues of German aggression, political leadership, the roles played by different participants, the impact of the war on peoples of different nations, the human losses, the widespread destruction of cities and towns, the outcomes. She realizes that for her Grade 10 students, the period 1938–1946 is the equivalent of "ancient history" and she is looking for material that will make the events of that period seem contemporary and relevant.

In *Cases for Teaching in the Secondary School* (Bickerton et al., 1991) she finds two cases that deal with World War II content. One, "The Case of the Nazi Art Purges" (Dart, 1991), concerns the control over art and artists in Germany during the Nazi regime. The second, "Welcome Aboard!" (see Appendix A; Wassermann, 1991b) draws on the theme of racial prejudice. It centers on the thwarted efforts of a group of 900 German Jews, who left Germany in 1939, on the ship St. Louis to find harbor in any North American port. Julie Briggs chooses the latter case. To her, the idea of ethnic cleansing, centrally related to World War II, is one of the "big ideas" she wants her students to examine in their studies of the era. She believes this case can serve to open inquiry into the major issues of that tragic historical period and relate to current events as well. "Welcome Aboard!" adequately meets her criteria for choosing an appropriate case.

CRITERIA FOR CHOOSING A CASE

Mesh with Curriculum Issues

In choosing cases for a class, there is, first of all, the mesh between the "big ideas" of a case and the major topics in the curriculum. Finding a mesh does not imply a perfect match. There is some flexibility. A single case will not, in the best of circumstances, deal with all the topics to be studied in the course. It doesn't need to. The case needs to touch on at least one topic, leaving the door open for further study through reading (texts, articles, stories), films, speakers, and other information-rich resources, as well as other cases. One case is a beginning point in the study of a topic. Each good case drives the need to know more.

Julie's selection of "Welcome Aboard!" is based on the "mesh" she finds in the big ideas and Notes to the Teacher (see Appendix A). She will be able to use the case as a way of breaking into deeper and more extensive studies of that historical period.

How does a teacher judge if the mesh is a good one? Perhaps in the same way teachers decide on other curriculum materials that find their way as "extras" into every classroom. Teachers choose films, for example, that they consider relevant to an area of inquiry, or books and stories that illuminate certain aspects of a particular topic. With these added materials, there is no perfect mesh. The materials are appropriate because they allow for examination of certain issues that the teacher considers significant to the ongoing study of the period. In making these determinations, teachers use their best judgment—which carries implicitly an informed wisdom about content, ideas of significance, and relevance.

Quality of Narrative

Some educators may argue that *Son of the Middle Border*, by Hamlin Garland, was a quality narrative, deserving of its place in high school literature programs 50 years ago. Students did not agree. It would not be an exaggeration to say that *Son* did more to turn Grade 8 students off American literature than if there had been a subversive conspiracy to do so. If this was literature, then give us the Hardy Boys! But, of course, that is ancient history in high school curriculum content. Between then and now, educators have learned a thing or two about choosing books that turn students onto, and not away from, literature of quality.

One important criterion in any piece of writing is the quality of the narrative. There is much junk that passes for literature, and much written that is junk. In choosing a case, the importance of quality writing is not a trivial matter. Quality writing has greater potential for hooking students' interest. Writing that is less than good panders to poor taste and implies that lower standards are acceptable. Characters that are not real do not give readers people to identify with and care about. A plot that is thin, or phony, gives no "meat." A plot that is too complex is too hard to follow.

How do teachers know if the case is an example of quality writing? How does one know if any piece of writing is good? What is one teacher's meat is another's poison. We all make individual choices in these matters; but there are nonetheless certain standards that apply across the board. Does the writing pull the reader into the narrative? Do the descriptive phrases allow for mental images of the people, the places, the events, to be formed? Are readers able to identify and to feel for the characters? Is the plot realistic? Teachers, I believe, are not strangers to these aspects of good writing.

The negative view also offers a means of judging. Is the writing trite? The prose "thick"? Do the eyes glaze over during reading? Does the plot bog down in too much information dispensing? Is the sequencing of events hard to follow? The story silly? The characters wooden? Teachers, I believe, are able to differentiate a poorly written case from a good one by applying good narrative standards.

Students will, of course, give their opinions truthfully, if they are asked. Since a good case opens the door to further study, whether the narrative "works" for students is a strong factor in judging its quality. Literary awards and teacher judgments notwithstanding, if the case narrative does not do the job of stimulating students' interest and thus their need to know, the case has failed in its primary function.

Readability

Particularly for students in junior and senior secondary classes, and for those new to written and spoken English, the question of readability of a case is another factor in choosing. Besides the factor of quality, teachers must also make choices based on their perception of their students' ability to comprehend the language, to decode the vocabulary, to find meaning in the issues.

Students who are unable to read the words will be at a total loss. Those who can decode, but whose experience with language circumscribes their ability to comprehend sentences and ideas, will not benefit from the case, no matter how well the narrative is written. Cases, therefore, should be chosen with their readability in mind as well. Once again, teachers are the best judges of how appropriate a case is for students' reading and comprehension levels and will have to find the middle ground between cases that are too difficult and those that challenge students to more advanced levels of growing and learning.

Heightened Feelings

Most good cases pack a wallop to the solar plexus, leaving the reader with a physiological "whoosh"—a rush of affect. This is not incidental to the narrative. In fact, narratives are constructed to deliver such a punch. In "The Case of Injustice in Our Time" (Chambers & Fukui, 1991), the Japanese-Canadian family is carted away, like criminals, children and parents in tears, taunted by cries of their neighbors, "Japs Keep Out!" In the case of "Barry" (Wassermann, 1993a), the boy who couldn't number, a teacher, in desperation, changes the answers on his math homework so that he will get a higher score, hoping that this will improve his diminished self-image. In the case, "I Felt As If My World Had Just Collapsed" (Hansen, Renjilian-Burgy, & Christensen, 1987), the teacher is enraged by a student's overt expression of racism toward a Latino classmate. These cases and others elevate passion and stir emotional juices. Few students are left untouched by these human dilemmas. The power of a case to pack such a punch is intimately related to its power to draw students into the content.

Sometimes, this heightened affect is misread as bias. A strong point of view, passionately felt by a character in a case, however, is not a polemic for or against an issue. The emotionality built into a case is intended to stir students' feelings—anger, rage, caring, concern, alarm— and thus bring normally "cold" facts and concepts to life. Instead of studying World War II as a list of names, dates, places and statistics, students look at it through a more human lens—what happened to people who lived during that time. In that way, students who read cases learn to care. History, economics, biology, geography, and mathematics become real, humanly connected courses of study, rather than disconnected from human experience. Students care about the people in the case, about the issues, about the subject matter.

Of course, the heightened affect in a case should never be used as propaganda to persuade students to embrace a particular point of view. Even though cases may seem to tilt toward a particular orientation, higher order questions and the teacher's neutrality during debriefing ensure that all points of view are examined respectfully, critically, and thoughtfully. Students have "equal opportunity" to examine issues from many perspectives, free of subtle or overt coercion to buy into "establishment" ideas. Cases, however good, may, like other good teaching tools, be used badly. But used effectively, the heightened affect in a case has great potential for stirring student interest and connecting learners to content.

Elevation of the Dilemma

One of the most irritating aspects of a good case is its "unfinished business." Good cases end not with a happy resolution, like a 30-minute TV sitcom, but rather with some nagging questions. The case narrative builds toward a climax that elevates the dilemma. What happens now? What should be done next? How is this going to be resolved? This aspect of a case is one more quality that spurs active pupil involvement in the study of the issues. The mind does not rest in the presence of this cognitive dissonance. It must find a way of resolving the dilemma. That cognitive processing demands student thinking.

A case that ends with a resolution may be seen as an editorial for a particular way of being, or doing things. Such a case would militate against open discussion or holding different points of view. Students would know they were expected to agree. Cases that end on the horns of a dilemma encourage open debate. We cannot know "what to do" or "what is the right way" until we debate, until we think, until issues have been examined in their complexity, until more data are gathered. It may well be the "hook" in a case that alerts students to the complexity of issues and steers them away from the simplistic, single answer that dominates much classroom discussion. If cases drive the need to know, it is the "hook" at the end of the case that works, like a magnet, to draw learners into spirited examination of the issues.

Teachers choosing cases will look for mesh—the relationship of the case to course issues—quality of narrative, readability, the ability of the case to generate feelings about the issues and provoke discussion about the dilemma. The question of which courses are more suitable for case method teaching is addressed in the next section.

CASES IN THE CONTENT AREAS

The social science and humanities seem like natural content areas for case teaching. It has been relatively easy to find and/or write cases that are rooted in historical, geographic, economic, government, legal, educational, business, and human relations issues. After all, social science and humanities are people-related subjects. It makes sense that cases should find their way easily into these subject areas and become useful and valuable tools in promoting student learning.

But what of the other content areas? Can cases be used in math, biology, physics, and chemistry? Is it possible that cases are also appropriate for content-laden, information-driven "hard science" courses?

Goodenough (1991), a professor of anatomy and cellular biology at the Harvard Medical School, describes how he and a group of colleagues developed the New Pathways Program, in which the "pedagogical high road" of lecturing was to be replaced by case method teaching in the training of doctors. Cases were written that incorporated material previously taught in courses like cell biology, histology, gross anatomy, and radiology. These cases were then presented in a reorganized curriculum consisting of courses emphasizing themes like The Human Body, Metabolism, Matter and Energy, Identity and Defense, Life Cycle, Information Processing, and Behavior. Goodenough writes:

> The power of group discussion in medical teaching suggests that the method is broadly applicable to other disciplines. This power has nothing to do with self-aggrandizement or adulation by students and peers. Rather, it is the power of meaningful interconnection among the students and teachers as they all learn and, in a very real sense, transcend themselves, adding a vital new layer to the growing coral reef of human understanding. (p. 98)

Greenwald (1991), in his essay, "Teaching Technical Material," points to several problems in teaching highly technical material. Students, Greenwald suggests, are typically anxious in the presence of highly technical material, and many of them have had limited experience with technically oriented content. Also, technical courses often demand modes of reasoning that are unnatural and/or nonintuitive. Consequently, it is easy for teachers to try to alleviate this anxiety by lecturing—presenting information

> clearly and carefully in a tightly controlled classroom environment. . . . That approach might seem to indicate a lecture format as the most appropriate way to present technical material. But my experience suggests that a discussion approach is more effective, particularly when students must ultimately apply their technical knowledge to practical problems. (p. 195)

Barnett's (1991) research in mathematics education used case narratives as a catalyst for discussion about teaching hard-to-comprehend concepts such as fractions, decimals, ratios, and percents. Barnett found that the pedagogy fosters thinking and reasoning skills applicable to mathematics teaching and concluded that case method teaching offers teachers opportunities to reflect on practice, as well as "breeds new knowledge through collaborative contemplation and deliberation" (p. 16).

A precondition for choosing cases in any course is the teacher's ability to see the course content as issue-bound—where students need to apply principles of understanding to solving problems, rather than merely collecting a vast body of theoretical information. If there are issues or concepts to be studied and applied to problem situations, then cases are a good tool for that study. As Greenwald (1991) writes:

> Successful discussion teaching forces students to go beyond learn-ing abstract principles and to apply them to the messy world of every-day reality. . . . These exercises help students appreciate both the value and the limitations of the technical skills they acquire. They learn not to be discouraged by the complexity, lack of information, and the time constraints of actual decision situations, and also to distinguish between the useful central kernel of the theoretical ap-proach and the peripheral details whose significance is swamped by the uncertainties and ambiguities of real life. (p. 196)

When teachers are clear about the issues or concepts in a course, and how these can be related to real-life problems, cases may be selected on the basis of their "mesh."

Present experience suggests that cases are as appropriate in the information-driven courses as they are in the social sciences and human-ities. As Christensen (1991a) put it, "I wouldn't keep this from a calcu-lus class."

RESOURCES FOR ACQUIRING CASES

Where do teachers find good cases? What resources are available in the different content areas? With interest in case method teaching grow-ing, more and more resources now exist, and even more are being gen-erated currently. What follows is a nonexhaustive list of possibilities from which interested teachers may begin their search.

For university coursework, the most extensive resource for locat-ing cases is the Case Clearinghouse at the Harvard Business School. Their catalogue contains a vast collection of cases for teaching all aspects of business (including the kind of technical content cases referred to by Greenwald, 1991), as well as "teaching cases"—those used for training in the art of case method teaching. The Case Clearinghouse catalogue also lists readings for those who wish to enrich their own understanding of teaching with cases.

Also at Harvard, the Roderick MacDougall Center for Case Development and Teaching is devoted to the development and encouragement of the use of case materials and the training of educational leaders. The Center offers cases for use in community and local politics, curriculum and instruction, facilities and financial management, human resource management, organizational development, personnel and labor relations, public policy, and institutional strategy. The Center's catalogue may be obtained by writing to Dr. Katherine Merseth, Director, 451 Gutman Library, 6 Appian Way, Cambridge, MA 02138.

Drs. Rita Silverman and Bill Welty of Pace University continue to add to their collection of cases for teacher education. Lists of cases available may be obtained directly from them, at Pace University in New York City.

In Canada, two additional case clearinghouse facilities offer case-based teaching materials. The International Case Clearinghouse offers cases in tourism and hospitality; business and teacher education for students in high schools, community colleges, and universities; and adult education and training programs. A bibliography of cases can be obtained from the International Case Clearinghouse, 37 Ebury Crescent, London, Ontario, Canada, N6C 3E1. The Case Clearinghouse associated with the Faculty of Education at Simon Fraser University is a repository of cases written for high school students and teacher educators. This catalogue may be obtained from the Case Clearinghouse, Faculty of Education, Simon Fraser University, Burnaby, British Columbia, Canada, V5A 1S6.

Two major resources of teaching cases and information on case method teaching are the seminal *Teaching and the Case Method* (Christensen & Hansen, 1987), and *Education for Judgment* (Christensen, Garvin, & Sweet, 1991). These two books are nonpareil for anyone who is seriously interested in teaching with cases.

In the field of education, several texts are available that contain cases for the study of issues in teacher education. *Case Studies on Teaching* (Kowalski, Weaver, & Henson, 1990) presents 30 cases that deal with issues such as teacher strikes, cheating, student behavior, ability grouping, and homework. *Case Studies for Teacher Problem Solving* (Silverman, Welty, & Lyon, 1992) include 28 cases dealing with issues of classroom management, learning, effective teaching, diversity, evaluation, and contemporary teaching issues. *Case Studies for Teacher Decision Making* (Greenwood & Parkay, 1989) offers 30 cases, categorized into curricu-

lum issues, instruction, group motivation and discipline, pupil adjust-
ment, conditions of work, and "additional cases." *Getting Down to Cases:
Learning to Teach with Case Studies* (Wassermann, 1993a) contains 26 cases,
grouped around issues centered in teacher-as-person, teachers and students, and the teacher and the curriculum categories. *Case Methods in
Teacher Education* (Shulman, 1992) offers valuable advice about using cases
to bridge the gap between educational theory and classroom practice.

An earlier work, *Case Studies in Human Relationships in Secondary
School* (Lloyd-Jones, 1956), presents 26 cases for studying issues related
to counseling and guidance of secondary school students.

For the examination of gender-related issues at the university level,
Kleinfeld's *Gender Tales* (in press) contains a wealth of cases. Also by
Kleinfeld (1989) is the series of teaching cases in cross-cultural educa-
tion, available individually from the Center for Cross-Cultural Studies,
University of Alaska, Fairbanks.

Teacher educators looking for cases in English education may find
useful the vignettes in *A Casebook for English Teachers: Dilemmas and Decisions* (Small & Strzepek, 1988). Thirty-three short scenarios are presented, each dealing with significant issues in the teaching of English,
language, and literature.

Cases for use in nursing education are referenced in Johnson and
Purvis's (1987) article, "Case Studies: An Alternative Learning–Teaching
Method in Nursing."

"The historical roots of the case method . . . lie in the field of law"
(Merseth, 1991, p. 243), and while law cases are numerous and the case
literature is vast, some good starting points for finding cases in this area
are Carter and Unklesby's (1989) "Cases in Teaching and Law," Zarr's
(1989) "Learning Criminal Law Through the Whole Case Method," and
Gerlach and Lamprecht's (1980) *Teaching About the Law*. For reading
about case teaching that is entertaining as well as instructive, Turow's
(1977) *One-L* is also recommended.

Bickerton (1993), a senior high school biology teacher, undertook
as her graduate research problem the development and writing of five
cases that revolved around senior biology concepts. Her graduate thesis demonstrated that by using certain case writing procedures, cases
could be constructed to serve an information-driven biology course. Her
cases include

- "A Shot of Reality"—examines issues of the functioning of the inter-
  relationship of respiratory and circulatory systems
- "Phantom"—examines how nervous sensation is carried from sen-
  sory endings to the central nervous system and decoded in the brain

- "Water, Water Everywhere"—examines osmosis as a process that moves water between body cells and the media in which they live
- "Do or Die"—examines how "superhuman" acts are the result of body systems working in concert
- "An Unwelcome Reaction"—examines how allergic responses are caused by contact with an allergic agent to which individuals respond differently

What distinguishes the Bickerton dissertation is her analysis of the process of how cases are developed in an information-rich course.

O'Shea and Wassermann (1992) piloted two mathematics cases for secondary school students. Their "Case of the Yahagi Maru" (see Appendix B) asks students to examine how coordinates are used to plot locations. "The Unbearable Ugliness of Subaru" (see Appendix C; Wassermann, 1992c) examines issues of how probability theory may be used to make determinations about the likelihood of a used car breaking down.

Additional sources for cases in other curriculum areas include

SCIENCE EDUCATION. Stakes, R., & Easley, J. (1978). *Case Studies in Science Education*. Urbana: University of Illinois, Center for Instructional Research and Curriculum Evaluation.

PHYSICS. Lowe, I. (1975). Using Case Studies in the Teaching of Physical Principles. *Physics Education, 10*(7), 491–492.

SCIENCE. Wheatley, J. (1986). The Use of Case Studies in the Science Classroom. *Journal of College Science Teaching, 15*, 428–431.

LIBRARY EDUCATION. Lowell, M. H. (1968). *The Case Method in Teaching Library Management*. Metuchen, NJ: The Scarecrow Press.

PSYCHOLOGY. Bromley, D. B. (1986). *The Case Study Method in Psychology and Related Disciplines*. New York: John Wiley.

LIBERAL EDUCATION. Goodman, D. M. (1982). Making Liberal Education Work in a Technological Culture. *Liberal Education, 68*(1), 63–68.

LIBERAL ARTS. Christensen, C. R., & Hansen, A. (1987). *Teaching and the Case Method*. Boston: Harvard Business School Press.

JOURNALISM. Graham, B. P., & Schwartz, S. H. (1983). Try the Case Approach in the Features Course. *Journalism Education, 38*(1), 45–48.

WRITING AND COMPOSITION. McCleary, W. J. (1985). A Case Approach for Teaching Academic Writing. *College Composition and Communication, 36*, 203–212.

AGRICULTURE. Nolan, A. W. (1927). *The Case Method in the Study of Teach-*

ing with Special Reference to Vocational Agriculture: A Case Book for
Teachers of Agriculture. Bloomington, IN: Public School Publishing Co.

ENGLISH AS A SECOND LANGUAGE. Pietrowski, M. V. (1982). Business as
Usual: Using the Case Method to Teach ESL to Executives.
TESOL Quarterly, 16, 229–238.

Cases aimed at secondary school students have been generated by
groups of teachers in British Columbia and cut across several curriculum areas. *Cases for Teaching in the Secondary School* (Bickerton et al., 1991)
contains 20 cases, in curriculum areas such as social studies, journalism, Western civilization, bioethics, and art. (This may be obtained c/o
Paul Odermatt, Centennial School, Coquitlam, BC, Canada V3J 6A8.)
Case Studies: The Cowichan Collection (1993) contains 17 cases dealing with
issues in government, law, business, history, health, and staff development. (The Cowichan Collection may be obtained from Diane Austin,
School District #65, 2557 Beverly St., Duncan, BC, Canada V9L 2X3.)
In production are numbers of single cases, written by secondary school
teachers throughout British Columbia and covering virtually every high
school curriculum area. This growing resource of cases is available through
the Faculty of Education Case Clearinghouse at Simon Fraser University.

The above list is far from complete, especially given that teaching
with cases is a re-emerging pedagogy and new materials are being generated even as this is being written. Since the work being done in stimulating case writing through the resources of the Faculty of Education at
Simon Fraser University is producing a burgeoning literature in cases
for diverse fields of study, readers who are seeking cases beyond what
is listed here may wish to contact me for further and more current information.

ALTERNATIVES TO CASES: MOCK TRIALS, SIMULATIONS, OTHER COGNITIVE CHALLENGES

In a text that extols the virtues of case method teaching, is there legiti-
macy to instructional tools that are not themselves *bona fide* cases? Are
case narratives the only game in town worth playing? Like most educational questions, the answer to both of these is, it depends. Points of
view vary from the more doctrinaire to the more liberal. At one extreme,
some would argue that no good alternatives exist for good cases; that,
in fact, unless a case narrative follows a particular form, it may not even
be considered a "case." A more flexible attitude is offered by Christensen

(1991a), who says that any "puzzle" may be used productively in lieu of a case. The more important question is not whether there are good alternatives, but rather what alternatives may give equally good results in building habits of thinking about the important issues in a course of study.

There are alternatives to good cases that can be (and have been) used as instructional tools. Some of these have similar ingredients to cases: They engage learners actively in the process of inquiry; they stimulate examination of issues in their complexity; they shun pat and simplistic answers; they elevate dissonance. With these alternatives, students must also wrestle with the dilemmas they present, and decisions, resolutions, and actions may be as diverse as the points of view represented by the players.

Mock trials offer such opportunities, and teachers have used these effectively in social studies and law classes. Mock trials, like cases, draw learners into the situation and enable them to examine issues from within the events. Simulation games are another rich resource that may be used like cases. For example, *Dangerous Parallel*, published by Scott Foresman, involves a simulation of international negotiations and decision making. *Democracy* (Webster) involves dealing with conflict in the legislative process. Other types of simulation games include *Carriers* (Parker Brothers), *Life* (Milton Bradley), and *The Stock Market Game* (Western).

Other cognitively challenging tasks found in texts dealing with the development of students' thinking offer a wealth of instructional materials in which pupils engage actively and that build habits of thinking. Cognitive challenges also draw students into the experience and generate enthusiasm for the undertaking. One sourcebook for activities that challenge pupils in these ways is *Teaching for Thinking: Theory, Strategies, and Activities for the Classroom* (Raths, Wassermann, Jonas, & Rothstein, 1986). Containing more than one thousand cognitive challenges in several secondary school curriculum areas, as well as elementary school subjects, the text offers a substantial resource for those who would examine the kinds of intellectual challenges that lie outside of the realm of case narratives but that may be used effectively and with good results.

The pedagogy used for case method teaching applies as well to alternatives such as mock trials, simulations, and other cognitive challenges. That is, pupils work in small study groups and engage actively in the exercise. Study questions follow the exercise, and they are used to generate student discussion of the "big ideas" in the exercise. This is then followed by debriefing, in which the teacher promotes further examination of the issues through selective questions and response strategies. Debriefing is followed by follow-up activities that allow for examination of issues from new and different perspectives. The big ideas examined in the initial round of activities (active engagement in the exercise, debriefing, follow-up) continue to be examined through a second round of related activities involving active engagement, debriefing, and follow-up—an instructional loop in which learners' understandings continue to evolve.

The alternatives to cases presented above are not the only ones that teachers might choose to serve students in cognitively challenging ways. Alternatives that offer opportunities to engage students actively in inquiry of complex issues, and that promote thinking about those issues, in a forum of open inquiry, will also yield productive results in building students' habits of thinking. Teachers will want to try cases—and determine for themselves how these work and to what end. They will want to try alternatives and compare the exercises with the results. In the end, teachers will undoubtedly make use of combinations of rich resources that serve their purposes of delivering on their most valued teaching goals.

4 | Writing Your Own Case

"I'm not a writer," he tells me, the second week into the staff development workshop in Teaching by the Case Method. "I'm afraid I don't
have the skill to write a case that anyone would want to read."

I am no stranger to this concern. Writing is a new adventure for
most teachers and, for some, poses what appear to be insurmountable
challenges. Lack of experience with writing makes us feel like begin-
ners on the ski slope, the blank sheet of paper as forbidding as a steep
downhill run, riddled with dangerous grades and curves. Yet, with a
bit of experience, writing, like skiing, can be exhilarating, challenging,
and enormously satisfying. Some of us even grow to love the experience.

Not every teacher will want to consider writing his or her own cases.
Teachers have other things to do with their time, and good teachers
hardly find adequate time to do everything they want to do in the first
place. There are lots of good cases already available for teachers to choose
from (see Chapter 3). Why should teachers consider writing their own
cases?

Teachers themselves have given their own reasons. Sometimes an
issue turns up in a course that warrants intensive examination, and there
are no cases available that will do the job. Sometimes, despite initial
anxiety about writing, teachers enjoy the new challenges that writing
a case offers. Sometimes teachers who thought they couldn't write find
that not only *can* they write, but the process of writing is pleasurable
and the end result a source of pride and accomplishment. Teachers have
also claimed that there is considerable satisfaction in teaching one's own
case—one's own creative energies having birthed something of value
to share with students.

Most teachers who are presented with the option of writing cases
begin with self-doubt and hesitation. Yet, most learn to write cases, not

because of any external pressure to do so, but because the challenge to write something creative is appealing. It takes only one successful attempt for teachers to see themselves differently—as case writers. "I'm not a writer," is exchanged for, "I'm beginning to see the potential for writing cases everywhere. It's exciting!"

This chapter does not represent writing one's own cases as a must in case method teaching. It is rather an invitation to those teachers who might consider such a creative effort within the realm of possibility.

CHARACTERISTICS OF CASE NARRATIVES

Teachers who have analyzed cases as a way of informing their own case writing have identified some attributes that they believe to be inherent in cases. Of course, the fundamental principle of all writing applies to writing cases: Good writing is good writing is good writing. Hansen (1987), in "Reflections of a Casewriter," comments, "In writing, especially narrative prose, less is more; pomposity is boring; and incoherence is a complete disaster. Orwell left me hypersensitive to the power of language to bamboozle and benumb as well as enlighten. Strunk and White left me terrified of being fuzzy or dull, and morbidly averse to the passive voice" (pp. 267–268).

Hansen's advice for case writing points to good writing techniques (pp. 269–270).

- Consider for whom you are writing. Write in a way that will "grab your readers and keep hold of their lapels until you're done with them."
- "Recognize the thudding passages in your own early drafts and either throw them out or improve them. . . . Soliciting a colleague's opinion at this point can make the difference between good, readable writing, and alphabet soup."
- "Reconsider the material from a reader's point of view . . . assume that the reader is every bit as intelligent, sophisticated, humorous, overcommitted, fatigued, irritable, emotional and generally human as you are."
- "Involve the reader's five senses, rather than simply the intellect, with imagery that stimulates fantasy."
- Use alliteration and assonance.
- Vary the length and syntax of sentences, using first a short one, then a long one, then perhaps a fragment.

- "Put the most important details at the beginning or end of paragraphs."
- "Check to see if too many paragraphs begin with participial phrases, or the word *he* or whatever."
- Remember that "repetition dulls the mind."

Good writing assumes the burden of making what is written intelligible to the reader. Good writing assumes the burden of being clear, comprehensible, intellectually honest, and artfully crafted. Writers owe at least that much to their readers.

We've all seen this kind of writing, and we marvel at its eloquence, its clarity, its poetic use of language. Because this kind of writing is such a pleasure to read, so clear that the words and sentences roll from the page, almost effortlessly into the mind, readers often make the assumption that "effortlessly" also describes the writer's ease in putting the narrative together. Would that it were so! What seems effortless to read is made that way through the writer's rigorous writing, editing, rewriting, editing, rewriting, editing, and on and on, ad nauseum—a process through which the manuscript is "tamed" until it attains near perfection. For many writers, this usually means dozens of drafts and considerable investment of time. That is a picture of "real life" for writers, and aspiring case writers should be alert to the fact that no good case ever fell from a pencil or word processor, in a perfect first draft, without having gone through the labors of the writing process.

Beyond the general rules for writing good narratives, cases have other narrative features that are uniquely theirs.

- *The opening of the narrative should draw readers immediately into the story.* Unlike other narrative styles, which may begin slowly, or with more descriptive passages, cases generally begin in an action mode. The idea is to seize the reader's attention, so that no student will respond, "Ho hum. Just another boring assignment," but instead, "Wow! What is this? I want to know more!"

"The Case of the Yahagi Maru" (see Appendix B; O'Shea & Wassermann, 1992), written for senior high school students to examine mathematical functions of measurement and the uncertainty associated with measurement, is an example of how this is done.

"My God!" he yelled. "We're sinking!" The captain searched the panel
of dials frantically, as if he could find the one that had betrayed him,
the one that had caused this terrible accident. The alarms through-

out the ship reached screaming intensity, as men scrambled to reach the lifeboats. In the background of the turmoil, the calls, "Abandon ship! Abandon ship!" repeated, like staccato drumbeats, marking time in the chaos.

Captain Tanaka, his face a gray mask, listened to the sounds of his ship breaking up on the iceberg, its jagged knives of ice cutting through the ship's jugular, spilling its cargo of oil and men into the icy seas. The disaster was incomprehensible. How did it happen? How could this fine, modern supertanker, with its cargo of 500,000 tonnes of crude oil, its state of the art equipment and technology—how could this ship have been defeated by an iceberg?

• *Cases are built around events of consequence.* Issues of substance provide the framework around which cases are written. A case about planting a garden would not get far; but a case about urban dwellers who were fighting for the right to use a vacant city lot to plant a neighborhood garden would involve issues of greater consequence.

• *Cases elevate tensions between conflicting points of view.* Because cases involve the examination of complex issues, there must be "many sides" to the story in a case. Good cases dramatize these tensions, so that readers are stimulated to discuss them. In the case "How Can I Make a Difference?" (Wassermann, 1993a), a teacher wrestles with his values about teaching in an urban slum school, while his best friend encourages him to "pack in the slum school and head for the suburbs" where life for teachers is much sweeter. A good case is never an editorial for one particular point of view, never a polemic for the "right way to think."

• *Cases are written so that readers grow to care.* The main players in a case are sympathetic characters, and even as they are drawn in complexity, we care about them, about their predicaments, about the events that are occurring around them. For readers to care, characters must be more than stereotypes. They should be multifaceted and be presented with human failings.

• *Case narratives must be believable.* In some ways, cases are more akin to good journalistic writing than to fiction. If the most important attribute of a case is its ability to stimulate discussion about the issues, the narrative must be closer to "fact" than "fiction." This characteristic allows readers to be drawn into the case. Readers are able to project themselves into the situation. "This could happen to me!" Such identification gives the case increased relevance for students.

• *Cases end on the horns of a dilemma.* At the end of a case, issues are not resolved. In fact, the opposite is true. The dilemma, or "hook," is left dangling. This, perhaps more than any other characteristic, is uniquely associated with case writing. This unfinished business gives cases considerable power and may explain why good cases, even years after they have been read and discussed, continue to plague the mind.

These characteristics of cases are not holy writ. Case writers will inevitably find their own style, their own voice, their own way into the process. That is one of the most attractive aspects about case writing—the process allows much flexibility, so many degrees of freedom in which to be creative. Another is that one does not have to aspire to be a Hemingway or to win the Pulitzer Prize for case writers. Students are enormously grateful for the cases they study in class. Perhaps it is because even an "average" case is so much more interesting than the material in the textbook. One develops skill as a case writer by writing cases. The only way that can happen is by sitting down to write and by offering what has been written to student study.

SITTING DOWN TO WRITE

What's the Big Idea?

At the heart of each case, whether in bioethics, teacher education, math, geography, or any other discipline, is a "big idea"—the central issue that the case will open to examination. Cases in teacher education may be rooted in big ideas such as teachers' resistance to change, classroom challenges of mainstreaming, teachers' rights to privacy, parental pressures on curriculum, fairness in evaluating pupil performance. Cases in mathematics may serve up the following kinds of big ideas for examination: using probability theory to make predictions; plotting coordinates in locating objects; error and uncertainty in mathematical measurement; using statistics to manipulate data. Cases in social studies might examine issues such as the relationship between immigration and the economy, the role of lobbyists in influencing legislation, the media as a force in shaping voter choice, the constitutional right to bear arms versus gun control legislation. These are only the smallest collection of examples of what "big ideas" look like. The range of big ideas underlying any course of study is vast. Big ideas point us in the direction of what we want students to study, to know, to understand about the course content.

A first task in case writing is choosing, from the array of "big ideas" in the course content, those that seem more significant; that would lend themselves readily to thoughtful, vigorous, intensive examination through a case narrative. Obviously, considerable class time will be spent in examining what is chosen, so the idea should be one of substance, one that is worth that kind of time investment.

There are several ways to approach this exercise of choosing a "big idea" for a case. One is to make a list of those curriculum concepts that are included in a course syllabus. Course outlines, syllabi, and curriculum guides are helpful in making these determinations, as are the tables of contents of required textbooks.

Even a partial list is a good resource. What is chosen from that list may reflect a teacher's own values; it may be chosen because the stirrings of a story are already felt; it may be an issue considered particularly relevant for certain groups of students. The criteria for choosing the big idea from the list are not as important as ensuring that the case is framed around an idea of substance related to course content that warrants considerable classroom examination.

Must the big idea be chosen before the case is written? Or may cases be written so that the big idea emerges afterward? There is no hard and fast rule about this. Some case writers prefer to begin with the big idea, which sits, like a beacon, to guide the shaping of the narrative. Other case writers begin with the story and extract the big idea from it. The danger in the latter course of action is that a wonderful story may emerge, but lack a central focus—a big idea related to the course content that warrants examination. In a case without such focus, study groups and debriefing are apt to meander and feel like a rudderless ship.

This is not to say that beginning with the story, rather than the big idea, will always be nonproductive. I have seen teachers begin with the story from which the big idea emerges like the moonrise. I believe that teachers who are able to work this way have an unconscious awareness of the big idea that guides their writing, and that the process of writing lifts the idea from the unconscious to clarity. This approach may be for the more intuitive case writer. The approach that begins with the clearly delineated big idea, however, may be easier to follow. Budding case writers are encouraged to find the pathway that is more productive for them. It doesn't matter as long as the end result is a case in which an idea of substance is at the heart.

What Is the Story?

At its best, a case is a darn good story. As you try to conceptualize your case, think about the story you will tell. If using statistics to manipulate data is the big idea, a story might come to mind about how this was done. Perhaps the story is about how research results are reported in television commercials to persuade buyers about a certain product. Perhaps the story is about how Nielsen ratings are generated about who is watching what TV programs.

If the big idea concerns immigration, perhaps there is a story about a family of Salvadoreans who were illegal aliens and were made to return to their country. Perhaps there is a story about a Mexican family trying to cross the border into California. Perhaps the story is about a woman who lost her job because her employer could get illegal immigrant help for less money than he had to pay her.

Newspapers and magazines are very good sources for ideas for case narratives. There are often articles that bear on issues related to a particular course. A newspaper article about the breakfast buffet set up for delegates to a leadership convention in an attempt to "buy delegate votes" led to the case of the "Cranberry-Orange Muffin Vote" (see Appendix D; Wassermann, 1992b). The news reports about the Exxon Valdez led to "The Case of the Yahagi Maru" (see Appendix B; O'Shea & Wassermann, 1992). Medical and technological breakthroughs that open issues of medical ethics inspire many cases in bioethics.

Textbooks are also good sources for case narratives. For example, while a science text deals with the depletion of ocean fish stocks as a factual event, the case writer used the data from the text to build a story about the dilemma facing a family whose income was dependent on salmon fishing (see Appendix E; Wassermann, 1993d).

Personal stories are often interwoven into case narratives. Teacher-case writers bring to their writing a vast array of personal experiences, which find their way into the stories. These personal events add real-life quality to cases because they have come from real-life experiences. There are many stories in the Naked City, and case writers will find ways wild and wonderful to incorporate them into case narratives.

Who Are the Characters?

Above all, the characters in a case must give the appearance of being real. This is accomplished by "breathing life" into them. People are complex; they do funny things. Sometimes they are irrational. Sometimes they are unpredictable. People also have certain attributes. They may like to eat pizza. They may like certain kinds of movies. They may enjoy wearing certain kinds of clothes. They may be shy, angry, sullen, anxious, scared. Breathing life into a character means giving that character a persona and developing him or her into a three-dimensional being.

Sometimes the budding case writer is too eager to "get on with the story" and tells the tale as a series of descriptions of events, leaving the characters undeveloped. Such a tactic diminishes the power of a case. Readers do not care about events. They care about people. Case writers must give readers people they can care about, and reasons to care about the characters.

Writers should be cautious, however, about developing a cast of players that begins to look like a Cecil De Mille film epic. If there are too many characters, readers may get lost among the multitudes. A writer has to know which characters are central and flesh them out. Which characters are nonessential? Would the case benefit more if they were dropped off the edge of the case world?

The characters should have interesting names. Smith, Jones, and Brown are overused and unimaginative. How about names like Kaliipio and Shugrue and Oz? The telephone directory is a wonderful source of names. However, if a character is patterned after a real person, the name, the character developed, and events around that character should be thoroughly disguised, to protect the anonymity of the original. The last thing a case writer wants is a libel suit.

What's the Dilemma?

A good case builds up to a climax, in which the central character confronts his or her dilemma. Most often, the dilemma hangs on moral or ethical issues. Sometimes, a decision needs to be made where some of the important data are unavailable. Sometimes, personal needs get in the way of a character's behaving as she thinks she should. Sometimes, pressures from outside sources cause characters to behave in ways that make them feel guilty and ashamed.

In facing issues of complexity, characters in cases wrestle with variables that confound them and make them wish for easy answers. These are the "hooks"—the unfinished business on which cases "end."

The dilemma of the case is the force that drives spirited discussion. When the dilemma is real, and is perceived by students to be real, when students are able to project themselves into a similar situation, that is going to add great power to the case. If the dilemma is contrived, phony, or false, the case will lose its power to draw students into meaningful dialogue.

Sometimes, a teacher-case writer has a strong, passionate point of view about a particular issue and is unable to free himself or herself from that bias in writing the case. What may happen, as a consequence, is that the case becomes a polemic for the teacher's bias, the dilemma is subverted, and the "right way to think" is embedded in the resolution. These "cases" are not cases at all, but rather "morality" stories that tell us what to do and how we should behave and what is right. They are especially visible around issues such as the "evils of smoking or taking drugs." If there is explicit or subtle manipulating of student thinking in a case, it is time to classify it as a short story, and either put it on the shelf or present it as a story rather than a case. The dilemma in a case must allow students freedom of choice and must provide for open examination of alternatives in making that choice.

Draft, Re-draft, Re-draft

The bad news is, there's no quick way to write a case narrative. Cases do not fall, without effort, from the mind to the paper. They must be crafted, like clay is sculpted, until the finished product is as close to perfect as it can be made. Sometimes this takes many, many drafts. Until a writer can accept the draft, re-draft, re-draft part of the normal process of writing, and until a writer can give up any illusions about producing a final copy in a first draft, the writing pathway is going to be full of frustration, unrealistic expectations, and disappointment.

A writer has to learn to love the process, as well as the product; has to see the process as satisfying as the end result; has to be willing to enter into that process ungrudgingly. A writer has to be ruthless about discarding false opening paragraphs and passages that don't ring true; has to be able to scrap an entire first draft and start again from scratch. Writers who are in love with every word they write are doomed; parsimony is the key to elegance; overwriting as bad as flatulence. Cut away all the fat; say what has to be said, and finish the sentence. There are no marks for word count. Less, as Hansen (1987) reminded us, is more.

If there are colleagues that can be turned to during the draft, re-draft process, who are able to give feedback on the case narrative, this will doubtless aid the process. Take care, though, who is chosen. Some colleague-critics may be overzealous and accentuate what they consider to be "wrong" and "needing fixing" in the case, failing to cite any good aspects. This can be extremely demoralizing to a budding case writer. But don't look for a colleague who merely offers unconditional praise, either. Choose one who has some sensitivity to good writing and who can give thoughtful and useful feedback that will help in thinking about subsequent changes.

At the end of the draft, re-draft process, it's the case writer who makes the final choices about the changes to be made. Decisions about changes in one's own work are never given over freely to outside critics.

Studying Other Cases

One good way to learn to compose in the Bach style, the music teacher told her students, is to listen to a great deal of Bach's music and analyze how he has constructed the pieces. One good way to learn to write cases is to read many good cases and to analyze how they are constructed. Sometimes, reading cases creates the "mind-frame" for case writing. Good cases, will, at the very least, serve as examples and as departure points for writing.

Sources for obtaining cases have been listed in Chapter 3. Several cases, however, are included in the Appendixes, to provide easy reference points for the aspiring case writer.

CREATING STUDY QUESTIONS

Most cases come with a list of study questions that call for thoughtful examination of the important issues raised by the case. Good study questions build habits of thinking in students. In formulating thoughtful responses, students gain experience in reasoning from the data, arguing a point of view, examining issues from more than one perspective, suspending judgment, differentiating between fact and opinion. What's more, good study questions allow students to enter the more complex world of understanding and appreciating what lies below the surface of events.

Study questions, like case narratives, also have unique characteristics. The first goal of study questions is to bring the important issues in the case under examination. One way of doing this is through sequencing, and this is discussed in more detail below. Sequencing of questions allows the examination to progress from the surface issues to the layer by layer uncovering of the deeper issues.

Yet creating good study questions involves more than effective sequencing. Study questions are framed in a way that encourages thoughtful examination. They also have a particular "tone." They invite, rather than demand; they are clear and unambiguous in what they are asking; they are neither too abstract, too general, or too leading; they avoid forced choice between "yes" and "no"; they avoid overusing the facile "why." The ability to create good study questions is a skill as demanding as writing good narratives. Experiences in writing other types of questions is not a guarantee of immediate success.

Sequencing Questions to Provoke Developmental Analysis

An important factor in the sequencing of study questions is their *relatedness* to what is happening in the case. What are the issues in the case? Who are the players? How did they behave? What circumstances contributed to these behaviors? What happened? Are the perceptions of what happened similar? How are they different? How are the differences explained? Questions begin first with an examination of the events, issues, and characters in the case—the particulars.

A second group of questions move students from the examination of the particulars to an analysis of what lies behind the surface of events. How is this event explained? What hypotheses can be generated? What data support the idea? What assumptions are being made?

A third tier of questions takes the student into deeper analysis. They are more generative and call for evaluations and judgments, applications, and proposed solutions. What plans are being proposed? How are such plans consistent with the data? What other plans are possible? Where might these plans derail? How are the plans alike? How are they different? Which is the best plan? What criteria are being used to make that determination? In some instances, a final study question will take the student into an examination of how an incident in his or her own life was similar to the incident in the case, in that way allowing for comparisons between the case narrative and a student's reality.

Sequencing of questions may be observed by comparing the questions in List A with those in List B. Both lists relate to the biology case "Old Age Ain't for Sissies" (see Appendix F; Wassermann, 1993b), which deals with the process of aging, specifically the deterioration of biological functioning that occurs in all living things. How this deterioration occurs in the family dog is the central issue of the case.

List A

1. What is your understanding of the aging process as it affects dogs? How did this work for Keela, the dog in the case?
2. What, in your understanding, are the biological conditions associated with aging? How do you see this process occurring in Keela?
3. Wrinkled skin, graying hair, and loss of hair seem to be a normal

part of aging, for animals and for people. What is your understanding of how this occurs in aging? How do you explain it?

4. Other conditions associated with aging include chronic diseases,
   like diabetes and arthritis. What is your understanding of these
   diseases? How do you explain the vulnerability of the old to
   chronic diseases?

5. Hearing loss, vision loss, and memory loss are also associated
   with the aging process. What is your understanding of how this
   occurs with age? How do you explain it?

6. If biological deterioration is a normal part of the aging process,
   how do you explain the variability in such deterioration among
   different individuals? What data can you give to support your
   ideas?

7. How, in your understanding, does pain enter into the process
   of biological deterioration? How does this work? What examples
   can you give to support your ideas?

8. What, in your view, might contribute to the retardation of the
   aging process? What are your ideas? What data support your
   ideas?

9. Dr. Wagner prescribed a vitamin supplement for Keela in this
   case. What is your understanding of the role that vitamins play
   in maintaining good health? What data support your ideas?

10. Tim, the boy in this case, has a hard time spending time with
    Keela, watching her be old. How do you explain the feelings
    people have about aging?

11. How do you explain our society's preoccupation with youthful
    appearance? What is your understanding of the various strate-
    gies that people use to try to "stay young" as long as possible?
    What is your understanding of how these strategies work physi-
    cally? Psychologically?

The first five questions in List A begin with a requirement to examine the aging process and the biological conditions associated with
aging. These questions deal with specific events in the case, and some
data about these concepts may be extracted from the case itself. These
five questions open the study of aging by calling for an examination of
specifics.

Questions 6, 7, and 8 require thinking that goes beyond the specifics in the case. These questions call for analyses to be made, for hypotheses to be generated, for concepts and principles to be extracted.

Questions 9, 10, and 11 are generative in that they ask students to
come up with new ideas, to conjecture, to theorize, to make judgments

that go beyond the case, to applications. While these questions use incidents in the case as departure points, they take the student beyond the case to examine issues from a broader perspective. Compare these to the questions in List B.

LIST B

1. What is your definition of diabetes?
2. What kind of diet should people eat to stay healthy?
3. How does our society treat the elderly? How should we treat the elderly?
4. How did Timmy feel when his dog died?
5. Why do people get bald?
6. What does it mean to be old?
7. What are the symptoms of arthritis?
8. Why do people get old?

In List B, while many of the questions may be of individual merit, they seem to leap around, like Mexican jumping beans, in a sequence that defeats developmental examination of the biological determinants of aging. Only Question 4 deals with the case itself. The larger issues in the case are bypassed, as the student is moved directly into more general issues. In the face of the List B questions, one might productively ask, "What was the case for?"

Keying Questions into the Big Ideas

In the earlier section of this chapter, it was suggested that big ideas lie at the heart of each case. When the big ideas in a case narrative are clear, it is easier to write study questions that call for their examination. It is helpful to begin by asking yourself, What ideas of significance does this case raise? What ideas are to be examined in the study questions?

In every case there are issues that are central; there are also other issues that are related, but in a tangential way. To get productive discourse on the more important issues, study questions are better written to examine what is central. Tangential questions may be deferred for later examination.

For example, in the case "It's Up to You, Mrs. Buscemi" (Wassermann, 1993a), a senior high school teacher of math is faced with the dilemma of having to fail a minority student, thus thwarting his opportunity to get into the college that has conditionally accepted him. The case revolves around four central issues: affirmative action; evaluation practices in teaching mathematics; equity in evaluating student performance; and teaching strategies and student learning in math. All of these issues are interrelated in this case and offer healthy possibilities for key-issue questions.

The following questions, adapted from the case, are offered as examples of how study questions are keyed into the issues:

- How would you describe the procedures used by the teacher in making an evaluative judgment of the student's work? What alternative procedures might have been effective?
- Where do you stand on affirmative action that would give students like this one an advantage that might help him to a better future?

These questions go to the heart of two of the big ideas in the case. They are markedly different from the following:

- What learning disabilities might encumber a student's performance in math?
- What are your thoughts about the relevance of the math curriculum for such students?

Although these latter questions are also of educational value, they are only tangentially related to the case. In putting together a list of questions, it is more important to keep to central issues. To go overboard and try to include everything dilutes the potential for the kind of productive examination that leads to understanding.

Phrasing Questions to Challenge Thinking

The way questions are worded can constrain student thinking and limit discussion. These questions lead students to "correct" answers, and discussion terminates as soon as the correct answer has been found. What's more, students quickly learn that original ideas are to be avoided, since only what is expected as "correct" is acceptable. These types of questions, often called "lower order," deal primarily with factual content and require the retrieval of specific information.

Phrased differently, questions can encourage thinking and discussion, opening the response range to include a greater array of ideas. How questions are written implicitly and explicitly affects the quality of student thinking and discussion about case issues (Wassermann, 1992a).

Here are some of the study questions from the case "It's Up to You, Mrs. Buscemi" (Wassermann, 1993a, p. 160). Each question is followed by an analysis to demonstrate how it is phrased to challenge students' thinking.

- *What is your assessment of Violet Buscemi as a teacher? What data in the case have you used in making this determination? What assumptions have you made?* These questions ask students to begin their examination of the procedures the teacher used in helping the student (Adam Wright) to master the math skills that were to be covered in the course. They also implicitly ask for an examination of the evaluation procedures she used in making her assessment of Adam's overall classroom performance. By asking for data to support positions taken in discussion, students are constrained to argue from data and discouraged from offering opinions based purely on personal whim. By asking students to question their assumptions, the teacher discourages them from making forays into unwarranted speculation, sweeping generalization, and positions that data do not support.

- *As you see it, what role did Violet Buscemi play in trying to help Adam Wright? How would you judge her effectiveness?* These questions continue with the examination of Violet's teaching practices. The case is silent on the classroom methods that were used; however, it allows for examining the assumption that a student's failure may be entirely his fault. Were the teacher's methods effective? What are effective methods? What might have been more effective? Less effective? The question calls for making observations about teaching practices and evaluating them according to criteria about teaching effectiveness.

- *How would you describe Adam Wright? Given the data in the case, how would you assess his performance in math class?* These questions call for observations and interpretations of the student's behavior. Was this just a stupid boy? Was he unable to comprehend the math concepts? Was he shirking in not accepting the teacher's offer to help him after class? Was he deserving of the kind of "boost" that the principal thought he should have? These questions encourage students to take a deeper look at their ideas with respect to student intelligence and performance in class. They also offer up to examination teachers' implicit prejudices about students that unconsciously color their perceptions of student performance.

- *How would you describe the procedures that Violet used in making an evaluative judgment of Adam's work? Is this a good way to evaluate students' performance in math? What are your views on it? What alternative procedures might have been effective?* At the heart of these questions is the examination of the reliability and validity of classroom evaluative practices that

bear directly on a student's future. Were Mrs. Buscemi's evaluation practices good? What was good about them? What might have been some
shortcomings? What assumptions have been made about her accuracy
in computing the scores? What assumptions have been made about the
"weight" given to different aspects of Adam's computation (e.g., did she
give full marks only for correct answers or did she give partial marks
for correct process with wrong answers?)? What assumptions have been
made about what Violet Buscemi has chosen to "measure" as a means
of assessing Adam's ability? Students are also asked to generate their
own ideas about alternative forms of evaluation in math.

• *Where do you stand on affirmative action that would give students like
Adam Wright an advantage that might help him to a better future?* In this
question, the issue of affirmative action is opened to students' examination. The question encourages students to examine their own values, take a position on the issue, and argue that position based on experience, data, and the examination of potential consequences.

• *Based on your own school experiences, what do you see as some inequities in evaluation practices? How does a teacher try to deal with those inequities? What strategies do you suggest?* In these questions, students are asked
to observe and evaluate issues of subjectivity and objectivity in evaluation practices. They are also asked to generate ideas for evaluation strategies that are more fair.

• *Given the data in the case, what do you think Violet Buscemi should do?
What do you see as some payoffs for those actions? What do you see as some
negative consequences?* These questions call for students to examine
teacher decision making. Teacher decisions are rarely uncontaminated
by pressures from outside sources. In this case, the teacher's decision is
swayed by the principal's concern that the student should not fail. Yet,
she is firm in her belief that Adam (regrettably) is getting just what he
deserves. Each choice to be made carries special weight—for the teacher,
for the student, for the principal of the school. Each choice is fraught
with consequences. When students discuss this question, they examine the values, beliefs, and institutional pressures that affect their own
educational decision making.

It is important to note that none of the study questions in this case
calls for "correct" answers; that none seeks "the right" solution; that
for each question, a wide range of possible answers is acceptable. That
means that each student must come up with his or her own answers
and often must do so through the process of thoughtful consideration
of how the data and personally held beliefs interface. It is not unusual
for students to change their minds about positions they have taken from

one class session to the next. This indicates that thinking about the issues is far from finished. One important byproduct of such unfinished business is that students learn that issues of consequence rarely, if ever, have any clear-cut answers; that more often it is a person's values, beliefs, and psychological needs that influence decision making. Students who learn to live with such ambiguity are far better equipped for the dissonance that real life offers than are those who are content with simplistic "answers" to life's most complex problems.

The way questions are constructed is also important. Some of the characteristics of that construction are identified below.

Questions That Invite Rather Than Demand

The way certain questions are worded makes them seem as if they are demanding that students respond. They are phrased in command words such as *Explain* the reason for his downfall; *Justify* your answer. While such questions may be productive in challenging students' thinking, the air of authority about them implicitly puts a barrier between teacher and students and creates tension around who has the power and who does not.

Questions that challenge do not have to command. Instead, they may invite; and this is done with a simple turn of phrase: How do you explain the reason for his downfall? Or, What data support your ideas? Worded in this way, the question is offered as an invitation to join in exploration, with the teacher and students as partners in that examination, sharing the power. Questions that invite, rather than command, make it safer for students to do their best thinking. This is not a matter of elegance or form, but rather a matter of creating the kind of climate in which teacher–student partnerships in learning contribute to more productive examination of issues of significance.

Questions That Are Clear

Sometimes, questions are posed in such a way that what they are asking is unclear. This not only results in student confusion; it also results in students' responding to a question different from the one the teacher had in mind. Examples taken from a "quiz" serve to demonstrate the point.

1. What was the extent and duration of the 1930s Dust Bowl drought?
2. What was unique about the Great Depression of the 1930s?
3. Where do you think the issue of self-esteem came from?

When words used in questions are subject to different interpretations (for example, "extent and duration" in Question 1; "unique" in Question 2; and "issue" in Question 3), students may cheerfully put their own spin on the meaning and give responses that are far from what the teacher had in mind.

Writing clear, unambiguous questions may take several drafts, until the questions reach the level of clarity that the teacher is striving for. A good test of whether the questions have reached that level is, once again, to submit questions to a colleague for feedback, or even try them out on a group of students to see if interpretations are consistent. Questions, like cases, profit from several drafts, to ensure that what has been written is clear and comprehensible.

What to Avoid

Questions to avoid are those that are too abstract, too general, too leading. All three types are counterproductive to thoughtful discussion. Questions that are too abstract or too general make it tough for students to zero in on the examination of the important issues. These questions reach way beyond what students are normally able to comprehend and are far beyond students' levels of experience. Of course, what is too abstract or too general at one level, might be just the right "size" for a different student group. But the criteria of high level abstraction and sweeping generality should be considered as potentially counterproductive in constructing study questions.

"How does the sound get on an audiotape?" is one example of a question that is too abstract and beyond most middle school students' conceptual grasp, although it is entirely appropriate for a group of engineers. "Why do some people become alcoholics?" may be fertile ground for a group of professional psychologists, but too complex for high school students to examine in depth.

Questions that are too leading are less than productive in another way. Implicit in the way they are worded is a tilting toward the acceptable response. Students are quick to pick up on questions that subtly force them into a particular response; and thus such questions constrain, rather than encourage, more independent student thought. They certainly diminish the potential for original ideas. Caution should, therefore, be exercised when questions begin to look like these:

1. Would guppies live in this kind of stream?
2. To what category would a creature belong that lives in a burrow in the bank of a river?

3. Where do you think this event takes place?
4. What would be the best way to measure the distance?
5. What are the most important things in these people's lives?

Another group of questions to be avoided, because they tend to constrain thinking, includes those that are set up to force a choice between a "yes" or "no" response. For example:

1. Is a parliamentary system better than a bicameral one?
2. Should we have zoos?
3. Was Robin's decision a good one?
4. Should we have more restrictive gun legislation?
5. Is affirmative action a good thing?

In such forced-choice questions contain seeds of more productive questions, and they can be re-created to encourage a greater range of responses, which is probably what has been intended. For example:

1. In what ways are parliamentary systems better than bicameral ones? In what ways are they less good? What are your ideas about this?
2. What do you see as some advantages of zoos? What do you see as some disadvantages?
3. How do you assess Robin's decision? What criteria have you used in making your judgment?
4. What do you see as some pros and cons of more restrictive gun legislation?
5. What do you see as some potential advantages of affirmative action? What do you see as some disadvantages?

Questions that begin with "why" fall more easily from teacher's pencils than almost any other kind. Yet, more often than not, "why" questions tend to be "too big" in that they reach for the examination of very sophisticated and complex issues, while the questions themselves tend to defeat such intelligent examination. The counterproductive underside to such questions is that they are framed by teachers, and heard by students, as calling for single, brief, and unambiguous answers. Through this kind of question and response pattern, students are apt to learn that there are quite simple answers for unspeakably complex questions, and they learn to be satisfied with such simplicity, even as adults. Examples of such "why" questions include

1. Why is there pollution?
2. Why did Hamlet kill his stepfather?
3. Why are people prejudiced?
4. Why do people not bother to vote?
5. Why are so many politicians corrupt?
6. Why does Japan have such a vibrant economy?

Given the reach of such questions, once again, it is better to reframe them, and thus tame them into questions that more productively encourage thoughtful examination of the big ideas. For example:

1. Tell about some of the ways you know in which pollution occurs.
2. What kinds of characteristics do you see in Hamlet that made it possible for him to kill his stepfather?
3. What, in your experience, are some examples of prejudice? How do you explain such behavior?
4. How do you explain people's reluctance to exercise their franchise? What hypotheses can you suggest?
5. What, in your view, contributes to the health of Japan's economy? What do you see as some essential conditions for a healthful economy?

CONCLUSION

The aspiring case writer will find that the best way to determine the effectiveness of a case narrative and its study questions is to test its power in the "marketplace." Teaching a case and letting students work over the study questions will give teachers a fair view of how well the case serves to promote examination of the important issues and concepts. Based on such field trials, teachers will be able to refine the narrative and to reframe study questions until they reach the point of working to the teacher's satisfaction. The case and study questions will, inevitably, go through several field test drafts; but when the process is completed, teachers will have greater assurance that both case and study questions effectively do the job.

A related discussion of questioning strategies is found in Chapter 7, which deals with questions and responses used in the oral forum of debriefing a case.

5 | Preparing Students to Learn with Cases

General math seemed to be an unusual arena for case method teaching, but Liam Wilson was convinced that case studies provided better opportunities for his students to understand general math concepts than did lecturing. Having observed case method teaching in other curriculum areas, Wilson was enthusiastic about its potential to enliven a traditionally spiritless class, where students "put in time" merely to get the course credit. He also believed that students who learned about math in a case study context would more readily see applications of math to their lives. Math, he hoped, would be lifted from routine pencil and paper assignments, done for the purpose of getting through the course, to a vital inquiry that had relevance and meaning in their lives.

After the first few days of classes, devoted largely to administrative matters, Wilson presented the students with their first case to read for homework. "The Case of the Yahagi Maru" (see Appendix B; O'Shea & Wassermann, 1992) is about the collision of an oil tanker with an iceberg and the subsequent inquiry to determine cause and culpability. Math concepts addressed in the case include measurement and measurement error, plotting coordinates, and other mathematical calculations involved in navigation.

To his delight, Wilson found that all of his Grade 11 students had read the case. He began the class by asking the students to form groups of five or six to work on the study questions and explained that he would allow 45 minutes for group work, which would be followed by a 45-minute, whole-class debriefing session.

Wilson observed from the sidelines the small group interactions. One group seemed very inactive, treating the study questions as if each were an infectious disease, to be kept at arm's length and given grudging attention. A group consisting of five boys who sat in the back, near the door, seemed to be having a wonderful time chatting, but Liam was certain that math in no way entered into the conversation. A third group of five moved from question to question, answering each dutifully with short answers that barely began to address the substantive issues. This group was concerned with getting the "answers" as quickly as possible, and proceeded through the list as if they were running the Boston marathon. In the absence of any discussion of mathematical concepts, this group "finished" all the study questions in less than 10 minutes, at which point they sat back in silence for the rest of the session. The two remaining groups seemed, at least, to have dug into the questions, and their discussions seemed productive and focused on mathematical issues. Liam Wilson was discouraged by what he had seen.

At 45 minutes past the hour, he called the groups together for a whole-class debriefing of the issues. Beginning with a facts-based question, "How would you describe the chain of events that led to the sinking of the Yahagi Maru?" he found, to his dismay, that students were focused on the issue of culpability, rather than on mathematics. No matter how he tried to bring the discussion around to math, students would finesse him each time. They wanted to confirm that the fault of the sinking lay with the captain. If the captain had not been sleeping in his cabin (even though it was 3:00 A.M.), he would have been able to prevent the disaster. Issues of calculating positions (e.g., the position of the ship, the iceberg), of error in mathematical calculation, of the math involved in navigation, gave way to the study of the human drama. Even there, simplistic judgments were tossed off as truths, without appreciation for assumptions being made. Intransigence in student thinking did not yield to examination of alternatives. Liam Wilson was buoyed by the intensity of the discussion, but disappointed by the content. He believed that the whole-class debriefing was a reflection of the limited range of discussion in the small group sessions. The students seemed unequipped to wrestle with the challenges that discussion of ideas involves.

In the last few minutes of class, Wilson shifted gears from debriefing the case, to ask the students to consider the teaching method. How did students respond to case method teaching? Liam perceived a distinct lack of enthusiasm in the responses. Students seemed perplexed. What did any of this have to do with math? One girl raised her hand timidly. "I liked this approach," she offered. "It shows us that math is more than just a bunch of exercises put on the blackboard. Math has application to real life." Some other students nodded in agreement, just as the bell rang. It was far from a universally shared view.

As students began to leave, one girl, hanging back, put up her hand.

"Yes, Marla?"

"Well, I just wanted to know, Mr. Wilson. What's the answer?"

Any teacher who has been in and around classrooms for any time is no stranger to students' dependency, their inability to function on their own, their needs to have "right" answers. Traditionally, educational settings, from kindergarten to graduate school, have perpetuated this dependency and fed this need. Classrooms in which teachers dominate and make all decisions of consequence, and assignments that are tilted toward single answers that are either right or wrong, with rewards and penalties meted out in direct consequence, do their jobs well in producing the kind of behavior seen in Wilson's class.

Instead of learning to think, students become "lesson learners." They believe that "answers" are the key to knowing; but, in fact, they are unable to use what they know in problem-solving contexts. Their understanding of the larger issues is hopelessly naive. These classroom conditions have produced a crop of students who are certain when suspension of judgment is more appropriate; who leap impulsively to solutions, where caution is called for; who are dogmatic about their ideas, where examination of alternatives is necessary; who are afraid to take the risks associated with advancing a new idea (Raths, Wassermann, Jonas, & Rothstein, 1986).

Teachers who are considering advancing case method teaching with an "untried" and "naive" group of students are likely to find many of the above behaviors surfacing in full flourish. These student behaviors are not only counterproductive to the ethos of case method teaching, they are also considerably vexing to teachers, for they do not disappear on command. Lesson-learners, no matter what their age, do not become serious thinkers by exhortation. Such paradigm shifts require learning experiences of a different type and a teacher's understanding that there are no shortcuts to the time it takes for students to grow from "naive" to "wise."

Preparing students to learn with cases is helped by a few familiar teaching strategies. These include

- Orienting students to the process—including informing and explaining about procedures, behavioral expectations, goals
- Encouraging effective study group work
- Involving students in systematic, ongoing evaluation that includes analysis of the process, students' participation, and suggestions for improvement

ORIENTING STUDENTS TO THE PROCESS

Before launching any new program, teachers usually take pains to introduce it to the students. A good teaching strategy, in any circumstances, it is particularly important when programmatic experiences will be markedly different from what has gone on in the past.

Orienting students to case method teaching need not be an arduous, long-term activity; but ensuring that procedures, expectations, and goals are clear will, at the very least, provide important information about the journey to the noninitiated travelers. The following list of suggestions should be considered guidelines to the what and the how of program introduction. Some of these are made explicit before the new program begins. Others will be an ongoing source of discussion, examination, and reassurance.

1. *Introduce students to the methodology by describing the what of cases, study groups, and debriefing activities, as well as the how.* Such descriptions might include reference to how cases work to promote examination of ideas, how study groups endeavor to work cooperatively in discussions, and how debriefing is used to further student thinking about the issues. Allowing students adequate time to raise questions about their concerns at this stage might forestall later problems.

2. *Let your students in on what you consider to be the benefits of case method teaching.* It may be nice to share your enthusiasms for this new program with your students —especially with respect to how you think it will benefit student learning. Students will appreciate knowing that you consider students' ability to see issues in their complexity, to learn to reason from the data, to make thoughtful, informed, wise decisions, to appreciate different points of view, to use their own initiative in securing data to support their ideas, as important as content knowledge. Students may need explicit information about how you see case method teaching as a means for realizing such learning goals.

3. *Communicate your appreciation for how case method teaching raises new challenges for students habituated to more traditional methods.* Teaching goals and student learning outcomes for case method teaching are different in form and substance from more traditional methods. Case method offers greater freedoms for students, but demands greater individual and group responsibility. Dependence on the teacher and on the teacher's directions is replaced by the expectation that students will function on higher levels of individual autonomy. It may be helpful to communicate your awareness about the new challenges that students are facing.

4. *Be explicit about your expectations.* For example:

- Students should be prepared by having read the case in advance of class and by familiarizing themselves with the study questions.
- Study groups (whether in or out of class) are expected to give serious attention to their discussion of the study questions.
- Whole-class debriefing also follows certain procedures in which individual students interact with the teacher in an extended examination of issues, and in which students' ideas are respected and given serious consideration.

In making expectations clear, it is important to stress the need for being prepared, for group cooperation, for respect for each other's ideas, for allowing that all points of view are heard, for a harmonious working group. It may be helpful to point out that effective small group work depends, to a great extent, on students' assuming responsibility for how the group work is conducted.

5. *Alert students to the shift in emphasis from "answers" to the "examination of ideas."* Especially in schools where students have been programmed in "single, right answer" methodology, teachers may find that students are having difficulty in making the transition from short answer responses to discussions of ideas. Being explicit about the differences in what is required, and helping students to make the transition, may ease their way into this more challenging arena of cognitive functioning.

6. *Provide students with information about how evaluation will be carried out.* At every instructional level, the issue of evaluation is of pivotal importance to students. Therefore, it will be reassuring for students to know, at the outset, what evaluative procedures will be used, what criteria are to be used in the process, and how grades will be determined. Consistency, fairness, and openness to students' concerns will go a long way in alleviating the stress around evaluation. Whatever assessment measures are chosen to evaluate students' learning must, of course, be consistent with the ethos of case method teaching. Otherwise, students will quickly learn that the behaviors necessary to pass the test (not those necessary for vigorous, intelligent discussion of issues) are the ones that really count.

7. *Be empathic with student difficulties in handling the freedoms.* An important requirement in case method teaching is that students assume more responsibility for their learning. Teachers are not overseers of every student action, every activity. Much freedom is given over to students

in trusting that they will work carefully, responsibly, and thoughtfully. Students may wish to know, at the outset, what these degrees of freedom involve—with respect to both parameters and ownership of consequences.

The freedoms that case method teaching offers students may, at first, seem like a "free ride." Not until one lives with those freedoms does one appreciate the responsibilities that are incurred with them. When the nature of their responsibilities hits home, students may understandably balk. There may be a longing to return to the security of a teacher-dominated program, in which students are told what to do, how to do it, and what answers are "right." Students may need to be alert to these stresses and strains of travel along the pathway of achieving independence, which are integral to the process of growing toward maturity. Empathy for the anxiety that case method teaching provokes, for procedures that lack clear, well-defined answers, may be reassuring to students who are embarking into the uncertainty of unknowns.

8. *Be sympathetic to students' impatience with the process.* Learning of any consequence (including knowledge, attitudes, skills, and appreciations) takes time to be planted, cultivated, and weeded, until it is seen in mature growth. The process of growing toward thoughtfulness takes time and careful nurturing. Students who are easily discouraged, who are fearful, and who find the process of inquiry unsettling may need to be reminded, from time to time, that the goals and outcomes of case method teaching are not easily won, but that there are important payoffs down the pike for students who engage seriously in the process and do not give up.

Teachers who have watched students struggle with the demands of new programs, new methodologies, and different expectations, will be sympathetic to the necessity for both good orientation strategies as well as patience on the teacher's part during the time it takes for students to develop the skills necessary for learning in these new ways. For no matter how effective the orientation strategies are, and no matter how skillful the teacher in using them, there is no magic zap that turns frogs into princes.

ENCOURAGING EFFECTIVE STUDY GROUP WORK

It is important to note that not every case teacher uses the convention of study groups as "advanced organizers" to precede debriefing. At the Harvard Business School, the exemplar of case method teaching, no study group mandate is made. Yet, either because of tradition, or because study group discussion is found to be essential in preparation for the rigorous whole-class discussion, students, on their own initiative, form their own groups that meet regularly throughout the semester. In some case method contexts, especially at the university level, students are launched directly from the reading of the case into whole-class debriefing.

While clinical data to support the use of study groups are limited, informed opinion, coupled with feedback from large numbers of students, makes a persuasive case for their use. And while study groups may be especially important for students new to case method teaching, this "rehearsal" stage of discussion seems to be a productive preliminary even for those students habituated to the process.

It seems clear that the small group, in which students discuss ideas with peers, is a safer context in which to risk putting ideas under examination. The practice students get in small group discussion contributes to more effective large group discussion. Ideas that have been tried out in a climate of safety can then be risked in a larger forum. Students grow less fearful about offering their ideas. They get more practice in developing more intelligent arguments. One graduate student used the term "washing through" as a way of explaining how study group discussion was a first stage in testing the validity of her ideas.

As informal practice sessions in which students' discussion skills are strengthened, study groups are more than worth the time they consume and the efforts given over to their effective functioning. Data from Adam's (1992) study confirm that study groups are seen to promote greater tolerance for the ideas of others, a willingness to listen to others' opinions, and increased comfort in expressing a point of view. Of course, these are some of the expected gains from case method teaching in the overall. However, the use of study groups is more than likely to intensify and increase the possibility of these growth gains.

It is also clear, though, that as study groups contribute to more effective functioning in debriefing, the process cuts both ways. Debriefing also contributes to the effectiveness of study groups. On one front, students who are immersed in debriefing sessions quickly learn that what occurs in their small groups has direct payoff for their discussions in the more rigorous, whole-class debriefing. On the other, the more challenging intellectual demands of whole-class sessions implicitly impose standards of inquiry in study groups. What's more, the modeling of teacher–student interactions and the nature of the discourse also point the way to more effective small group process.

Forming Study Groups

Where teachers are going to use study groups, there are at least two courses of action: prearranged groups and ad hoc groups. As in most choices teachers make, both have advantages and disadvantages, and teachers will likely choose what seems more appropriate to their level of instruction and to the nature of the student group.

Prearranged groups give teachers the option of ensuring that the student "mix" is a productive one; that "talkers" and "nontalkers" are evenly distributed; that each group contains a core of more highly functioning students; that students who are "bad pairs" are split up. These are considerable advantages for students who are new to working together in unsupervised small group settings and may be especially appropriate at the secondary school level. That students' choices are preempted may be a small price to pay for more effective group functioning. Teachers who choose initially to prearrange groups may offer students more options for choice later in the semester. Effective group size is between four and six—enough for a critical mass, and not too many to interfere with adequate individual participation.

Ad hoc groups (where the teacher simply directs students to "form groups of approximately four to six") allow for greater student choice with respect to who will work with whom. Ad hoc groups have the advantage of flexibility; students may change their groups from week to week, thereby exposing themselves to a wider range of student opinion and behaviors. Students also have the option of freeing themselves from "low functioning" groups, since the flexible memberships automatically change group dynamics. The downside of ad hoc groups is that the teacher has very little control over group arrangement. Yet, for teachers who are able to give up control over who belongs in what group, the open choices of ad hoc groups are particularly attractive, especially at college and university levels of instruction, where open choice of working partners seems to be a more respectful approach.

Prearranged and ad hoc groups work equally well in both in-class and out of class arrangements.

Deciding on In-Class or on Out of Class Groups

As with prearranged versus ad hoc group formations, choices about whether study groups are to work during scheduled class time or as out of class assignments are once again a matter of teacher discretion. In making that choice, teachers will have to weigh factors of class scheduling, numbers of class hours per week, overall deployment of class time with respect to all class activities, and logistics of out of class arrangements. Obviously, if it is virtually impossible for students to gather for out of class study groups, that would necessitate some form of in-class arrangement.

Where study groups can work within the existing class schedule, teachers are able to observe group functioning and individual student behavior, and use those data to their advantage. (The nature of teachers' supervision of study groups is discussed in more detail below.) Teachers will, of course, want to assess whether the use of class time for study groups is worth that expenditure of time.

Where there is adequate time in the semester for the big ideas in the course curriculum to be addressed in class through both small group discussions and large group debriefing, the choice is obvious. If a teacher's battle with the course curriculum and the clock makes impossible the use of in-class study groups, the choice is again obvious.

When logistics seem to present obstacles to either form of arrangement, it is time for the teacher to sit down, perhaps with a helpful colleague, and problem-solve ways of dealing with whatever obstacles appear to stand in the way of forming the groups. Any strategy tried and found wanting can always be changed, and that kind of flexibility allows teachers considerable freedom to learn about what can be made to work for them.

Providing Guidance During Initial Study Group Sessions

Guidance and support offered during the beginning stages of study group work may be more overt or subtle, depending on a teacher's style. Style, however, is not to be confused with the nature of the support offered. Support may not be too directive, lest it perpetuate student dependency. Nor may it be too off-hand, lest it not provide sufficient structure and grounding. The art lies in finding the middle ground—using strategies that encourage and are empathic, but avoiding stepping in to take charge, helping students to answer the questions, or giving the teacher's points of view. This is especially difficult when teachers see groups who are stuck and cannot function on their own.

For students with limited experiences with study groups, an introduction to the "rules of the game" is a good idea. In such an introduction, the teacher clarifies expectations about group discussions and responsibilities. At this stage some teachers offer advice about group process; others leave it to the groups to wade through the initial "group grope" stages and into more productive procedures. For teachers who choose to provide advice, the following are suggested as guidelines for student study groups:

Listen carefully to each other's ideas.

Work at trying to understand what is being said.

Treat all members' ideas respectfully.

Don't interrupt.

Be tolerant in listening to ideas that are different from yours.

Don't be a silent participant. Make sure to offer your own ideas.

Raise questions when you don't understand. Ask for examples.

Never put down another member for what she or he has said.

Keep the discussion focused on the issues.

During discussions, be alert to avoid sweeping generalizations, value judgments that pass as facts, extreme statements, simplistic conclusions, and conclusions that are not supported by data.

Alternatively, study group guidelines may be generated by the class, under the teacher's direction. However, even with clear and explicit guidelines, it is more than likely that some groups will, at the beginning stages, flounder and find productive discussions difficult. Off-task behavior, extreme dependency, dysfunctional members, and absence of "harmony" indicate group malfunction, and strategies for working with these behaviors are suggested below. While these apply primarily to in-class groups, whenever possible teachers might consider "visiting" with out of class study groups, by prior arrangement with the group. While this means extra work for the already overcommitted teacher, the payoff may be well worth the extra time. Sitting in with a group, as a silent, nonparticipating observer, offers all the benefits of in-class observation plus the opportunity to use the suggestions offered in the previous section, as needed. Group visits should be rotated, so the teacher has a chance to visit all groups several times. Visits may not be necessary once the groups are fully functioning; yet students might like to know that the teacher is available for visits, on call.

Handling Group Problems

Off-task groups. Where the teacher observes that a study group is off task, a subtle reminder to the group is the teacher's presence nearby. Manley-Casimir (Manley-Casimir & Wassermann, 1989) used this strategy with a group of undergraduate students in an education class.

> Some study groups had a great deal of difficulty focusing on the study questions. In these groups, one or two participants would pick up the ball and run with it—to South America. In some groups, students were unable to use group process skills to keep discussions on track.

As they grew to know each other better, students (like water) began to seek other students "at their own level" gravitating toward the same students each week. This tended to produce groups that we thought of as "higher functioning" and others that functioned on lower cognitive levels. In the lowest functioning groups, the silent, but physical presence of an instructor helped to bring the group back on task. (p. 290)

It may be tempting to consider addressing an off-task group directly with a reprimand that condemns inappropriate behavior, but it is not a strategy that is recommended here. Although appearing to do the job of "behavior management," such a move explicitly widens the breach between teacher and students—and is inconsistent with the ethos in which teachers and students are partners in learning. Groups rarely assume responsibility for their own behavior without the psychological freedom to do that.

While it has not been my experience to find groups that never shift from lower to higher levels of functioning on their own in time, it is certainly conceivable that some students' entry behaviors might be so counterproductive as to warrant more intrusive strategies. In that event, the teacher's presence as an active group member—not the authority, but a collaborative inquirer—might be a helpful procedure.

Teachers are cautioned, however, to be obviously available during the in-class study group sessions. It is easy to be tempted to use that time to do chores, to get on top of accumulated paper work. But such behavior sends to students a clear message of teacher disinterest in the groups and in their work. The teacher's availability during the study group sessions is reassuring. The students know the teacher is there, if needed. The presence of the teacher indicates interest, psychological support, and caring, and is a strong deterrent to off-task behavior.

Very dependent groups. Students who have been programmed into extreme dependence on their teachers may try to manipulate the teacher into being more directive. Questions like, "What do you want us to do here?" and "What do we do next?" tip the teacher off to such dependency behaviors. Responding to such questions with new directives (e.g., "Do it this way") is a sure way to perpetuate dependency behaviors. Alternatively, the teacher can be empathic, encouraging, and nondirective, letting the group struggle through the process on their own. For example, if a student in a group says, "I'm not sure what you want us to do," the teacher may reply, "I recognize that these questions are hard and different from what you have been used to. But I'm interested in learning what you think about these issues and I'm sure you have some ideas to share. I have confidence in your ability to rise to these challenges."

Groups with dysfunctional members. The silent observer role of the teacher offers other advantages. It allows for studying the functioning of individual members of groups. Which students tend to monopolize the discussion? Which students never contribute? Which students are authoritarian in their positions? Which repeatedly interrupt other speakers? Which resort to "put downs" of others' ideas? Teachers may use these data in private conferences with students after class, not as a means of reprimand, but rather as observations about group functioning, the objective being, How might I help this student become a more productive group member?

Groups that don't harmonize. Some mixtures of students just seem to create disharmony. The students are unable to get past personalities and into the issues. Where the teacher has observed that a particular mixture in a particular group is simply not working, there is always the option of shifting students around and changing the mix. This is especially useful where one student has become a particular nuisance and occasionally shifting that student tends to "spread the burden" around to be more equally shared. In ad hoc group arrangements, this situation is likely to resolve itself as group composition changes.

Examining the Functioning of Study Groups

Reflection, after experience, provides an opportunity to analyze what has occurred and offers insight into how improvements may be made. Involving students in a post hoc discussion about the functioning of their study groups is an effective strategy in evaluating process and identifying remedial procedures. Five minutes at the end of each class might be all that is needed to address questions such as

> How did the study groups work today?
> What procedures did you use to ensure productive discussion?
> How did the discussion get sidetracked?
> What ideas do you have for improving the quality of the discussion for next time?

It is essential, during these reflective examinations, that teachers remain neutral, allowing the students to offer their views. Should teachers try to impeach student ideas, condemn suggestions, be sarcastic in their comments, or in any way undermine or devalue student statements, the process of reflective examination is doomed.

Evaluative sessions can be abandoned when the teacher is assured that study groups no longer profit from post hoc examination because they are at last productive discussion cohorts.

Providing Affirmation of Growth

Everybody likes to know that he or she is doing well, and this is especially true when students have risen to new challenges and have worked hard to do so. When the teacher remembers to appreciate students' efforts, and acknowledges their progress in becoming more thoughtful members of small and large groups, students are further encouraged and affirmed. Of course, such affirmation must be both honest and sincere; phony sentiments will work against both teacher and students in this developmental process.

INVOLVING STUDENTS IN REFLECTION
ON THE CASE STUDY PROCESS

Some study groups may "take off" quickly and move to highly productive discourse in a short time. Others may need more time to grow toward more thoughtful examination of issues. Where habits of thinking and intelligent discourse need time to grow, such growth does not occur overnight, nor does it happen in response to command. Yet, intelligent discourse is a primary goal of case method teaching and teachers should expect no less.

Experience with thinking and opportunities to reflect on experience build habits of thinking (Raths, Wassermann, Jonas, & Rothstein, 1986). Case method teaching is, of course, a consistent and continuous challenge to student thinking—and the individual and collective growth that occurs as a result of such experience has been well documented (Adam, 1992; Ewing, 1990; Raths et al., 1986; Wassermann & Ivany, 1988). Involving students in ongoing reflection on the process takes students a giant step toward such growth.

"We love this class," one of my sixth-grade students once told me, "and we are having a lot of fun. But I'm afraid we aren't learning very much." While I was astonished and chagrined to hear such sentiments (after all, I thought I had been doing an excellent job!), the experience alerted me to inquire further and uncover several assumptions that both

I and the students had been making. Students who, throughout earlier grades, had learned about "how learning was supposed to occur" from an entirely different set of experiences, believed that learning activities had to follow those forms to be of value. Group projects, class discussions, designing investigations, self-evaluation—well, all of that stuff was quite nice, but what did any of it have to do with "real" learning? I, as teacher, had assumed that the benefits of learning in these different ways would have been obvious to my students.

When I left public school teaching and joined the academy, I was even more astonished to find that many adult learners had similar appreciations for "how learning is supposed to occur." Adult learners too, need to be involved in examination and analysis of the process— to help them see what the benefits of such different forms of learning are, and how they, individually and collectively, are in fact benefiting.

Inviting students to enter into the activity of reflecting on and examining the how and the what of their learning with cases benefits them in several ways. First, it allows them to discern and appreciate how their thinking is being challenged. Second, they are helped to see how their knowledge grows, even without the teacher at center stage transmitting information. Third, it provides the means for enabling them to see how the process builds their habits of thinking. In addition, they will be able to see how they are becoming more assertive and independent in their functioning. Suggestions for how to involve students in reflection on the process are offered in Chapter 7.

A group of Grade 11 students who were asked to reflect, in retrospect, upon the impact of case method teaching on their learning, offered the following responses:

> The case study method in the classroom allows you to listen to other points of view, consider them, and then form an analysis of the issue using these other points of view. A better understanding and examination of the issue is possible.
>
> The use of the case study method has broadened my way of thinking on certain issues.
>
> I listen to others better now before I respond.
>
> The case study process gives the students an atmosphere and surrounding where they feel comfortable. This increased my ability to communicate and understand other people's points of view, which is critical out in the "real world."
>
> I think more about how others will be affected by my decisions.
>
> I think more about the issue before coming to a conclusion. Not just jumping automatically to a conclusion.

I am making choices in what I believe and not backing away from it.

The case study method teaches you to consider all points of view and all possibilities before you form an opinion. This makes for better decisions. You start to use this way of thinking in everyday decisions. (Adam, 1992)

Preparing students to learn with cases may require some effort on the teacher's part; yet good preparation is critical in helping students to be more comfortable, and thus more willing to accept the challenges of learning with cases. With students playing active "studenting" roles, there is greater likelihood that case method teaching will serve them well in building their habits of thinking and preparing them to use these habits in their lives. However, the teacher who sets about preparing students to learn with cases is cautioned to remember Paul Winchell's (1954) advice to budding ventriloquists: "Don't rush. Don't get impatient. Don't get discouraged. Don't ever give up."

6 | Preparing to Teach with Cases

"It's very intimidating," Roger Beauchamp tells his colleagues as he contemplates teaching with cases. "You can't plan for it in advance like you do when you are preparing a lecture. Lots of things could go wrong when you have to respond 'on the spot.' I'd feel more comfortable if I knew how to prepare for teaching a case."

Despite McAninich's (1993) disclaimer that teaching with cases "can't be planned out in advance" (p. 101), effective case teachers can and do engage in a series of planning steps that contribute to more productive and satisfying classroom results. Even highly experienced case teachers who have taught the same case many times have been known to prepare extensively in advance of a class session. The notion that a case teacher simply rolls into class, sheds his jacket and tie, and launches spontaneously into a brilliantly orchestrated case discussion is as inaccurate and misleading as the Hollywood version of Elizabethan England.

Good advance preparation is never a guarantee that everything will go as it should—that is, that the teacher will be able to respond to every student's statement productively; that students will be eager to volunteer their ideas; that the teacher will be able to keep the discussion focused on the big ideas and not allow it to get sidetracked onto tangential pathways. But preparation will, at least, minimize potential problems and provide the teacher with a clearer framework for helping students examine issues of consequence.

GUIDELINES FOR PREPARING TO TEACH WITH CASES

The following suggestions are offered as guidelines for teachers who understand that good advance preparation is one key to successful case teaching.

Know the Case

The first step in preparing to teach a case is intimate acquaintance with the case itself. This requires more than merely reading the case in advance. It requires perhaps several readings, and the kind of study that puts all the case details at one's fingertips. The more knowledgeable the teacher is about the facts in the case, the more he or she is able to use that information in raising questions for student analysis.

Obviously, the more times teachers teach a case, the more familiar they will be with the details. Yet, familiarity should not preclude a teacher's *a priori* thoughtful review of the case, its details, nuances, and overall arc.

Know the Issues

Each good case raises several issues that beg for examination. In some cases, the issues are made explicit by the author in a "Notes to the Teacher" section. For other cases, teachers are on their own in lifting out, from the case and study questions, those issues to be examined in class discussion.

Teachers who find issues identified in "Notes" are not constrained to discuss the case from those perspectives only. They may find other big ideas that are equally applicable to the case and more relevant to the classes they are teaching. For example, in the case "Old Age Ain't for Sissies" (see Appendix F; Wassermann, 1993b), while the "Notes" call for examining issues related to the biological determinants of aging, appropriate for study in bioscience classes, the case is equally applicable to family life classes, where examination of issues relating to the death of loved ones may be just as profitable. Whichever the context, teachers who are clear, in advance, about the issues they wish students to examine in case discussion, will have an easier job of keeping the discussion on track and focused on those issues.

In preparation for teaching the case "It's Up to You, Mrs. Buscemi" (Wassermann, 1993a), Laura Farrell identifies those broad perspectives around which she will generate questions for students' examination. She knows she wants her students to look at this case through the lens of affirmative action. She also wants students to examine fairness and equity in evaluation practices, as well as validity of classroom tests. Finally, she hopes to give some attention to the teacher's autonomy in making a decision about a student's grade. Having identified these issues in advance, she has a clear framework to build the pathways down which her questions will travel. She knows which issue will begin the case discussion and which she is prepared to drop if the discussion of other issues becomes very productive. She also may arm herself, in advance, with some prepared questions that highlight certain aspects of the issues.

One of the more intriguing aspects of cases is their flexibility. Unlike a series of facts that are intransigent, a single case may be used to examine different issues. This means that teachers who have used the math case "Yahagi Maru" (see Appendix B; O'Shea & Wassermann, 1992) to examine issues of plotting points on a graph may, after time, shift perspectives and use the same case to examine issues of accuracy in measurement. This flexibility allows an experienced case teacher many advantages. Cases used many times in the past take on new life; and good cases' potentiality to open new avenues of awareness makes their teaching life extensive. Whichever way the big ideas in a case evolve and shift, the teacher never ignores that aspect of preparation that requires clear identification, in advance of the session, of the perspectives to be examined in class discussion.

Prepare Good Questions in Advance

Raising the "right" questions in response to a student's statement is a cultivated art. Knowing which question to ask and when; how to frame it with clarity and precision; and how to ask it so that it invites, rather than intimidates, are skills born of years of practice. The ability to think on the spot (McAninich, 1993), formulating questions that productively engage students in intelligent examination of the issues, is arguably one of the most complex aspects of case teaching, and Chapter 7 is devoted to the "how" of mastering these skills. However, preparing questions in advance may work to teachers' advantage in keeping the discussion focused on the issues of consequence.

Where good study questions exist for a case, debriefing questions may be "lifted" directly from these. They may be a rephrasing of study questions; or they may combine study questions in a special way. They may depart from study questions, calling for student thinking beyond what was discussed in study groups. However they are constructed, they should, at the very least, reflect those issues of significance that are being called into examination.

Preparation of questions in advance helps to keep the debriefing on track, and it is helpful to write these out, so that they may be referred to during the discussion. Preparing questions in advance also gives practice in framing them with clarity and with a gentleness that bespeaks invitation. The practice of writing good questions eventually translates to speaking on the spot.

Debriefing questions progress in tiers of escalating difficulty, much as they do in study questions (see Chapter 4). The opening questions, or first tier, may be survey questions; for example, What issues of significance did this case raise for you? They may call for data: What do you know about this teacher? What do you know about [this particular] style of architecture? They may be questions that call for identification of what students see as the central dilemma: Where do you see the primary source of conflict in this case? All three types of questions may be used in the first tier, that group of questions that opens the examination of the issues in the case.

Second tier questions begin the call for analysis: What is your analysis of this teacher's evaluation practices? How is [this] style of architecture different from [that]? How do you explain the student's inability to perform well in the subject? What do you see as the social conditions that contributed to the famine? What do you see as some inequities in the situation? What assumptions are being made?

Questions in the next tier raise the level of challenge to student thinking. These call for evaluations to be made and for the proposal of plans of action. For example: What is your evaluation of this teacher's methods? What criteria are being used to make that assessment? What should she have done instead? What plan would you have used to improve the situation? How do you see the goals of the plan as consonant with the means? What are some potential consequences of what is being proposed? Which plan is the best? What should [the person] do now?

A final tier of questions addresses more global issues. For example: Where do you stand on the issue of affirmative action? What is your position on the patient's right to choose his or her own method of treatment? What do you see as this country's role in providing access to immigrants whose lives are in peril?

Rosmarin (1985) describes how the "driving and directional energy of any good discussion class comes from the teacher's questions" (p. 37). In her profile of C. R. Christensen and his work in the Harvard "discussion leader" seminar, she writes:

> The best questions are those that seem as spontaneous as they are probing, that seem to be spur-of-the-moment responses to the classroom drama. In other words, they are the very questions that seem most immune to pedagogic analysis. Christensen, however, showed

us that this spontaneity can itself be conceptualized and planned. Hence, his "typology of questions." First, the exploratory questions: What are the "facts"? What went wrong? What can be done? Then the challenge or testing questions: Are these solutions or interpretations adequate to the problem? Are others possible? Where might these plans go wrong? Next, the contextual and relational questions, the "weaving devices" that at once broaden the perspective of the class and begin the process of tying things together: How is this solution like that solution? How is it different? What kinds of solutions do we have?

Then come the "priority" questions: Which is the best solution? Why? Finally, the concluding and conceptualizing questions: What have we learned? What are the principles involved in the choices we've made? How do they relate to choices we've made in previous classes? The most important thing to remember about questions, however, is this: "A good question is never answered." It always has offspring. It always engenders more questions and thus more thought. (p. 37)

As in most decisions case teachers make, the choice of which questions to use and how they progress is an indvidual one. But it is an informed choice, based on a preconceived idea of which questions have the potential of digging out the key elements of the case, and of challenging students' thinking about issues of consequence. While questions prepared in advance need not be adhered to faithfully, they seem to keep the discussion centered, and become like "money in the bank" for the teacher caught up in the intensity of debriefing.

Know the Students

How students respond (or, indeed, whether they respond at all) may be the single most important variable in the success of discussion teaching. A helpful strategy is to know the students—whether they are resistant, even hostile; whether they are singularly unresponsive; whether their responses are lackluster, banal, arrogant, defensive (all of which are more than likely and have the potential for "making or breaking" a good discussion). This strategy is not unique to case teaching. It is a strategy used by good teachers everywhere, no matter what the pedagogy.

In the very first instance, teachers should know students' names and call them by their names. In a large lecture hall, name cards, with names clearly visible to the teacher, are placed on students' table tops. In some classes, students are asked to keep the same seats, giving the teacher a better chance at remembering who is who. Gathering biographical data about students is easier in the secondary school, where such information is accessible through office records and exchanges with other teachers. At the university, such data may be requested from students in the form of a bio-sketch, for the teacher's personal reference.

Knowing the students is, of course, not a guarantee that they will be more responsive. But it certainly helps move a group of resisters toward becoming more forthcoming. Being able to call students by their names will go a long way toward building a classroom community in which it is safer for students to respond. Talking with students after class, individually and on a personal basis, will demonstrate the teacher's caring about them as people and as learners. Using biographical information thoughtfully and responsibly can be enormously helpful in building teacher–student relationships.

Students are unresponsive for good reasons. They may feel insecure or inadequate in expressing their ideas. They may be unaccustomed to the demands of thinking their own thoughts, having been habituated to "right answer" learning. They may have been programmed early in school to believe that their ideas are "wrong" or "stupid." They may be timid, fearful of speaking in public. They may be inarticulate, lacking experience in communicating their thoughts. English may not be their first language. Knowing the students as people provides entry into those background factors that contribute to students' unresponsiveness. Knowing students provides the data and therefore the means for helping them cross the bridge into more thoughtful and active participation.

Knowing the students also allows teachers to draw on students' strengths as they lob questions into the students' court. Christensen (1991a) writes:

> I tried arriving [in class] early to see what that might teach me about my students. The exercise proved valuable. Talking with students and watching them enter the room revealed much about their lives and interests—who played sports before class, who was under the weather or visibly fatigued that day, who had special interest in the day's topic (or conversely, an apparent desire to hide). Coming to class early also allowed me to prepare a genial, cooperative atmosphere by welcoming students by name, and it gave me an opportunity to note students' subgroups. (p. 103)

In preparation for case teaching, students need to be studied as extensively as cases. The more the teacher knows about the students, the better equipped he or she is to help them rise to the challenges that case teaching involves.

Know Yourself

It has been said that the best teachers embark on a journey of self-discovery that begins with their first day on the job and endures until they leave the classroom forever. From those very first moments facing a group of students, teachers are thrust into a self-examination process that occurs, simultaneously, on a variety of dimensions.

> Will I know the material?
> Will I know the answers to their questions?
> Will I have enough material to keep them busy for a whole semester?
> Will I be able to manage the group?
> Will I be able to teach them anything worthwhile?
> Will they like me?
> Will I be able to earn their respect?

Good teachers are constantly looking at themselves in their metaphorical mirrors, comparing their expectations of self-as-teacher with their actual classroom performance.

> How could I have done that better?
> What went wrong?
> What should I have done instead?

This self-scrutiny, painful at best, is the source of much hard-won professional growth. Through the process, teachers get to know themselves a little better: their strengths, limitations, hang-ups, biases, emotional push-buttons. In the best of circumstances, they learn to draw on their strengths, find help to compensate for their limitations, and deal more effectively with their biases and hang-ups. For extra measure, they also grow as persons.

Preparing to teach with cases means that teachers enter into partnerships with students. The "us and them" attitude that historically has shaped teacher–student relationships—where teachers are authority figures and students remain unconditionally submissive—gives way to new forms. Teachers and students become partners in the examination of issues, searching together for deeper, more intelligent understanding. Partners are helpers for each other. They are not divided by status or assumption of perfect wisdom. The teacher who would enter such a learning partnership must give up any defensive posture that might serve as a protective barrier. The teacher is more open, more nondefensive, more genuine. The engagement in partnership is not a role played out by a manipulative teacher. It is a genuine stance.

It is in the area of personal biases that we teachers need to look long and deeply in our work with cases, for these are the demons that get in the way of nondefensive functioning. Every teacher, without exception, has biases. We teachers enjoy and appreciate students who are "smart" and who get their assignments in on time. We hold certain values about democracy and freedom of speech very dear. We (understandably) think our own children are the most handsome and clever of all. We need not give up these biases. We need, rather, to know which ones "operate us" and cause us to behave in judgmental ways toward others who do not share our views. We need to learn to "operate them" —to stand apart from them when teaching with cases, so that we can maintain a more open attitude to different points of view. This is not always possible; but at least we can make a good effort to move ourselves in that direction. Preparing for teaching with cases is helped by recognizing those areas where our own biases are strong and trying, insofar as possible, to remain neutral when such issues are under discussion.

What does it take for a teacher to do this? The process of knowing oneself is the key, and it is the starting place for a life journey.

Gather Relevant Follow-up Activities

One of the most compelling forces of effective case teaching is the way cases drive the need to know more. Well-taught cases provoke what Festinger (1957) called "cognitive dissonance." Because students are thus provoked, because issues are not resolved, because different points of view appear to carry equal weight, students are put in the challenging position of having to find more information. Readings from texts, novels, newspapers, magazines, journals; films, both commercial and documentary; resource people—all serve as valuable resources to provide background information and open new perspectives on the issues.

Some cases come with lists of potentially valuable follow-up resources (see Chapter 8 for an extended discussion of follow-up activities). In other instances, teachers may need to generate their own lists. Of course, the more times a case is taught, the more the list of follow-up activities is likely to grow. Given an array of potentially fine post-case activities, teachers will be able to select from among many options those resources that will continue to inform, as well as broaden and deepen, student understanding of the issues in a case.

TEACHING WITH CASES:
AN INSTRUCTIONAL LEARNING LOOP

Discussions of case teaching in this book have, to a large extent, treated the different parts of case teaching experience. For example, there are sections devoted to cases, study questions, student and teacher preparations, discussion teaching. This fragmentation of parts may seem familiar to someone who has studied the piano, where one learns parts such as scales, arpeggios, fingering, trills, and the like, in separate exercises that appear initially to have little to do with real music. However, at one point in the wannabe pianist's musical studies, the student is finally presented with a Beethoven piano sonata. Now it is clear that all the fragments studied are found interwoven in the whole of the music. The parts studied contribute to understanding and skill in playing the whole, but the whole is the musical experience.

The whole of the experience in case study teaching appears in the form of an instructional learning loop, with learning experiences that build, one from the other, in a series of stages that allow for the evolving of understanding. In an earlier text (Wassermann & Ivany, 1988), I labeled this learning loop "play-debrief-replay" to describe the progression of learning experiences that fold back on each other and lead to new understandings. A more sophisticated labeling would suggest: "experience-debriefing-re-experience." The labels are not important; what is important is what happens in the progression and how the stages of experience re-create student understanding.

Student experience with the case narrative is the beginning point. The study of the case allows for students' beginning awareness of the key issues. Small group work on the study questions takes students to new levels of examination and understanding, but rarely in a linear progression. Small group work may produce a backward movement. Students may have discovered, for example, that ideas they had formed are no longer tenable. They must rethink, reconceptualize.

Large group debriefing is the next step in the progression, but once again the thrust is not to take the students down a linear pathway to a particular destination, but to build conceptual awareness along the way. Students make their own meanings from their experiences with the case. The creation of cognitive dissonance in the minds of the students does not allow for direct forward motion. It demands re-examination, and once again rethinking and reframing of ideas.

Based on teachers' perceptions of how best the issues may be further examined, the teacher selects one or more follow-up activities, where meanings are tested in new experiences. These new experiences may include films, readings, discussions with resource people, field trips, projects. Students continue to gather data, and examine ideas in a climate of continued, provocative, intellectual engagement. Work on follow-up tasks may be as extensive as the teacher wishes. Once again, the nature of this stage of the journey is not to forge ahead, but to move in a way that individual or group work dictates: some forward, some downward, some sideways. Understanding of principles and concepts continues to evolve, as experience is followed by reflection on experience, which is followed by data gathering, leading to new, but related, experience.

The whole-class debriefing that occurs after the follow-up activity, continues the process of examination. These debriefings may, of course, move the students along the pathway, take them more deeply into the issues, or take them sideways, along related pathways. It would not be unusual to find, at any given moment on the journey, that different students were in entirely different locations on the pathway, in terms of knowledge acquired and understanding achieved. In this instructional loop, students engage in a continuous process of meaning making. Meaning continues to evolve out of growing experiences in which students are always actively engaged.

When the teacher determines that the journey of inquiry on the learning pathway must be concluded, so that new journeys addressing new issues may be undertaken, students are asked to participate in some culminating activity, demonstrating through individual or group performance their ability to apply concepts learned in some new, creative way. While termed a "culminating" activity, these evaluative tasks do not assume the completion of the journey. Unlike destinations, culmination leaves the door open for the inevitable personal odysseys to continue, because the absence of closure provokes just such ongoing reflection.

Traditional teaching–learning pathways seem to follow a linear progression, with a beginning, a middle, and an end. Before beginning a lesson, the teacher is clear about the specific content to be covered. The beginning is marked by dissemination of information by the teacher; the middle, by acquisition of content by the students; the end, by an evaluation to determine the extent to which students have acquired the relevant knowledge. This linear progression is often embellished by activities along the learning pathway, for example, readings, trips, projects, small group discussions. But the purpose of the journey along the linear pathway seems concerned with the destination—that is, students' acquisition of specific knowledge. Thus, "covering the curriculum" becomes a metaphor for the teaching–learning experiences along the linear pathway. In this particular vision of instruction, once the destination has been reached and student knowledge assessed, the journey is terminated, so that new linear journeys may begin.

In the instructional loop of teaching with cases, the learning pathway is far from linear. It folds over upon itself, backs up, returns to retrace steps, in a series of many investigatory stops along the pathway. Instead of destination (acquisition of specific knowledge) as the first learning priority, it is the *journey* (evolving understanding) that plays the key role. At culmination, nothing is really finished. No student is ever likely to say, "Oh, yeh. Functions of the human body? We *had* that in Bio 11." Along this more zig-zag learning pathway are a series of interrelated experiences that allow for the reframing of personal meanings, so that students are continually challenged to add each new life experience to their developing cognitive frameworks and deepening understandings.

Teachers who are accustomed to seeing instruction in linear-sequential ways may, at first, find the instructional loop of case teaching methodology confusing. Experience in teaching in the loop, however, may reveal its exciting potential for promoting the kind of learning experiences that stimulate students' thinking and lead to richer understanding about issues of consequence.

CONCLUSION

The instructional loop described above was not conceptualized in a university laboratory, nor was it invented at the Harvard Business School. It is, in fact, a methodology used by many teachers, in classrooms at every instructional level, where students' active, experiential participation is the primary instructional step in the learning progression and where subsequent experiences allow for the extraction of meanings. Bruner's (1985) research and the developmental concepts of Piaget (see Furth, 1970) pointed to the significant effects of experiential learning for young children. But it is in the educational theories of John Dewey (1964) that the roots of the instructional learning loop are found.

> The explorer, like the learner, does not know what terrain and adventures his journey holds in store for him. He has yet to discover mountains, deserts, and waterholes and to suffer fever, starvation and other hardships. Finally, when the explorer returns from his journey, he will have a hard-won knowledge of the country he has traversed.

Then, and only then, can he produce a map of the region. To give the map to others (as a teacher might) is to give the results of an experience, not the experience by which the map was produced. Although the logical organization of subject matter is the proper goal of learning, the logic of the subject cannot be truly meaningful to the learner without his psychological and personal involvement in exploration. (p. 350)

Dewey goes on to write:

There is, then, nothing final about a logical rendering of experience. Its value is not contained in itself; its significance is that of standpoint, outlook, method. It intervenes between the more casual, tentative, and roundabout experiences of the past, and more controlled and orderly experiences of the future. It gives past experience in that net form which renders it most available and most significant, most fecund for future experience. The abstractions, generalizations and classifications which it introduces all have prospective meaning. (p. 351)

Teaching with cases requires teachers to challenge themselves in new and different ways. Preparing carefully in advance means greater potential for successful classes. Seeing the whole of the process, the instructional loop of case teaching, gives the teacher greater insights into the process and thus greater understanding of how to "make music" in the art of case teaching.

7 | Teaching a Case

The choice to teach the case "Old Age Ain't for Sissies" (see Appendix F; Wassermann, 1993b) at the teachers' workshop on case method was not made lightly. Factored into the decision was consideration of the nature of the participants (i.e., their individual and collective professional needs; their entry levels as case teachers); the applicability of the case to learner needs; the ability of the case to "showcase" case method; the "power" of the issues in the case to charge study group discussions and fire the debriefing.

"Old Age . . ." was newly written and had not, at that point, been field tested. But the poignancy of the issues, their universality, and the example of a case written in a subject area other than the humanities, had considerable appeal.

The teacher-participants were asked to prepare by reading the case prior to class. On the morning of the class, study groups of five or six teachers each, met in designated areas to discuss the study questions. Because the big ideas in this case concern the biological determinants of aging, most of the questions dealt with science issues. Two questions, however, went beyond the boundaries of science, to deal with sociocultural aspects of aging in Western culture (see the study questions for the case in Appendix F). A full hour was allocated to study group discussions. During this time, the discussion leader did not intrude herself in any way into the small group discussions.

Following the study group sessions, 38 participants crowded into the classroom that had been prepared in advance to accommodate a large group debriefing session. Tables and chairs were arranged in a horseshoe, so that each participant could see and hear everyone else. Space was left so that the discussion leader, Roxie Barnett, could easily maneuver around the horseshoe to approach students when they spoke. Tagboard name cards were positioned on each of the tables, so that they stood up and were easily read from all angles of the room.

Because most of the participants were new to case teaching methodology, Roxie began the debriefing by making explicit the guidelines for discussion.

1. Participants were asked to raise their hands if they wished to volunteer an idea. This would prevent the kind of free-for-all discussion in which many speak at once and students respond argumentatively, barely listening to each other. All ideas, then, were to be directed to the discussion leader, who would work with them in a one-on-one exchange with that participant.
2. There would be no "cold call" of any participant. Only those who wished to volunteer their ideas would be called on.
3. In any part of the one-on-one exchange, a participant was free to say, "I pass" or some other comment to indicate that she or he wished to "get off the hook." There would be no penalty for this.
4. Participants were also asked to speak loudly enough so they could be heard by others in the class.

Having laid out the guidelines, Roxie began the debriefing with the following question: What is your understanding of what happens in the process of aging?

PREPARING FOR CLASS

The day before the debriefing, Roxie began her preparations by studying the case. She made certain that the big ideas, outlined for the case in the Notes to the Teacher section (see Appendix F), were at the forefront of her mind. She was clear that the framework for discussion would be built around those biological issues.

In her study of the case, Roxie used a highlighter to mark certain facts, so that these would be fresh in her mind during the debriefing. It is always awkward, and even embarrassing, when the discussion leader is ignorant of even the most minute facts in a case, which sends a clear message of unpreparedness to the students.

Using the big ideas, the case content, and the study questions as a springboard, Roxie then conceptualized the "science lenses"—those key science issues that would focus the discussion. The "science lenses" for this case were

Normal aging processes involve biological deterioration.
Certain chronic diseases are associated with the aged.

> Biological deterioration is variable among different individuals.
> Certain steps can be taken to diminish, but not vanquish, the effects
>   of aging.

She also included Western culture's preoccupation with youth as a sociocultural perspective that would be examined.

These lenses gave rise to a list of prepared debriefing questions that
would help Roxie keep the discussion on track and centered on the big
ideas, thereby avoiding the "disquieting patterns" that Sykes (1989) has
written about in class discussions in which "there is nothing more than
the swapping of opinions" (p. 7). She did not expect that the 75 minutes scheduled for debriefing would allow for extended discussion of
each question, but these, she knew, would set the stage for continued
examination of the issues in subsequent study and debriefing sessions.

Writing the questions in advance helped Roxie to arrange them in
the tiers described in Chapter 6, allowing for progressively more challenging examination of the issues.

1. What is your understanding of what happens in the process of
   aging?
2. What do you suppose chronic disease has to do with aging? How
   do you explain the physiology?
3. How do you explain the limited "shelf life" of living beings?
   What, in your view, limits "shelf life"?
4. How come the aging process plays out in different ways among
   different individuals?
5. What role do vitamins play in keeping you healthy? What other
   preventative measures are used to mitigate the "going downhill into old age" process?
6. How do you explain our culture's preoccupation with youthful
   appearance?
7. How do you explain our culture's distaste/avoidance of the
   elderly?

Aspects of aging mentioned in the case (e.g., graying hair, wrinkled
skin, slowing down) were reviewed, as were those ailments mentioned
(e.g., arthritis, diabetes, hearing loss, vision loss, memory loss, diminished muscle mass, tooth loss, diminished cardiovascular efficiency, joint
deterioration).

Early the next morning, Roxie went to check on the classroom to
be sure that the tables were arranged appropriately, windows open,
notes on her clipboard easily at hand.

DEBRIEFING THE CASE

Roxie's initial question, "What is your understanding of what happens in the process of aging?" was met with a wall of silence. She had heard that response before. She smiled, looked around the room hopefully, and waited. Some students said afterward that she opened her hands in a gesture of invitation, but she was not aware of it at the time. After what seemed to be a long time, but was in fact only a few moments, two hands went up.

"Yes, Doris," she invited, a random choice. She also recorded in her mind that Brian was being put "on hold" and would have the next turn.

"Well, one of the things that happens is that you get wrinkles," Doris volunteered.

Roxie pulled at the sagging skin around her neck, laughed, and said, "You mean like this?" Doris laughed along with the others in the class. Roxie had chosen this response consciously, to bring an air of levity into the high-risk chamber and to break the ice.

"Doris," she said laughing and approaching her, "I was hoping you wouldn't notice." More laughing. Doris sat back in her chair and seemed to relax. Roxie had let Doris off the hook quickly and thanked her. She considered it to be too soon to challenge further. She then turned to Brian.

"Brian, thank you for waiting. What would you like to add?"

"You can see that the hair turns gray." Brian pointed to his head. "That's because the hair follicles lose their pigmentation."

Roxie moved across the inner area of the horseshoe toward Brian. "Turning gray is a result of loss of pigmentation. Is that what you're saying?"

"Yes."

Someone from across the room called out, "That's a science teacher talking." Laughter. Roxie signaled with her hand, held behind her back, to the talker to "hold it" and moved even closer to Brian.

"How do you explain the relationship of loss of pigmentation in the hair follicles to the aging process, Brian? Do you have any ideas on that?"

Brian's face became a question mark and his eyebrows turned into s-curves. "I'm not sure—but I have a theory about it."

Roxie opened her hand out, in a gesture of invitation to Brian's theory. "It may be a wearing out process—maybe pigmentation has a particular 'shelf life'—like the wearing out of a bicycle tire." Brian's expressive eyebrows once more signaled his uncertainty.

"The pigmentation gets used up. It has a limited life. That's your theory." (Yeh.) "Thanks, Brian. I want to return to the original question. What are some other examples of what happens in aging?"

Lucinda put her hand up. "In the case we read, the dog developed arthritis. I can see that as related to aging." She held up her hands, showing a disfiguration of joints and fingers.

"Arthritis is a disease associated with aging." Roxie paraphrased Lucinda's idea. (Yeh.) "Do you want to say anything more about that, Lucinda?"

"Only that it's a damn nuisance." Laughter.

"Old age ain't for sissies, eh?" Roxie smiled. Laughter. "Dave, your hand is waving about there."

"I'd just like to say that arthritis is not necessarily associated with aging. Lots of young people get arthritis," Dave offered.

"It's not a disease that's exclusively seen in the older population. It's found across the population." (Yeh.) "I'm wondering, Dave, if you'd care to speculate which population would show a greater proportion of people afflicted with arthritis?"

"I'd have to guess it would be the elderly."

"More of it among the elderly? How do you explain that?"

"They're around longer."

"So if you're around long enough, arthritis is going to catch up with you eventually?" Roxie pushed. (Yeh.) "There seems to be a suggestion here that certain diseases are 'out there' waiting, and the longer we live, the more susceptible we are."

"I don't agree," Tilly quickly countered. "I don't think it has to do with just being around. I think there's a question of vulnerability. Some people, as they age, become more vulnerable."

Roxie moved in closer to Tilly and caught her eye. "This is a kind of challenging question, Tilly, but I'm wondering if you'd be prepared to say how, with aging, our physical selves become more vulnerable?"

Tilly paused a moment, then offered, "Well, like Brian says, it has to do with 'shelf life,' I think. Physical condition just wears down—like bicycle tires."

"We just begin to wear out from all that use," Roxie paraphrased. (Yeh.) "You know, it seems to me that there is a great deal of variation among the elderly with respect to this 'wearing down' theory of yours, Tilly, and Brian. I'm wondering if anybody has any ideas that might explain that? Yes, Rob?"

"I think it has a lot to do with how we take care of ourselves, our bodies. If we take good care of our physical equipment, it will tend to last longer."

"Maybe there are things we can do to take care of our physical equipment," Roxie restated Rob's idea. (Yeh.) "For example?"

"Exercise, for one. Diet, for another."

"Exercise and diet, according to your theory, play a major role in keeping ourselves healthy," Roxie reflected. (Yeh.) "Would you go so far as to say they are key in preventing the chronic diseases associated with aging?"

Rob took a long pause. "Yeh. I believe so."

"You seem to be less than one hundred percent certain," Roxie responded by interpreting Rob's pause. "Am I reading you correctly?"

"Yeh, not one hundred percent certain," Rob explained. "But from all I've read, the likelihood is that they do contribute in a major way."

"I'd better get out there and do some more jogging, would you say?" Roxie smiled.

"I think it keeps your body more flexible, more limber. When the muscles aren't used, they tend to atrophy," Rob responded.

"The muscles atrophy. They lose their power." (Yeh.) "There's something else I'd like to add to the equation. In this case, the vet prescribed vitamins for the dog, as a diet supplement. What about vitamins? Do they help?" Roxie pushed the question level to the next tier.

Patsy volunteered, "If you have a good diet, you don't need them. We get all the vitamins we need from a healthful diet."

"I disagree," Alice jumped in. "We can't get everything we need, even from a good diet. Vitamin supplements are very important."

Roxie pointed to the difference. "We have a split opinion here. Patsy says, 'not necessary if the diet is good.' Alice says, 'important.' Whom should I believe?"

Patsy grumbled, "You can take them if you want to. They certainly won't hurt you."

"But you are not recommending them." Roxie moved closer to Patsy as she attempted to interpret her statement.

"It's a waste of money," Patsy said without equivocation.

"They won't do anything for me," Roxie reflected and then turned to Alice. "Alice, what do you say?"

Alice was quick to respond. "Look at what we have done to our foods. The impurities, the additives, the poisons. Take those vitamins!" (Laughter)

"You two seem to be offering two different points of view here. Now, I want to know, what data do you have to support your ideas? I mean, whom should I believe?" Roxie once again elevated the discrepancy.

"Take them if they make you feel good," Patsy said.

"But what about data, Patsy? I'm a researcher. Convince me with data," Roxie challenged her.

"It's just my opinion. From my experience," Patsy said.

"You've evidence from your own experience suggesting vitamins are useless," Roxie reflected. (Patsy nodded.)

"And Alice disagrees," Roxie raised the point of disagreement again.

"I take megadoses of vitamin C for a cold. It always works for me," Alice's voice grew strong in her defense of her position.

"Your cold goes away." (Yeh.) "So based on a sample of one, I should do it," Roxie challenged.

"Well . . ." Alice hesitated.

"It should work for me if it works for you," Roxie challenged again.

Alice was unyielding. "It works for me."

"Thanks, Alice and Patsy." Roxie chose to leave up in the air and unpursued at this time, the question about supporting data. "And thank you for letting me push you a bit on those questions. I want to shift gears now to the question of our society's preoccupation with youth and youthful appearances. Where does this come from? How do we get this way?"

"It's the media," Marla offered. "Look at all the ads, in magazines and TV, youth and beauty. It's a national obsession. We all want to look like movie stars, to keep the image."

"It's a cultural obsession. Our culture is oriented to youth and beauty," Roxie reflected. "Yes, Malcolm? You want to get in here?"

"Wait a second. We can't just blame contemporary culture. Romans and Greeks also worshipped youth and beauty. It's not just us."

"It's not just our culture, the media hype. It goes back a long way— this preoccupation with youthful appearance," Roxie paraphrased Malcolm's statement.

Marvin made his first foray into the discussion. "We don't want to think about getting old. We want to keep that far away from us. Growing old means we have to face infirmity, dying, death. It's too hard. Too painful. We want to believe that we can stay young forever."

"Maybe I'm reading too much into what you are saying, Marvin, and please tell me if I am. It seems that if we distance ourselves from the aged and aging, we can pretend that it's never going to happen to us," Roxie approached Marvin to speak to him directly.

"Exactly," Marvin told her.

"We've just about run out of time for today's session. You have in your binder, following this case, an article about diseases of the elderly. I'd like you to read that before next class, when we'll be looking at some of the chronic diseases associated with aging, and particularly the physiology of those diseases. So thanks very much to all of you for your ideas and I'll see you tomorrow."

After the teacher-participants left the class, Roxie sat at the desk and made notes about which of the ideas would be examined in the next debriefing session. She also made notes about those students who participated, particularly what was said and by whom, and how the ideas were supported by data. She then reviewed her role as discussion leader—which questions she used; what she felt about the discussion climate; what she might have asked; the pacing; the students she called on to participate; her listening, attending, and paraphrasing skills; whether she moved too early to challenge; if she interrupted a student. She made notes about what would be highlighted for discussion the next day, which would follow the reading of the article and would examine both the biology of aging and chronic disease.

THE INTERACTIVE PROCESS OF DEBRIEFING

What interactive skills does it take to debrief a case?[1] How does a teacher learn to use these skills in the full orchestration of a large class discussion? How does a teacher avoid the problems described by Sykes (1989) in his comment, "Too often, I fear, my class traffics in 'anecdotal knowledge,' because I am unclear about the larger conceptual apparatus that might invest cases with significance. And since I am unclear, I cannot convey such meaning to students through case analysis" (p. 9).

Those teachers who have studied the art of interactive teaching have pointed to several skills used in concert to bring students' ideas under examination. These are not all the skills used by a discussion leader, but to those who practice debriefing in their classrooms, they seem to be the ones considered minimal for a successful discussion. In debriefing a case, the teacher does all of the following:

• Listens, attends, and apprehends students' statements
• Comprehends the message the student is giving
• Selects, from a range of options, the type of response to be made, with

---

1. The material on questioning strategies has been adapted with permission from Wassermann, Selma. 1992. *Asking the Right Question: The Essence of Teaching.* Bloomington, IN: Phi Delta Kappa Fastback.

full appreciation that different responses have different cognitive and affective effects
- Chooses questions that put the big ideas of the case under examination
- Asks questions that promote cognitive dissonance

While all of these skills are discussed in separate sections in the following pages, it should be noted that these occur in concert, in each moment of debriefing, smoothly and seamlessly, in fractions of seconds. This orchestration is an important attribute of the art of debriefing.

Listening, Attending, and Apprehending

The skills of listening and attending are evidenced in behavior. The teacher turns full attention to the student. Body language, face, and eyes indicate, "I'm with you. I am listening to what you have to say." Attending means shutting out all extraneous noise, concentrating totally on what is being said. Listening is more than just hearing the words. It includes observing all behavioral cues as the words are being spoken; hearing nuance and voice inflection; observing particular words chosen to express certain ideas; noticing where the statement is given emphasis. When all of that occurs in listening and attending, the teacher is doing what Freire (1983) calls "apprehending"—taking in and making meaning of the totality. This meaning making allows for greater understanding and thus provides the material from which a response may be constructed.

Listening, attending, and apprehending require a full and conscious effort to tune into the how and the what of the student's idea. They require freeing the mind, so it is open to hear and observe. One cannot listen and attend if one is, at the same moment, thinking of a good response. That part must wait until afterward. Nothing may get in the way of full concentration on the student and the student's statement.

Texts dealing with the development of interpersonal skills (Bramer, 1979; Carkhuff & Berenson, 1983) identify nine conditions associated with attending, and it is suggested that ability to attend thoughtfully and intelligently increases as the following conditions are met:

- Making and holding eye contact with the student speaking
- Listening to and communicating respect for the student's idea
- Being free from the need to evaluate the student's idea, in either word or tone
- Avoiding reactive comment on the student's idea; avoiding presenting one's own thoughts

- Apprehending—making meaning of—what the student is saying
- Being aware of tone of affect (verbal or nonverbal) being communicated
- Being especially aware of indicators of stress being shown
- Formulating responses that accurately and sensitively reflect the meaning of the student's statement
- Being able to make the student feel safe, nondefensive, and nonthreatened throughout the dialogue

The ability to listen, attend, and apprehend provides the teacher with the information needed to formulate intelligent responses. It also creates the climate in which respect for students and for their ideas is palpable and makes it safe for students to offer their ideas. Even more, it contributes to the essential condition of interactive teaching, that is, the teacher and students engaging in a dialogue in which all parties together are searching to understand. The teacher's skill in listening, attending, and apprehending is basic to the art of discussion teaching. It is on this foundation that all the other skills rest.

Comprehending the Student's Meaning

In the film *Now, Voyager* (1942), Bette Davis plays the role of a repressed spinster, dominated by her demanding and controlling mother, Gladys Cooper. When Davis has a nervous breakdown, she is treated by psychiatrist Claude Rains, who brings her out of her shell and allows her to take control of her own life. When the transformed Davis returns home, mother Cooper immediately sets about to take charge of her daughter's life again. In the scene of their first confrontation over who will hold the power, Cooper tells Davis that she is to shed her fashionable clothes and wear again the sensible clothes that Cooper bought for her before Davis became ill. The dialogue between the two women occurs on two levels. There is the surface exchange of words.

COOPER: You'll take off those clothes and put on the dress I bought for you.
DAVIS: But mother, I've lost 25 pounds.
COOPER: I've had Martha [maid] take all your clothes in.

Listening and attending allow the viewer to apprehend what is going on beneath the surface of the spoken message. Cooper's face is stern, unyielding. When she talks of Davis's fashionable clothes, her voice is dripping with contempt and condemnation. The implicit message is that she is once more establishing herself as the one who will decide what clothes Davis is to wear and, implicitly, who will have control over Davis's life. So the real message is not about clothes. It is about control. Hence, Davis's response, "But mother, I've lost 25 pounds," becomes pathetic. It does not respond to the real message being sent.

In the real world of the classroom, teachers do not have the camera's eye to point out the visual clues needed to discover the hidden meanings; nor do they have the director's behind-the-scenes suggestions to the actors that point us in the direction of appropriate interpretation of meanings. Teachers are very much on their own. The process of making meaning of a student's statement, however, is greatly helped by the ability to listen, to attend, to apprehend. Using both visual and auditory cues helps teachers to discern the surface and below-surface meanings. A moment of reflection—what is the student saying?—enables a teacher to process and then to understand.

Sometimes, when the student's thinking is muddled, the message may be incomprehensible. "Would you run that by me again?" is fair game, when it is clear that the teacher is "right there," making every effort to understand. The student needs another chance to say it in a way that is comprehensible.

More often, a student's message may be extensive, with several ideas packed into a lengthy statement. The teacher is put in a position of having to choose the one, from among the many, that will bear further examination.

Hearing the student's idea is the beginning of the exercise. The student's statement is then processed, mentally, so it is understood. This must occur before the teacher is in a position to begin to consider an appropriate response.

Selecting a Response

There are dozens of ways in which teachers respond to students. Teachers may choose to agree or disagree with what a student is saying. They may offer their own ideas; give explanations; provide examples; give information. Responses may be directive or judgmental. Even an absence of response is a response of a kind. None of these, however, has much to do with the kinds of responses teachers use to bring students' ideas under examination. This is not to say that such responses are never used, or that they are "wrong." They are appropriate in other contexts, of course. But they are singularly inappropriate in debriefing a case.

Those who have studied the kinds of responses that encourage stu-

dents' thoughtful reflection upon their ideas have suggested three increasingly more challenging categories of responses in teacher–student
interactions (Raths, Wassermann, Jonas, & Rothstein, 1986): basic responses that encourage students' re-examination of the idea; responses
that call for analysis of the idea; and responses that challenge.

Basic responses that encourage students' re-examination of the idea.
These are called "basic" because they are fundamental to the interactive process. They have the power to communicate to the student
that his or her idea has been heard. They also "say the idea back" in
some new way, reflecting the idea in a verbal mirror, so that the student has an opportunity to re-examine it from a new perspective. Basic
responses are minimally challenging, so that students feel safe in offering their ideas for examination. Liberally used, they build trust in
the interactive relationship and do the basic work of promoting reflection.

Basic responses that encourage students' re-examination of their
ideas include

- Saying the idea back to the student in some new way
- Paraphrasing the idea
- Interpreting the idea
- Asking for more information (e.g., "Tell me a little more about that,"
  "Help me to understand what you mean.")

The more closely a teacher's response mirrors what a student has
said, the less the challenge to the student in the interaction. This is the
safest response of all. But, it is immediately recognized that maintaining the response level at "saying the idea back" will not take the student far on a journey of deeper examination. The more one challenges,
however, the more potential there is for trouble. The artful teacher must
balance the scales between responses that make it safe for the student
to examine, and responses that challenge the student more in examination. There is, of course, no formula that the teacher can follow to
make these choices. This is where listening, attending, and apprehending pay off. But caution about challenging students is an important rule.
The more challenge, the higher the risks and the less the climate of safety
in the discussion.

The following are examples of how different basic responses may
be used debriefing "The Case of Injustice in Our Time" (Chambers &
Fukui, 1991). The response actually chosen by the teacher is marked
with an asterisk.

TEACHER: Tell me what you see as some important issues raised in this
   case. Yes, Sylvie?
SYLVIE: The government showed discrimination against the Japanese.
TEACHER: [Options for responding]
   • The government showed discrimination against the Japa-
   nese. [Says the idea back.]
   • The government was prejudiced against the Japanese. [Says
   the idea back in some new way]
   • Japanese-Canadians were being discriminated against.
   [Paraphrases]
   • The Canadian government, in its actions, showed its preju-
   dice against Japanese-Canadians. [Paraphrases] This was an
   important issue for you. [Interprets]*

LAUREL: Well, I think it was strange that the government picked the
   Japanese as potentially dangerous and left the Germans alone.
TEACHER: • The Germans could keep their lives intact. It was the Japa-
   nese who were uprooted and sent to the camps. [Paraphrases]
   • That puzzles you. [Interprets] The Canadian government
   picked the Japanese as potentially dangerous and left the
   Germans alone. [Paraphrases]*

Teachers who are embarking on a course of learning debriefing skills
may, at first, consider these basic-level responses unworthy and want
to move quickly to more challenging responses, to move the discourse
forward rapidly. Basic-level responses should not be underestimated,
however, in their ability to generate productive examination of issues,
and there are good reasons to spend time studying them, mastering
them, and using them generously in debriefing a case. First, they are
the most natural to master and use. Second, they allow for practice of
listening and attending skills, without having to worry about formulating more complicated responses. Third, they are useful in promoting
effective examination of issues. Fourth, they contribute to a safe classroom climate; nobody feels threatened or challenged confrontationally
in the presence of these types of responses.

Teachers who are working to develop discussion teaching skills
should not underestimate the power of basic responses to promote students' examination of the issues. Here's an example of a transcript in
which the teacher uses only basic responses to move students to deeper
examination of their ideas.

A class of preservice teachers is involved in a debriefing of the film/case,

Miracle Worker. *The lens through which the discussion is focused is "the power of a teacher to make a difference."*

TEACHER: What are your thoughts on how this teacher influenced her student's life?

KIM: She was able to take the girl, Helen, from a borderline existence, into a world where she could communicate with others.

TEACHER: You see Helen as initially in borderline existence. [Paraphrases]

KIM: Yeh.

TEACHER: Tell me more. [Asks for more information]

KIM: I think that without the ability to communicate, you can't be a part of this world. You can't communicate with others; they can't communicate with you. Well, you are living a marginal existence.

TEACHER: Without the ability to communicate, you are hardly in the world. [Paraphrases]

KIM: Yeh.

NOREEN: Can you imagine what it must have been like for her? Helen? To be trapped without the means of telling anyone what she thought or felt? A terrible prison-like existence. Worse.

TEACHER: She did not have the ability to tell what she was thinking or feeling. She was in a terrible trap. [Paraphrases]

NOREEN: No wonder she was wild. Her behavior was wild. Her frustration must have been unimaginable.

TEACHER: Her frustration was enormous. This produced her aggressive behavior, which her parents saw as wild. [Paraphrases; interprets]

NOREEN: Yeah. The frustration-aggression theory.

TEACHER: You've read about that. [Interprets]

ROSS: That's the gift of that teacher. Annie Sullivan. She gave Helen the gift of communication. In this case, the gift of life.

TEACHER: What she gave Helen enabled her to break out of the trap. [Interprets]

ROSS: Without it, she would have been doomed. But it sure wasn't easy.

TEACHER: Helen didn't make it easy for her. [Paraphrases]

ROSS: Not Helen, not the parents.

TEACHER: Annie didn't seem to have much support for what she was trying to do. [Interprets]

ROSS: I don't know how she did it.

TEACHER: She had a lot of courage. [Interprets]

ROSS: Beyond belief. I don't know if I could have stuck it out.

TEACHER: Sometimes, the gifts teachers give take a lot of courage. Annie never seemed to lose faith in herself. [Paraphrases; interprets]

JENNIFER: It seems to me that teaching requires courage. Teachers do give gifts, but these are not easy to deliver, nor are they appreciated.

TEACHER: Teachers have gifts to give, but giving them is not easy. Teachers have to work hard to give these gifts. [Paraphrases]

JENNIFER: It would be nicer if they were appreciated more.

TEACHER: There's some sadness in your voice when you say that, Jennifer—like it's a thankless profession. [Interprets]

JENNIFER: Sometimes, I think it is.

JOAN: It may be sometimes, but look at the gift Annie got in return for what she gave.

TEACHER: Say more, Joan. [Asks for more information]

JOAN: The satisfaction. Can you imagine the satisfaction that she felt when Helen made that breakthrough?

TEACHER: There's nothing like that feeling, eh? [Interprets]

JOAN: That's why we want to be teachers. To know that feeling of satisfaction. I think that drives all of us to teaching.

TEACHER: So teachers give gifts, but we are gifted in return. Those are the rewards of teaching. [Paraphrases]

JOAN: You bet.

Learning and mastering listening, attending, and paraphrasing is the very first step on the pathway to successful and artful debriefing.

Responses that call for analysis of an idea. At a level slightly more challenging than basic responses are those that call for analyses to be made. These responses require deeper examination and go beyond surface observations. These include asking

> That examples be given
> Whether assumptions are being made
> Whether alternatives have been considered
> For comparisons to be made
> For supporting data
> Where the idea came from

This, of course, is far from an exhaustive list of examples in this category, but they reveal the kinds of questions used in calling for analysis. Note, too, that while all basic responses appear in the form of declarative statements, these responses appear more often in the form of questions. That is one reason that they are more cognitively challenging and therefore pose greater risks for students to offer their ideas.

Another is that they require the student to take his or her idea further—to examine some new aspect of the idea.

Responses that call for analysis have the possibility of taking the inquiry into new territory. When, for example, in the debriefing of "Old Age Ain't . . ." Rob is asked to give examples to support his statement about caring for our bodies and he responds with "exercise and diet," the discussion leader, Roxie Barnett, is at an interactive crossroads. Should she pursue how exercise and diet perform the function of keeping bodies healthy? Or should she remain on the original pathway and continue with the examination of how physical functioning deteriorates with aging? These choices present intriguing possibilities for the discussion leader, who is ever mindful that a fork in the road leading to a highly productive examination of related issues is taken only at the expense of leaving the discussion of the original ideas behind. One cannot have it both ways. So when a teacher chooses to follow a new track in the discourse, it's best to be alert to what may be gained as well as what may be lost in the process. Questions that call for analysis present these discussion crossroads, and the teacher needs to be always mindful of how a response is bound to lead students down one pathway or another.

One helpful guideline in choosing a question from this category is to make certain that the question chosen is going to add an important new dimension to the examination of the issues; that the question will take teacher and student to where they want to go. Questions are never chosen haphazardly; they are always chosen after reflection on their possibilities to move the discussion in a productive direction. Another helpful guideline is to diminish the challenging effect of these questions by framing them as declarative statements whenever possible. For example, the confrontational effect of, "What examples can you give?" can be diminished by saying instead, "You may have an example to illuminate your idea," which is offered as an invitation to respond rather than a command.

The transcript below demonstrates how questions that call for analysis are interspersed with basic responses in a debriefing of the case "The Cranberry-Orange Muffin Vote," used with secondary school students (see Appendix D; Wassermann, 1992b). The debriefing is focused on the various factors that influence voters' decisions in the electoral process.

TEACHER: What are your views about how voters choose the "best" candidate?
JUNE: I think the media influences our opinions. We tend to go for the candidate that has the most media appeal.

TEACHER: Say a little more about that, June. About how that works. [Asks for more information]

JUNE: I think the media plays a big role in presenting a candidate favorably. You know, how he (or she) appears on the camera, what clothes are worn, how the person smiles, or doesn't smile. These are the factors that seem to count. Never mind what the person is talking about.

TEACHER: You believe that what the person looks like is more important to the voters than what he or she is saying. [Paraphrases]

JUNE: I think it's sad, but true. People don't listen. They are just looking.

STEVE: I don't agree. In my family, we discuss the issues. The issues are important to us. We don't make decisions based on whether the guy is wearing a Brooks Brothers suit, or if he's got a $200 haircut.

TEACHER: In your family, it's the issues that count. Appearance is not an issue for you and for your folks. [Paraphrases] To what extent do you consider your family to be typical, Steve? [Asks for analysis]

STEVE: I can't say. I hope that we are typical, but I'm afraid that June may have a point. Other families may go for surface issues.

TEACHER: You're not sure how typical your family is, but you are guessing that for other families, appearances would enter heavily into the decision making. [Paraphrases]

MELANIE: I think there's more to it than just the issues. I think it's how people interpret what the issues are. I'm not sure that people are really interested in the issues; they're more interested in the slogans that represent the issues.

TEACHER: Slogans pass as issues? Could you give some examples? [Paraphrases; asks for analysis]

MELANIE: Well, for example, the free trade issue. I mean, how many people have gone deeply into the issue of free trade, and read all the literature? How many are just out there with their picket signs, like "down with free trade"? I think people just sign onto an issue, without really considering what's behind it.

TEACHER: People may make choices about candidates based on incomplete knowlege of the issues. [Paraphrases]

MELANIE: Yeh. There's a lot of media hype and then the issue gets reduced to its simplest terms. Like, remember George Bush, "No New Taxes"? That's an example of signing onto a hot issue, without fully understanding its implications.

TEACHER: The candidates and the media are guilty of provoking the voters' passions with these slogans. [Paraphrases] Voters then tend to

vote with their passions, instead of with their intelligence? Have I gone too far in making an interpretation of what you have said?
MELANIE: No, you haven't. That's just what I meant.

The combination of basic responses and questions that call for analyses to be made has the effect of promoting examination of surface issues and progressing to deeper levels. When questions calling for analysis can be framed as declaratives, they take some of the sting out of the challenge.

Responses that challenge. At the most demanding level of the cognitive hierarchy is that group of questions and responses that require the generation of new ideas. These ask students to extend their thinking into new and uncharted territory, to come up with ideas that go beyond what has been seen or heard; to take data and manipulate them into new configurations, so that something new and different is revealed. These responses put students at the highest cognitive risk. Understandably, they are used sparingly during a debriefing session. These responses include asking

> That hypotheses or theories be generated
> That data be interpreted
> That principles be applied to new situations
> That evaluations be made and criteria be identified
> That predictions be made about what is theoretically possible
> How theories might be tested
> That plans of action be originated
> That decisions be made and their consequences examined

These examples, of course, do not exhaust the list of what is possible to ask in this category, but they do present a picture of the kinds of questions that constitute such challenges, as they demonstrate the sophistication of what is being asked.

Teachers who are new to debriefing often make the mistake of thinking that challenging questions run the show in good discussion teaching. However, that is not an accurate perception. Challenging questions are merely one tool in the teacher's response repertoire. Like hammers, which are no better tools, in the abstract, than screwdrivers—invaluable when used effectively and with the potential of causing irreparable harm when used ineffectively—the tools of challenging questions are best used with the following caveats in mind.

Challenging questions, by their very nature, shift the discourse onto new and wholly different pathways. A result of using several challenging questions in rapid succession is that the discourse begins to appear fractured and disjointed as each idea is immediately abandoned for a new idea. It is the basic response that grounds the discourse and permits a slower, more studied examination. Challenging questions need to be used thoughtfully, sparingly, and wisely, and only when the teacher wishes to take the discourse onto a new level of inquiry.

Since challenging questions are more cognitively complex and require the generation of new ideas, they are infinitely more fraught with risk. Students may be stumped by them, especially students who are new to thinking about complex issues. Challenging questions may frustrate students and cause them to "feel stupid" and "dummy up." These caveats should be as red flags to teachers who may fall into the trap of using challenging questions indiscriminately, or those who may misguidedly believe that the greater number of challenging questions used, the more productive the discussion.

Once again, faced with the choice of using a challenging question, the teacher may consider phrasing it as a declarative statement, thereby lessening the "sting" of the challenge. Students seem to feel less intimidated by, "You may have a suggestion for an alternative plan of action, William," than they do under the gun of the more confrontational, "What can you suggest that would be more effective?"

In raising the issue of challenging questions, several words need to be added about the use of "why" in the interactive discourse. This question is perhaps most frequently heard in classrooms in the form, "Why do you think so?" or sometimes, "Why, or why not?" This question is intended as a challenge and its purpose is to have the student defend an idea, a principle, or a proposition with data. Teachers who have worked with debriefing tend to use "why" questions sparingly for several reasons. First, "why" is both confrontational and highly challenging. Second, "why" covers a vast amount of territory, which can be only partially answered in a student's response. Third, teachers seem to fall back on "why" questions when they are unable to frame a more productive question. It is not that reasons are not important or that students should not be asked to defend their ideas with supporting data. It's rather that there are more productive ways to get at that information. For example:

What reasons do you have for those suggestions?
What data support your ideas?
What examples can you give?

The "what" questions tend to narrow the field and give the student a better handle on framing a response. They are also less confrontational. Used selectively, they seem to add more to the quality of the thinking in a discussion than do the more wide open "why" questions.

The transcript below provides a picture of how all three response types are used in debriefing the case "It's Up to You, Mrs. Buscemi" (Wassermann, 1993a) with a group of teacher-participants. This portion of the transcript examines the issue of affirmative action.

TEACHER: What do you think? Should Adam Wright be given a chance by getting a passing grade?

BILL: I'm against it. It's not fair to all the other students if he gets his grade boosted, when others don't get that advantage.

TEACHER: So the issue of fairness is the one that concerns you, Bill. [Paraphrases] If Adam gets a boost, it's not being fair to others who earned their grades. [Paraphrases] Anyone else?

MARCY: I agree with Bill. I think that boosting his grade 20 points is asking a little much. If it were a matter of five points, I'd consider it.

TEACHER: You'd go for five points, but not for 20. [Paraphrases] The issue for you is the discrepancy between the passing grade and his final mark. [Interprets]

MARCY: I think teachers weasel students' marks a bit; I think we all tend to give a student a bit of a boost if the grade is near passing. But this boy is nowhere near passing.

TEACHER: A few points is okay, in your book, Marcy. I want to push you a bit on that with respect to your cutting off point. You'd go for a boost on five points. Well, what about six? [Challenges]

Marcy nods.

TEACHER: What about seven? [Challenges]

Marcy nods again.

TEACHER: What about 10? [Challenges]

MARCY: I was afraid it would come to this. [She laughs] I don't know. I just don't know.

TEACHER: You don't know the cutoff point. The point at which you are prepared to say, "This is my limit." [Paraphrases]

LAURA: I'd like to say something here, please. Based on my experience, Adam deserves a boost up. He's a good kid. He's tried hard. He's not shirking. Giving him a boost up may mean a life and death difference in his life. I mean, what are we talking about here? These are just numbers. We're talking about a kid's life.

TEACHER: You want to give Adam a chance at something better in his life. [Interprets] You think that that chance is more important than the grades. Grades are just numbers to you. [Paraphrases]

LAURA: I think that more kids would get a better chance if teachers wouldn't take the numbers so seriously. Kids are more important than marks.

TEACHER: I'm going to raise a question that is a bit challenging for you, Laura. How about the question of standards? Where do you stand on that issue, with respect to boosting Adam's grade? [Challenges]

LAURA: I haven't thought that out. I recognize that we've got to have standards in schools, that without them, schools would lose their reputations. But right now, I'm staying with my position that Adam needs a chance more than he needs to fail math.

TEACHER: You're conflicted about the pulls between standards and giving a deserving boy like Adam a break. [Paraphrases] You haven't thought it out yet and you'd like more time to consider the issues. [Paraphrases]

MARK: He's a boy from the projects. If he fails, loses his chance for college, what predictions can we make about his future?

TEACHER: Given that he's a boy from the projects, this has implications for your decision, Mark. [Paraphrases]

MARK: You have to know what life is like in the projects. Most of us don't know that.

TEACHER: Can you give some examples of what you mean? [Asks for analysis]

MARK: Well, drugs are sold openly, for one thing. People are armed to the teeth. There are killings almost every day. That is, if Adam's project is like the one I knew in New Orleans.

TEACHER: Life in the projects, as you know it, is cruel and terrifying. [Interprets] He wouldn't have much of a chance, if his teacher did not give him the boost. [Interprets] You seem to be making the assumption that all projects are alike in these ways. [Asks for analysis]

MARK: I'm not sure they all are the same. But I think many of them are the same.

TEACHER: I want to get back to the issue of fairness. If the teacher chooses to give Adam a boost on his final grade, what about the other kids? And what about the issue of fairness? [Raises a related issue]

The three transcripts presented above give short vignettes of how different teacher-response levels are used to encourage students' examination of the issues in a case, and how, with increased challenge, responses promote reflection on deeper issues. It is taken as a given that the criteria identified for good study questions in Chapter 4—that is, to invite, rather than command; to be respectful of students and their ideas;

to be clear about what is being asked; and to proceed with questions in a developmental sequence that allows for progressive deepening of understanding—all apply in the oral form of debriefing as well.

Choosing Questions That Address the Issues

A favorite story about using appropriate questions was told by a teacher whose first graders were having "show and tell." Donald, age 6, had the floor and was showing a game that his grandmother had given him. Donald spent several minutes describing the game, and the children were attentive and interested in his presentation. When he finished, he asked, in good teaching strategy, "Are there any questions?" At this point his classmate Terry raised his hand to ask, "What's your grandmother's name?"

There is much more to the art of questioning than merely making interrogative demands. If debriefing discussions are to be productive—that is, promote students' intelligent examination of the big ideas—not only must questions be sensitively framed, respectful, articulate, and inviting; they also must be conceptualized to allow the discussion to get at the heart of the real issues. This requires the teacher to have a clear idea of what those "real issues" are, in advance of teaching the case. This also requires an understanding of how the questions are sequenced, to allow for progressive uncovering of issues.

This sequencing of questions is, of course, guided by the teacher's goals for the case debriefing, that is, the important ideas that are to be put under examination. But knowing how best to move questions from (a) to (b) to (c), to uncover the issues layer by layer, gives the debriefing a richness and fullness that makes it feel complete.

Christensen's (Rosmarin, 1985) "typology" of questions is a helpful guide. The first-tier questions are exploratory, bringing the surface issues under examination.

> What are the important issues as you see them?
> What can be said about the key players? About their roles in the incident?
> What is seen as the nature of the dilemma?

The second tier of questions call for analysis.

> Why do you suppose that [people behave that way]?
> What do you see as some limitations to the approach used?
> How do you see the context of this situation making a difference?

Questions in the third tier call for the generation of new ideas and the evaluation of plans.

> What plan would you recommend?
> How do you see that plan as adequate to the problem? What makes you think so? Where might that plan derail? What other plans are possible?
> How should the teacher be supported during this time? What do you recommend? Where might that plan derail? What other plans are possible?
> Which is the best plan? How did you make that determination? What assumptions are being made?

Finally, the concluding tier of questions reflect on the process.

> What has been learned in this process?
> What principles/values underlie the choices?
> What principles/values of your own are protected in the choices you are recommending?

As in most other aspects of case method teaching, there are no hard and fast rules about the sequencing of questions. Each effective case method teacher is likely to have his or her own typology; but some rational system of how the sequencing will progress ought to be planned before the debriefing begins. This will help discussion leaders avoid the "off the top of the head" questions that come spontaneously, without connection to each other, and leave the students feeling as if they have been on some kind of speed trip, without a clear idea of either what the journey was about or what destination they have arrived at.

Ask Questions That Promote Cognitive Dissonance

In addition to the criteria identified above that guide a teacher's choice of what questions to use during debriefing a case, there is also to be considered how questions are used to promote cognitive dissonance. When students make dogmatic statements, when they are certain where they should be circumspect, when they are assertive where they should be cautious, promoting cognitive dissonance is a productive way of bringing the student's ideas under examination.

Finding the "right" question—the one with the capacity to rattle a student's closed-minded view is one way of piercing dogmatic thinking. If the mind can be envisioned as a giant cognitive jigsaw puzzle, with trillions of connecting pieces that make patterns or pictures that shape thinking (Snygg, 1966), the "irritating" question becomes like a grain of sand in an oyster shell, a troublesome, prickly thing that jars already framed cognitive patterns and weasles its way into the interstices between the pieces, looking for someplace to fit. The mind must work to free itself from such a cognitive burden.

This freeing occurs in several ways. An extremely closed-minded person is likely to reject the question outright, discarding the irritant by denial or distortion, leaving the cognitive map in place (Rokeach, 1960). The more open-minded person is more likely to view the discrepant idea, turning it this way and that, trying to see how it fits. Such refitting means a reshaping of the pieces in the cognitive jigsaw, so that new patterns are made, leading to new perspectives. When that occurs on a larger scale, it is sometimes referred to as a paradigm shift.

Students whose ways of thinking fall somewhere between these two polar opposites do not reject the irritating question outright; nor do they immediately see its possibilities. They must do some more cognitive wrestling, to find a means to reduce the dissonance. Those who wrote about conceptual change theory (Posner, Strike, Hewson, & Gertzog, 1982) suggest that the creation of cognitive dissonance is required to modify conceptual frameworks. The question that has that capability forces students "to recognize the discrepancy between their present beliefs or knowledge and the alternatives" (Sykes & Bird, 1989, p. 493). Presenting examples and suggesting alternatives, the data suggest, do not lead to change, since students are likely to distort or deny the discrepant data.

Questions that aim at piercing students' cognitive frameworks may not be too irritating, lest students become so overburdened with the discrepancy that they will move to reject. In the overall, these questions present students with conflicting data, show up inconsistencies, present examples that do not fit a student's paradigm. They can also inquire into the extent to which a student believes the statement (e.g., "Would you bet a nickel on it? a dollar? a thousand?"). They must, of course, also meet the other criteria for good questions—to be inviting, respectful, nonjudgmental. Here are two examples of how "irritating" questions are used to provoke cognitive dissonance:

Scenario 1:
STUDENT, with authority: "Children who commit serious crimes *should* be tried and punished as adults."
TEACHER: At what age would you draw the line, then, between children and adults?

STUDENT: I'd draw it at 12.

TEACHER: What about 11?

STUDENT: It would depend upon the crime.

TEACHER: So if the crime was serious, you would recommend a child of 11 be tried and punished as an adult.

STUDENT: Yes.

TEACHER: What about 9? Would you go for 9?

STUDENT: I'm not sure.

TEACHER: What's the difference between 9 and 11?

STUDENT: Nine is too young.

TEACHER: But 11 is old enough. You'd put an 11 year-old who committed a serious crime in prison with adults, but you would have different treatment for 9 year-olds.

Scenario 2:

STUDENT: The Japanese education system is far superior to ours.

TEACHER: How come, then, that this country outperforms the Japanese in Nobel Prize winners?

Reaching for just the "right" nettlesome question is one of the most challenging tasks facing the discussion leader. I have often spent long hours revisiting a discussion, contemplating what questions I "might have used more productively"—knowing that somewhere, just beyond my reach, lies just the *right* question that is sufficiently disturbing to jar a student's smug assertion and bring his or her thinking under re-examination. It is, of course, in those mental replays that one also practices these skills and learns a little more about questions that promote cognitive dissonance.

When the Student's Response Stumps You

In the openness of the interactive forum, students are likely to, and often do, make statements that are baffling, infuriating, breathtaking, painful, provocative. Even an experienced case method teacher may feel inclined to respond, "How could you say such a thing!" Yet, even under the gun of an outrageous student statement, the case method teacher frees the mind from the punitive retort and stops to ask, What is this student telling me? And, what response can I use that will allow him or her to re-examine or examine in a deeper way the implications of what has been said?

During a debriefing of The Cranberry-Orange Muffin Vote (see

Appendix D; Wassermann, 1992b), one teacher-participant who was talking about the limitations of political decision making said, "It made me have some doubts about democracy." This she said with considerable affect in her voice, and there was nothing frivolous in her tone. What response should be made? How is her idea best brought under examination? There are, of course, many choices, each with singular consequences.

The choice I made in that particular context was to say, "Democracy has some serious limitations for you. You seem disappointed that people in power make decisions based on what appear to be frivolous criteria."

I chose that response, rather than raise a question ("What do you see as some of the limitations of the democratic process?") because I was much moved by the sadness in her tone—as if she had discovered for the first time a very disappointing aspect of the democratic process that she had heretofore held in high regard. I wanted to show, in my response, some empathy for her feelings. I also wanted to elevate the idea that even the democratic way has imperfections, leaving the door open for taking the next step. Further, I chose a declarative, rather than an interrogative, response because it seemed to be more respectful of her feelings.

Later, in the same debriefing session, another teacher-participant said, "I'm not that interested in politics," and sat back in his chair as if to dismiss the case and all the issues raised in it. What does the teacher say then? ("No wonder we've got the government we have! You nerd!" Tempting, but definitely unacceptable.) Once again, the choices are vast, and the response selected will invariably bear the trademark of the teacher's particular style elevating the issue that the teacher sees as imperative. Cognitively editing out the impulsive/judgmental response, I chose the more neutral, "Politics is an area that you've distanced yourself from"—using "distanced" as a way of pointing to his verbal and nonverbal behavior. Even then, he shuffled in his chair and looked around, as if for support, before he nodded his head in affirmation. I then pursued him with, "There are more important things in your life than politics," said in a neutral, nonconfrontational tone, but allowing the response to confront his personal choice. He had, now, to reflect on some of his values and do this in a public affirmation. He did, of course, have the option of making his own choice.

Teachers who are beginning to try the interaction skills in their classrooms often ask, "How do you respond when a student says such and such?" referring to some outrageous, inappropriate, or perhaps hostile remark. The best response I can give is: respectfully. Students who are consistently treated respectfully in debriefing sessions soon learn that what they say is taken seriously by the teacher and, moreover, that their ideas will be put to the rigorous test of re-examination. That debriefing ethos goes a long way toward promoting the kind of thinking-before-speaking that teachers long for in student commentary.

CREATING A CLIMATE FOR REFLECTION

Underlying all the response and questioning strategies is the tone that the teacher sets in the discussion classroom. Whatever questions and responses are used, certain aspects of tone contribute substantially to productive and safe discussion.

Inviting Rather Than Commanding

"Defend your answer!" Her voice is raised, her finger pointed at the student under the gun. The student blanches, gulps, responds, "Aaaaggg-rrrhhh," and slinks down into his seat, while others laugh. "It does them good," she says, defending her practice. "They know that they must support their ideas with data."

No one would question students' need to learn to reason from data. Yet, certain actions in calling for such reasoning may be very costly, in terms of creating a climate in which students feel unsafe to respond. It doesn't take any more effort to ask: "Tell me more about how you arrived at that idea, Brendon." Or, "You may have some data to back that up, Gwynne." The advantages to the softer, more inviting approach are great. Students are encouraged to reason from the data, but they are also treated with considerably more respect. A teacher–student partnership, where both parties are engaging in a process of learning more, has little room for the arrogant and authoritarian commands of a teacher, which implicitly carry the order for the student to obey.

Remaining Neutral

One important condition in creating a safe climate is the teacher's ability to resist the tendency to evaluate each student's response. Teachers who have become habituated to using evaluative statements such as "Good idea, Margie," "That's interesting, Marshall," "Not quite right, Gaylord," may claim that students need evaluative encouragement to stimulate further participation. However, such responses are more likely to cut off thoughtful examination than to facilitate it.

Teachers who have tried to let go of evaluative responses, for even one class, have seen evidence in their students' responses of the positive effects of such trials. Students have said:

> "We felt safe to express our own ideas. We felt freer to volunteer our ideas without having to worry about being wrong."
>
> "Even if I had a wild idea, I could raise it without worrying that it might be inappropriate. I can be more creative in my thinking and I can stretch my mind in a wider way."
>
> "I always felt shy about speaking in class. It took me quite a while before I could feel brave enough to say what I think. But I know the teacher would listen and would not put me down."
>
> "Everyone's ideas have value, in some way. It makes me appreciate the ideas of others, even though they are different from mine. We learn to listen to each other, too."
>
> "It makes me feel good about my contribution. I feel I have something worthwhile to say and that my ideas will be heard." (Adam, 1992, pp. 64–86)

Letting go of the evaluative response does not mean being unappreciative of students' ideas. But there is considerable difference in both intent and impact between "Good idea, Marvin" and "Thanks for letting us hear your ideas, Marvin."

Being Consistently Respectful

To respect students, and their ideas, is perhaps the greatest gift that teachers can offer students. Being respectful means taking students and their ideas seriously. It means listening to what they have to say with courtesy; it means treating them as you would guests in your home.

It's hard to know where educators got the idea that students need to be dominated; that they need to learn obedience to the rules; that they must follow, unquestioningly, the teacher's commands. Where the teacher plays the role of authority, all power is taken from students. They have no rights, and they have no say in the important goings on of the class. In this climate, students learn that authority holds power; and that in order for them to get power, they must rise to positions of authority. From such positions, they then will be able to dominate others. That is the implicit message communicated when authority rules and students learn by domination. This is not a climate conducive to critical examination of issues. This is a climate in which students learn that the authority's role is never challenged.

It's not enough for teachers to say, "I respect my students." Respect is seen in behavior; it is seen in the ways teachers treat students. To treat students respectfully means using invitations, instead of commands. It means freeing oneself from the authority role when responding to students' ideas and opinions. It means avoiding making positive or negative judgments about students' responses. It means being flexible and open and nondefensive in the presence of student challenge. To behave in ways that are truly respectful of students and their ideas takes a predisposition to the idea that students deserve respect. When such behavior is exhibited in case discussion, the results can be powerful.

Watching for the Effect

"How do you suppose those mountains got there?" she asks the fifth-grade student. She watches him as he hears the question; there is the briefest flicker of the eyelids and a shutting down. "I don't know," he answers, with an emphasis on the "I"—as if to say, "How do you expect *me* to know *that*?" The effect of her question teaches her something important: The question is too challenging. He may be hearing it as a call for the correct answer. He has shut down and resisted coming up with even a single hypothesis.

Given her "reading" of his response, she is able to repair the damage.

"I was wondering if you have any theories about it?" Introducing the word "theories" opens up some possibilities for him. He doesn't have to know the answer. He is being invited to conjecture.

"Well," he offers, "I think they get there from rocks." He is beginning to formulate his theory. The idea is to keep the thinking line open. He may not be habituated to offering original ideas.

"How does that happen? Could you help me to understand?" He begins to unravel his "small rock" theory, in which small rocks, over the years, grow into mountains. He does have ideas to offer, given the right conditions. If the "machinery can be oiled" he will even venture forth to give them. His theory may be naive, but at least he has taken the risk to offer one. A first step.

Every question asked, every teacher response made to a student, has both cognitive and affective power. Students will feel that power and their subsequent responses (or lack of response) will be affected by it. Learning to "read and interpret" the effect of a response on the subsequent response of a student is an immensely valuable skill in making it safe for students to respond and in building a climate of trust. A look of bewilderment may be mitigated by, "Perhaps I didn't make myself clear. Let me ask that another way." A lack of response may require support, "That was a tough question. You may want some time to think about that. Let me know when you want me to get back to you." A muddled response may be helped with, "Help me to understand. I'm losing the thread of what you are telling me."

The interactive dialogue is not a game in which the teacher is the "hunter" and the student the "fox." It is a partnership in which two people engage in examination of issues, leading to more informed meaning making. The teacher who is able to apprehend fully and be cognitively and affectively aware of all the nuances in the interactive process will be able to draw on those resources to the benefit of all participants.

WHAT DO THE OTHER STUDENTS DO?

Teachers have asked, "What do the other students do in a whole-class debriefing, while I am working, one-on-one, with a single student?" The implication is that students will be bored; that their attention will wane; that they will be disinterested in the discussion that is going on in another part of the room. These concerns come from teachers who have not as yet used case teaching in their own classrooms; they do not come from those who are using cases successfully. To the latter, these are nonissues.

Anyone who has taught with cases successfully will find that students are truly interested in the discussion that is taking place, even when the discussant is on the other side of the classroom. Students seem to follow those discussions closely. They do not need to be reprimanded to pay attention. Perhaps they are interested because ideas of significance are being discussed. Perhaps they are interested in hearing different points of view. All of these reasons have been suggested by students who have been in case method classrooms.

Evidence of students' attention to the discussion is manifest in what happens in their study groups over time. Whereas at the beginning of a semester students fail to listen to each other, are argumentative, and show poor interpersonal and discussion skills, after time study groups reveal the same kind of discussion strategies used by the teacher in the large group debriefing. Students are found to ask each other for supporting data; to examine assumptions; to give examples. Such growth could not come unless students were, in fact, observing closely what was happening during the whole-class debriefing, when their teacher was using just those discussion skills.

Students have said, "Even though I'm not talking myself, I am listening closely to what others are saying and processing those ideas in my own head." The suggestion is made that even when they are not themselves speaking, their minds are working. While the evidence that this occurs is anecdotal, rather than clinical, the comments from students are persuasive.

CONCLUSION: LEARNING THE ART
OF DISCUSSION TEACHING

Orchestrating all the strands of debriefing a case demands a high level of performance from the teacher. Obviously these skills are not learned in a day. Case method teachers may devote a lifetime of serious self-scrutiny to their questioning and responding styles. Like other important teaching skills, this is learned more on the job than in any preparatory program.

At the very top of the list of suggestions for teachers who would aspire to this "lifetime of self-scrutiny" is to learn to "listen to yourself" in the interactive dialogue. This is about the equivalent of learning to listen to yourself play, if you are learning a musical instrument. Without being able to hear not only the wrong notes, but the nuances, the shading, the smoothness of the line, the quality of the sound being produced, there is little hope of mastery. How you learn to listen to yourself in the discussion is key to evolving success. From listening, and from discerning the effects on students of what has been said, you learn about what you are doing well and what needs correction. You learn to build in those corrections in the next sessions. This building process moves you toward mastery.

Also at the very top of the list of suggestions is coming to the awareness that you do not become a discussion teacher through the "short course" of exposure to interactive teaching. This process does not have an "end." It is not like learning some finite skill, like the times tables. It is more like learning to play the Bach Preludes and Fugues. You never stop learning them. You never finish studying the art of discussion teaching.

For enduring self-study, there is the help of a colleague—a co-teacher, who may be co-opted to visit your classroom, comment on what is being observed as you conduct your debriefing sessions, and perhaps even script the interactive dialogue for later analysis. When two teachers work together, this partnership can be enormously additive. Teachers can provide support for each other, help examine each other's interactive style, and together make plans for further professional development.

More intensive self-examination is made through the tool of a tape recorder—audiotape for the more cautious, videotape for the more intrepid. In replaying the tape of a classroom discussion, listen for the kinds of questions being asked; the sequencing of the question; the amount of teacher talk; the kinds of responses being made; the amount of student talk; the quality of student responses brought by your questions. In analyzing the tape, make suggestions to yourself about "wrong notes" and where change in approach or style is required. Make additional notes about how the changes are to be built into subsequent discussions.

Teachers who want to make an even fuller commitment may do so by taking on the arduous task of making a verbatim transcript of a tape of at least 10 minutes of classroom dialogue and subjecting that transcript to critical analysis. While it is very tedious to write out everything that is being said, even in a 10-minute interval, there is great value in the minute examination of every word and question, of tone and nuance, and of the effect of each teacher response or question on students' subsequent responses.

If there is a single preparatory reading to recommend to teachers who wish to study the process, it surely must be C. R. Christensen's (1991a) "Every Student Teaches and Every Teacher Learns: The Reciprocal Gift of Discussion Teaching." This remarkable essay describes with insight and profound wisdom the journey of one teacher's mastery of the art of discussion teaching.

Should teachers commit to such a course of study in learning the skills of debriefing? Should teachers take steps that move them in the direction of more effective classroom discussion? It's like asking whether it's a good idea to study the violin. The course of study may be arduous; but it is the only way I know to learn to make music.

8 | Beyond Cases: Expanding Perspectives with Follow-up Activities

Scott Wylie had just finished debriefing the case "Let's Have a War! That's a Good Idea!" (Gluska, 1991) with his Grade 11 social studies class. This case deals with the issues of patriotism and the call to arms, juxtaposed with the killing, human suffering, and aftermath of the battles in World War I. One of the questions the case raises is whether the sacrifice was worth what was ultimately gained.

World War I had always been a remote event for his students in previous classes, but the case "Let's Have a War" seemed to bring the event into reality for them. The case generated considerable passion about the issues. The students identified with the protagonist in the case and felt his grief over his personal loss. They were horrified to read about the explicit recollections of loss of life and limb during battle. They were stunned to learn of the numbers of casualties among all the countries involved. One student told that her great grandfather had been gassed in the trenches, and he had been disabled all his life. He had come back from the war a broken and depressed man, and this had been a part of her family history for as long as she could remember. She was vigorous in her antiwar arguments and scornful of other students' views that it was a citizen's patriotic duty to enlist in this war. These students maintained that citizens had an obligation to enlist, to protect and defend their country from the aggressor.

As students began to examine the reasons that brought about the initiation of hostilities, they were not able to pin down, in any way they could comprehend, how countries could so easily come to armed warfare that was so destructive of so many. Nor could they begin to comprehend what was gained. At the end of the debriefing, students were more confused and more unsettled. Instead of answers, they were full of questions. The study of issues in and around World War I had barely begun.

It has been said several times throughout this book that a case "drives the need to know." Teaching a case—including study group examinations of study questions, followed by debriefing—is the initial experience in the instructional learning loop, a series of learning experiences that require students' continued critical examination of issues from emerging and evolving perspectives. Beyond debriefing, the teacher selects follow-up learning experiences, each with intent to inform and build knowledge; each subject to subsequent debriefing, so that the process of critical analysis continues. As each subsequent learning experience is added, students become immersed in the examination of basic and related issues, studying these from new and more informed perspectives. This instructional learning loop has been described in Chapter 6.

Beyond the case "Let's Have a War!" Wylie made selections from several different kinds of media, to build his follow-up activities. Information-rich related readings were given as homework assignments. One article about the methods of propaganda used by government and the media to build popular support for the war was written by the teacher and based on primary sources of data. Another article was selected from a history text. Two films were chosen to be viewed in class: *Gallipoli*, the feature film of a futile World War I campaign against the Turks on the beach at Gallipoli; and *Life and Nothing But*, in French with English subtitles, about a French army officer who is assigned to put names to the scores of nameless dead on the French battlefields of the war. Wylie also considered *All Quiet on the Western Front*, a poignant, powerful film of German soldiers' experiences, and *The Guns of August*, a documentary made of old newsreel footage, but put these "on hold" lest too many films overpower the other activities.

A list of novels and nonfiction books was presented to the students, from which they were to make at least two selections. This included *A Farewell to Arms* (Hemingway, 1929); *All Quiet on the Western Front* (Remarque, 1957); *The Guns of August* (Tuchman, 1962); *The Great War* (Barnett, 1978); *The Outbreak of the First World War* (Lee, 1975); *My Grandfather's War* (Matheson, 1981); *Poetry of the First World War* (Hudson, 1988); *Legacy of Valor* (1986); *The Courage of the Early Morning* (Bishop, 1967); *The Long Fuse* (Lafore, 1965); *Marching to Armageddon* (Morton & Granatstein, 1989); *The Zimmerman Telegram* (Tuchman, 1958).

In-class activities included film viewing; study groups on new questions related to articles, films, and texts; and subsequent debriefings. At the end of 2 weeks of studies, students were given options about choosing some culminating activity that would provide a form of closure to their studies and also give Wylie a way of assessing the kind of understandings students were taking away from their experiences. (Suggestions for evaluation activities are discussed at length in Chapter 10.)

Before bringing the studies on World War I to a close, Wylie asked the students to participate in an analysis of all of their experiences. This was to be an evaluation of the teaching–learning process, in which students would respond to such questions as

- What did you observe about the process?
- How did study groups work to inform your thinking?
- What observations did you make about how debriefing promoted your intelligent examination of the issues?
- How did you see yourself benefiting from case study work? What problems did you experience?
- What have you learned about the topic?

The students responded to questions thoughtfully. They saw considerable benefit to learning with cases. Study groups, they said, tended at first to be argumentative, but eventually the members began to listen to each other more and to have more respect for each other's ideas. Study groups also made it safe for them to express their ideas. They learned, they said, to communicate their ideas more clearly and to be unafraid to speak. Debriefing, they told Wylie, made them accountable for what they were saying. It forced them to think. They couldn't just "run off at the mouth. They had to defend their ideas with data. Debriefing makes us work hard to think." Students also pointed to Wylie's nonevaluative role as a discussion leader. They attributed their willingness to speak, in large group discussions, to the absence of his evaluative judgments of their ideas. What Wylie heard in his students' analysis of the process was consonant with Adam's (1992) findings in her study of Grade 11 students.

MATERIALS FOR FOLLOW-UP ACTIVITIES

If a case "drives students' need to know," this opens the door for a variety of follow-up activities that feed that need. While a few books containing cases come with suggestions for follow-up activities (see, for example, Bickerton et al., 1991), most teachers are faced with having to make their own follow-up resource list. In this section, follow-up activities such as related readings, films, novels, original source data, speakers, and field trips are discussed from the vantage point of their usefulness and how they are obtained. These categories of follow-up activities do not represent all the possibilities; they do, however, give a wide spectrum of what is available and what can be used to build students' perspectives on the issues and expand their knowledge base. To what extent, and how, teachers use follow-up activities is a matter of individual choice. Ideally, however, teaching strategies used for follow-up work ought to be consistent with case method teaching, for obvious reasons. It is recommended, therefore, that insofar as possible, follow-up activities move through the same pattern of experience-debriefing-re-experience.

Related Readings

Related readings include information-rich essays, articles, or other textual material that gives background information on events or issues under examination in the case. Related readings are used in lieu of teacher lectures. They present data that "fill in" the knowledge gaps. Students who do the readings are expected to be more informed about the issues.

Teachers may, of course, compose their own essays to follow up the cases they use. There are certain advantages to this. Information that the teacher believes to be particularly relevant can be included and highlighted. Language used may be more appropriate to the reading level of the students in the class. The teacher has more control over what material is included and how that material is presented. Length and accuracy are also under the teacher's control. This is the good news.

The disadvantages are obvious. Teachers will need to create these resources, and as in the creation of any good curriculum material, this requires yet another out of class time commitment on the part of the already overburdened teacher. It may be of some comfort to realize that the creation of teacher-written essays is done only once. These essays are then used each time a particular case is studied.

Another route to acquiring related readings is to draw on what others have written. Here, teachers will have to make choices based on some criteria, for example:

- Does the textual material present information about issues relevant to the case?
- Does the textual material provide background information that is necessary to broaden students' knowledge and deepen students' understanding?
- Is the textual material the "right" length (i.e., not overly long) to sustain students' interest?

- Is the writing clear, coherent, easily understood?
- Does it present information from a balanced point of view? Does it avoid subtly or overtly pitching a particular position or point of view?
- What steps need to be taken to duplicate this material legally, so that all students may have their own copies? Is permission to duplicate a legal possibility?

Material for related readings may most easily be found in required and supplementary classroom texts, where there is no problem of duplicating copies if there are enough texts on hand. School and public libraries provide access to a host of other books, journal and newspaper articles, and other information-rich reference materials from which readings may be drawn. Once again, when these related readings have been gathered for a case, the job of gathering need not be done again, unless there is some reason to update the material.

Here is an example of how one teacher gathered and used related readings with her Biology 12 class. Following the case "An Unwelcome Reaction" (Bickerton, 1993), written to promote examination of the process of allergic response, especially severe anaphylactic shock, the teacher needed a reading about the causes and effects of anaphylactic shock. A good discussion was found in the Grade 12 biology textbook, which then served as the related reading for this case. Another reading presenting information about homeostatic mechanisms in the body that work to restore body systems to normal was also deemed necessary. Material for this was obtained from a supplementary science text.

Cases for social studies, history, geography, economics, government, and Western Civilization might make use of original source material as related readings. For example, the Declaration of Independence, Canada's Charter of Rights, the Magna Carta, the Balfour Declaration, and other similar documents present information to enlighten students' further discussions of issues.

The use of related readings provides background information for students who learn with cases. These follow-up written materials provide important ways of presenting data that enrich students' understanding of concepts and principles and broaden their knowledge about the issues. In the absence of teacher lectures about content, follow-up readings offer the teacher the means of promoting knowledge acquisition in a case method classroom.

In staff development workshops on case method teaching, some teachers have questioned why information-rich readings come *after* the initial discussion of the case. "Wouldn't students' discussions be more informed if they did the readings *before* they got into the discussion of the case?" That is the way many teachers do, in fact, teach: the input of data first, prior to the actual or vicarious experience. That is perhaps why so many students forget the information quickly after the lesson is over. There has been no relevant experience to build the cognitive frameworks on which to "hang" the data.

Cognitive frameworks are developed from personal, meaningful experiences. That is what the study of the case does and that is why information comes *after* the case study. The information in the related readings fills in the gaps left opened by the unanswered questions in the case discussion. Frameworks are built in the discussion, and information that comes afterward is then woven in where it is needed. This instructional concept of information *following* experience did not originate with case method teaching. Formulated in the work of John Dewey in his seminal work, *Experience in Education* (1938), it was further developed by the cognitive psychologist Jerome Bruner (1966) in his theoretical constructs of learning. Donald Snygg's (1966) cognitive field theory of learning also made a substantial contribution to the thinking in this field. Snygg writes about the "good" student "who learns the required material for examination purposes but keeps it from entering and changing his view of reality by dividing his field into two parts, 'reality' and 'school,' the latter having nothing to do with real life. This is the game that has given the word 'academic' its connotation of impractical futility" (p. 86). Snygg notes that a learned concept is "perceived as part of reality only when it has been discovered by the student as part of the reality of his own experience, in his own perceptual field" (p. 86).

What these developmental theorists have told us is that meaningful learning is "extracted" from experience. This is contrasted with transmission-type school learning, in which information is fed to students prior to, or in the absence of, experience. These are some reasons for the readings to come *after* the case discussion. Does it work? The data from teachers who use this approach are persuasive. Will it work for you? You will need to use your own classroom experiences as evidence to see if it does. If students are not learning successfully, and if learning does not endure, then whatever instructional method you have chosen must be modified.

Films

The use of films—documentary and commercial—to enrich and enliven students' learning experiences is as "old hat" to teachers as pencil sharpeners. Films have been used in classrooms for at least 50 years, since audiovisual departments made both the films and technology available for classroom use. With the advent of videocassette recorders, the range of what is available has increased a thousandfold. The medium of film has many and considerable advantages as follow-up activities to cases.

Films are, in one sense, other forms of cases. There are characters to identify with; narratives with considerable dramatic power; issues that bear examination. Some teachers have, in fact, used certain selected films *as* cases, and using case teaching methodology have found considerable success with them (Manley-Casimir & Wassermann, 1989).

Those who would consider films as potential resources for follow-up activities will find an embarrassment of riches. The emergence of the videocassette industry has produced several fine film guides—reference books that contain alphabetical listings of thousands of commercial films. Canadians will be familiar with the National Film Board of Canada, whose catalogue is available in most school media centers in Canada. These films are also available in the United States through the National Film Board offices at 1251 Avenue of the Americas, New York, NY 10020. Noncommercial television stations, like the CBC in Canada and PBS in the United States, have extensive lists of made-for-TV films, listed by subjects, making it easy to find out what's available in the subject area you are searching for. Each listing comes with a brief description of what the film is about, including the running time.

Commercial and made-for-TV films listed, for example, in the impressive *Movie and Video Guide* (Maltin, 1993), are, unfortunately, not categorized by subject, and in searching out films that are relevant to a particular topic, teachers need to resort to their own devices. A knowledgeable film buff, acquainted with classic films as well as more contemporary ones, will be a valuable ally.

While videocassettes are easily found and cheap to rent, keep in mind that it is illegal to show rental cassettes in classrooms. These are specified "for use in homes only." Keep in mind, too, that for a modest purchase price, these can be bought and kept on hand for classroom use, whenever needed. Of course, it is not necessary for teachers to do the legwork in acquiring films. Most school media center personnel will be glad to do the job.

Certain case topics will yield a plethora of film possibilities from which teachers will have to select, unhappily, only those few that time allows for. For the case "Welcome Aboard!" (see Appendix A; Wassermann, 1991b)—a narrative of a Jewish family trying to escape from Germany in 1939—literally dozens of films are available that present haunting and horrifying stories of the plight of the Jews in Nazi Germany. These include: *Shoah; Playing for Time; Sophie's Choice; Garden of the Finzi-Continis; Au Revoir, Les Infants; Dark Lullabies; Two Men; Wallen-*

berg: A Hero's Story; Judgment at Nuremberg; Inside the Third Reich; and the celebrated *Schindler's List*. (See Appendix A for the full documentation of these films.)

In making selections of films, teachers will wish to choose only those that bring to light those issues related to the case that warrant more extensive examination.

Books

Teachers who have taught a particular subject before will already know at least some of the books, both fiction and nonfiction, that can serve as supplementary teaching material. To follow up case narratives, it is suggested that both novels and nonfiction texts be considered resources in the social sciences and humanities, as well as in the sciences. There are several suggestions for building up a reading list for a case, beyond a teacher's own personal resources.

1. Consult with the school and public librarians. Explain your quest and ask for suggestions about locating relevant literature.
2. Consult the card catalogue files (most libraries now have these on computer), particularly the subject classification.
3. For nonfiction titles, spend some time searching the shelves that house the books listed in your subject classification.
4. Visit two or three of the best bookstores in your town. Consult with the salespersons and, more important, search the shelves in those subject classifications related to your case.

Of course, selection of titles for your list presupposes your first having read and sanctioned a choice as appropriate to your class needs. Whatever other criteria enter into your choice, the first ought to be how the book is related to the issues in the case. It is always a good idea, in promoting critical analysis, to include material that presents different sides of issues, and lists of books ought to represent the best quality thinking from several perspectives. Such diversity exposes students not only to the different ways in which different people perceive issues, but to the lack of agreement, even among "knowledgeable" individuals, about issues of substance.

It is not being suggested that students read all the books on a list; in keeping with the spirit of case method teaching, students will have choices about what books are selected and how what is read might then be shared in the wider forum. (See Appendix A for the list of books related to the case "Welcome Aboard!")

Magazines and Newspaper Articles

The discovery of the newspaper clipping file in my local public library was, for me, a blessed event. Even in that modest neighborhood branch, the clipping file was extensive and covered subject areas chronologically. It was more than adequate for my needs in building a clipping resource for the case "Where Have All the Salmon Gone?" (see Appendix E; Wassermann, 1993d).

In a larger, urban library, the clipping file should be overflowing, offering much choice, a diversity of points of view from editorials and op-ed essays to news reports. Clippings ideally should come from several newspaper sources. It is healthy to have different viewpoints represented, and worthwhile for students to see how the same news is reported from different perspectives in different papers and news magazines. The reference librarian more than likely will be pleased to "show you the how and the what" in locating clippings, and my experiences with these excellent people has always resulted in much more material than I could ever practically use.

If the clippings needed antedate what is in the clipping file, let the librarian introduce you to the microfilm or microfiche file. In some libraries, whole newspapers are now stored on microfilm or tiny microfiche negatives, which are viewed on a large, computer-like screen. For newspaper and magazine articles that are more than a century old, once again consult with the reference librarian about how you might get access to these sources. Your school librarian should also be a valuable resource and ally in acquiring what you need. Consider, too, the possibility of writing or phoning newspapers or magazines directly, to inquire how to obtain information that they published over a century ago. The *New York Times* is especially simpatico to requests and is extremely helpful in locating information.

It is true that searching for the documents is time intensive. Perhaps your school has some funds to support student-workers, who may then be enlisted to do the reference legwork. Avenues for support help might be explored to lighten the load of personal involvement in the task of acquiring newspaper and magazine resources.

Original Source Material

Several years ago, a company called Jackdaws (Grossman Publishers) went into the business of publishing reprints of historical source material that teachers could use as reference for particular social studies units. Included in these packages were copies of original documents, such as the Declaration of Independence; the U.S. Constitution; a letter written by Louis Pasteur to his first patient; a page from one of Shakespeare's books, Russian Civil War posters, and various eyewitness accounts of historical events. These primary data, written and reported in the language and the context of the times, became powerful support materials in the study of history, economics, and government. These are, unfortunately, no longer available for purchase, but school libraries may still have them in their curriculum materials section.

Original source material need not be limited to historical documents. Posters, maps, photos, and pages from newspapers headlining events of consequence are also good resources. Advertisements from the early 1800s selling land for $3.00 an acre; recruiting posters from the American Revolution; early Sears and Roebuck catalogues; posters of slaves for sale during the Civil War era are examples of the kinds of materials available through local, state, and national historical societies, town and city museums, and state and national parks at minimal cost. Also available from those sources are letters, diaries, paintings, telegrams, and cartoons.

Photos are excellent sources of primary data and offer insight into time, place, people, and events. Historic photos are easily available through local historical societies and natural history and anthropological museums.

Tools and relics made centuries ago may also be added to the list. What did early American medical and dental equipment look like? What equipment was used to store and cool food? What did children's toys look like? Dolls? What kinds of shoes were worn? What sports equipment was used? What musical instruments? What tools? A hunt through the junk shops on "main street" will yield surprising bounty for small cost.

Where original material is not available either because it has been lost or because it is too valuable to be brought to school, drawn-to-scale illustrations may be used in their place. In that way, illustrations can provide source material to inform about the artifacts used in Greek and Roman civilizations, early Native cultures, Oriental cultures. Check natural history museums in your city for what they have available in materials and artifacts for school use. Many teachers use reprints of the art masters in the examination of historical events, for example, the Bayeux tapestry and the art of Vermeer, Rembrandt, Bruegel, to give cultural evidence of life during those times. There is a wealth of original source material, which, like related readings, once collected should have a long shelf life. Not to be neglected in the search for these is the school's or college's curriculum resource center, which very likely stocks the more recent publications in the curriculum material field.

Speakers

A teacher in California who each year undertakes with her senior history class a simulation of the Nuremberg trials, has, through local organizations in her community, been able to contact a Holocaust survivor who has become a resource person for her classroom work. The mock trials have become identified with this teacher; and each new semester all her students look forward to their participation in this simulation. Over the years, the teacher has accumulated a file of letters from former students, pointing to the powerful effect of the trials on their attitudes and on their behavior as adults. At the end of each semester, after the long process of preparing for and carrying out the trials is over, she formally requests the Holocaust survivor to come and speak to her class. The woman she has chosen is, by now, in her late sixties. She was a child when she was taken to the concentration camp. She is soft-spoken and reflective, and the tattooed number is still prominent on the inside of her forearm.

By the time of the mock trial's end, the students are convinced that they have become intimately acquainted with virtually every event and every scenario leading up to and during the Nuremberg trials. Their guest speaker, however, brings a living example, a piece of reality documenting the horror and the barbarism of that terrible time. There are ten thousand new questions to be raised after she has spoken. Where there was satisfaction in the closure that the trial's finish brought, now there is turmoil. One small, frail, elderly woman has put a new face on what they have learned.

If a speaker is to be chosen as one of the follow-up activities to a case, the speaker should do more than just represent his or her own opinion about the issues. He or she should be chosen because there is something of significance to add, something that will elevate students' awareness beyond what has already been considered. The speaker should have firsthand knowledge about the issues in the case and should present a point of view from "someone who has been there." This might be the judge or lawyer in a real courtroom case; the young man who had the allergic reaction to nuts; the doctor who was in the emergency room when the boy who was shot was brought in; the man who must sell his boat because he is no longer able to earn a living fishing; a Japanese who lost his property and his freedom during his internment in the U.S. or Canadian camps in World War II; a businessperson whose business went bankrupt, or one whose small business made a million dollars in its first year of operation; a psychotherapist who treats compulsive eating disorders.

Not all cases will lend themselves to a speaker as a follow-up activity. But when a case can be followed up through a real person's experiences, the issues in a case take on new meaning.

Field Trips

If a field trip is chosen as a follow-up activity to a case, the experience of the trip should have the power to illuminate new dimensions about the issues. It should be much more than just a good time, a holiday away from school. While field trips go beyond the ordinary in case classrooms, the significance of what is offered in a trip may make the complex preparations for the occasion more than worthwhile.

"The Case of Donald Marshall" (Wassermann, 1991a), the Micmac Indian lad who was wrongly accused and who spent 11 years in jail, might be extended by students' visits to a courtroom to witness a real trial. The case "Where Have All the Salmon Gone?" (see Appendix E; Wassermann, 1993d) may lead to a field trip to a fishing town or cannery, if the school is in a coastal city or town. The case "To Care or Not to Care" (Wassermann, 1993c), about the placing in foster care of an abused child, may lead to visits to social service placement agencies.

Field trips are expensive in several ways. They are costly in terms of time—to make all the arrangements and take the trip itself. They are costly in terms of resources used, of energy spent, of finances. Therefore, field trips should be planned only when the net result of going is anticipated to be greater than the sum of the costs. When these gains are justifiably expected, the primary experience of being there and experiencing the situation firsthand will deepen understanding and raise questions that lead to ongoing, reflective consideration of issues.

REFLECTION ON THE PROCESS

It is not necessary that students be asked after the study of every case to reflect on the process of their experiences with learning from cases. But reflection on experience can lead to important insights about what students see as happening to them, in terms of knowledge, attitudes, and skills built. What's more, such reflection on experience can affirm for students exactly what they are learning: what they are discovering about how they process data; how they are becoming intelligent consumers of data; how they are learning to suspend judgment; how they are learning to deal with the absence of closure; how their need for simplistic answers to complex problems is diminishing; what knowledge they are acquiring.

From my own teaching experiences, and from the experiences of colleagues who work in similar ways with adult learners in college and university classrooms, it is clear that even adult students in a more student-centered classroom do not necessarily understand much about the process they are engaged in. Some might even consider this more student-directed process as "less demanding" in terms of academic rigor. "Why can't we be sitting in rows, copying notes from the blackboard, and getting reams of homework, like the other sixth graders in Mr. Biot's class?" one of my sixth-grade students complained to me a long time ago. My students then believed they were having too much of a good time in school. Learning needed to be tough, even unpalatable, if it was to be worthwhile. Never mind that they outperformed the other sixth-grade class on the Stanford Achievement Test at the end of the school year. They thought this happened "magically"—certainly not as a result of the projects they had been doing in cooperative learning groups; the "thinking activities" that they thought were great fun; the choices they had in selecting their own books to read; the science experiments carried out; the continuous engagement in firsthand experiences, with opportunity to extract meaning from experience. It is frequently the case that adult learners share these naive views.

Opportunity to reflect on the process should help students to realize more about the kinds of cognitive struggles they are making in order to comprehend complex and serious issues. They should be able to see how their learning, within this process, is enhanced. They should be able to point to the gains that occur from learning with cases, in their own performance skills, their knowledge, their attitudes.

Reflection on experience does more than dramatize, for the students, in clear and explicit ways, what the process has given them, both individually and collectively. It makes articulate how the experience has done this and in that way takes the mystery and the magic out of the process. It brings to life and to reality the way case method teaching works to enhance their learning.

For those potential gains, the time spent in such reflection on experience is well worth it. Questions should be posed that probe for insights into learning. Following are some examples, not all of which are intended to be used in a single session:

1. How did you see your work in the study group help you in your thinking about the issues?
2. How did you see the debriefing help you in your thinking about the issues?

3. What is there about the way a study group works that helps you to think more about the issues?
4. What is there about the way the debriefing works that helps you to think more about the issues?
5. In what ways does case teaching help you to understand these issues?
6. How does case teaching work to improve your communication skills?
7. How has this methodology contributed to your respect for the ideas and opinions of others?
8. What responsibilities does a learner have in a case study classroom?
9. What do you see as the teacher's job in a case study classroom?
10. What do you see as some important benefits to you, personally, as a student in a case method classroom?
11. To what extent do you see this method as helping you academically?
12. How does case method teaching help you to become a more independent learner?
13. What are some of your frustrations with case method teaching? What do you see as some causes of those frustrations?
14. How could the class work on the next case be improved? What suggestions do you have for the class?
15. How could the teacher's work with the class on the next case be improved? What suggestions do you have for the teacher?

CONCLUSION

Teaching a case is the beginning point of students' inquiry into the issues. The case itself, study groups, and debriefing take students into their initial experiences of examination. Beyond teaching the case lie numerous possibilities for follow-up activities selected by the teacher to deepen and enrich students' understanding. What activities are chosen, the extent to which follow-up activities are used, and how much time will be spent on follow-up activities are all matters of individual determination. What is important in selecting experiences beyond cases is that students' inquiries continue to unfold in the intelligent examination of issues of consequence.

9 | Evaluation in the Case Method Classroom: Setting Standards

Teachers have long known that evaluation is the "tail that wags the curriculum dog." The nagging question, "Is this going to be on the exam?" defines what really matters in the world of teaching and learning. While noble goal statements, curriculum innovations, creative pedagogies, and new resource materials may hold considerable promise for student learning, what makes *the* difference to what teachers do in classroom practice is dictated by what is mandated in the assessment of student learning. In the wake of every educational reform movement of the last 10 years, with the objectives of preparing students to live productively as citizens of the twenty-first century, it is arguably the how and the what of evaluation of student learning that, more than any other force, effectively enables, or disables, progress toward those reforms. As one senior high school biology teacher anguished, "I believe in case method teaching. I want this kind of learning for my students. But until they change the provincial-wide exam, with its oppressive emphasis on recall of specific information, I cannot see how I can use cases to prepare students to learn this gargantuan collection of facts and definitions."

Where teachers are constrained by assessment policies and practices that militate against the goals of case method teaching, there may be little they can do. They are caught between what they believe to be right and good in classroom practice, and district-mandated policies that not only constrain, but seriously undermine, the positive effects of what they seek in student learning. This chapter does not have answers for teachers so boxed in. I can only recognize and commiserate with the frustrations and the stress that fall upon teachers in such unsatisfactory teaching circumstances.

The materials found in this chapter and the next are for teachers who are not so constrained—those who are in the happier circumstances of being free to choose evaluation methods that are more in keeping with the goals of case method instruction.

DETERMINING THE EVALUATIVE CRITERIA

A preliminary task in assessing student performance is the setting of standards—the criteria against which students are measured in order to determine the extent to which they have achieved certain learning gains. In many public school systems, the standards are implicit and the measurement criterion is set by a number, for example, 65%, or the "passing grade." Implicit in the number are hidden criteria that teachers use to make their determinations that students have attained or failed to attain the numerical standard. Where standards are implicit, whatever a student's score, it is difficult to know to what extent different criteria, such as effort, performance on various tasks, understanding of the larger concepts, skills, attitude, class participation, and other variables, are weighted in computing that student's attainment of the standard. It is also impossible to know if each of the hidden criteria is given equal weight in evaluating all students in the class. It is already a given that criteria for making such numerical determinations vary widely from teacher to teacher (even among those teaching the same subject in the same school). Students know in advance that Mr. Blue is an "easy" marker, while Mrs. Mauve is a "tough" one.

In some classes, teachers do let students in on how different aspects of their classwork is to be weighted, for example, 20% for class participation; 40% for assignments; 40% for exams. However, even if the distribution of weight is explicit, criteria may once again be hidden. For example, what does class participation include? Frequency? Quality of contribution? Both? How is quality determined? Even in the presence of clearly identified distribution weights, the standard for assessing student performance is likely to be variable from teacher to teacher, and even a single teacher has been known to apply criteria flexibly to different students in a class. Whoever said evaluating students was easy is either a fool or has never been faced with the rigors of the task.

Wrestling with the problems of evaluating students in their case method classrooms, a group of secondary school social studies teachers met to discuss their concerns. Maureen Adam, Rich Chambers, Steve Fukui, and Joe Gluska[1] saw two major impediments to using traditional assessment procedures for case method classrooms.

---

1. The materials in this chapter and the following chapter originally appeared in the resource book, *Evaluation Materials for the Graduation Program* (1991), developed collaboratively by Maureen Adam, Rich Chambers, Steve Fukui, Joe Gluska, and myself. We were supported with funding from the British Columbia Ministry of Education. The materials have been adapted with the permission of the authors.

First, they had no explicit standard—no agreed upon criteria—that would identify those learning goals that combined significant aspects of social studies and case method learning. It was not enough for criteria to be implicit. Making criteria explicit would increase reliability as well as validity in assessing student performance. It would also make explicit to students what teachers considered to be their highest expectations for student performance in their classes.

Second, the teachers pointed to the inadequacies of the tools they had been using in previous teaching years to assess student performance. These short answer tests were no longer viable. They did not allow for the measurement of those aspects of student learning that were believed to be achievable through case method teaching.

This chapter describes how these teachers developed a standard of performance—*The Profiles of Student Behavior* (Adam et al., 1991). The *Profiles* make explicit the criteria they would use to identify significant learning for their students. While the *Profiles of Student Behavior* were originally intended for use in social studies classes, their applicability to virtually all subject areas is immediately seen. Chapter 10 presents examples of assessment tools—ways of determining the extent to which students have attained the standards—also developed by these teachers.

What is the postsecondary teacher to make of all of this? What relevance does a standard for secondary school students have for college and professional courses? While not all of the 20 *Profiles* may be useful in assessing university level students, it will be seen that most of these criteria of intelligent classroom functioning are equally applicable to students in case method classrooms at higher levels of education as well. At the very least, they serve as examples for the kinds of criteria that can be developed to assess student growth in more comprehensive ways. Professors in faculties of education are also referred to the *Profiles of Teaching Competency* (Eggert & Wassermann, 1976), which, like the *Profiles of Student Behavior*, identify standards and criteria for assessing the performance of preservice teachers.

DEVELOPING THE PROFILES OF STUDENT BEHAVIOR

In developing the *Profiles of Student Behavior*, the teachers agreed that students' classroom behavior is evidence of what and how well students have learned. It is also evidence of students' growth or lack of growth. If a way could be found to identify those classroom behaviors considered representative of the most desirable qualities of intelligent functioning in learning situations, they would have a "standard" to assess student growth. In other words, rather than examining the small details of subject matter knowledge, the teachers wanted to find a way to determine how what students were learning was seen in the way they functioned in the classroom.

The questions—What should student behavior look like, from the most promising perspective of achieved learning? What are the very best examples of students' high level functioning on learning tasks? What is it teachers hope to see in students' behavior as a consequence of their very best teaching efforts?—were used to generate a list of about 60 behavioral characteristics that suggested that learning of quality was occurring. This list was then refined and reduced, characteristics grouped and further categorized, yielding 20 behavioral standards (see Figure 9.1). These standards are not subject specific. They represent what teachers hope students will become as they move through the school programs and become more "educated." This is what teachers hope to see in student behaviors as a consequence of their best teaching.

After these behavioral standards had been identified, "profiles" were written to describe how the behaviors were seen in the classroom. The profiles take the behavioral standards to lower levels of abstraction, making them more concrete, and thus allowing greater accuracy in assessment. Each profile is offered in both a negative and a positive view. On the positive side are the indicators of higher quality functioning. On the negative side are those behaviors that are seen as counterproductive to learning. The 20 profiles are not the *only* behaviors that teachers may look for as evidence of how students act in class, but they are cited by teachers as those behaviors considered to be representative of students' ability to function intelligently as citizens in a democratic society.

In addition to setting standards, the profiles reveal, with clarity, those areas where students need help and what kind of work is needed to promote student growth. Used as a diagnostic tool, the profiles pinpoint students' performance strengths and weaknesses as well as providing a focus for writing evaluative reports and conducting parent–teacher conferences.

The *Profiles of Student Behavior* were developed in two forms. The Teacher Form (Form A) allows for teachers' assessments. However, the need to involve students in self-assessment was also considered to be an important and valuable aspect of furthering student learning. Therefore, a Student Form of the *Profiles* (Form B) was also developed. In carrying out classroom assessment, it is recommended that teacher and student each complete a set of *Profiles*, which are then compared and discussed in an evaluation conference. When teacher and student perceptions on each of the profiles can be examined in nonrecriminatory

Figure 9.1. Standards for Student Behavior

A. INTELLECTUAL DEVELOPMENT

1. Quality of thinking
 1.1 Sees the big idea
 1.2 Shows tolerance for the ideas and opinions of others
 1.3 Differentiates between opinion and fact, between assumption and fact
 1.4 Shows tolerance for contrary data
 1.5 Gives examples to support ideas
 1.6 Makes intelligent interpretations of data
 1.7 Is original, inventive, creative in work
 1.8 Embraces thinking as a way of life

B. SKILLS

2. Communication of ideas
 2.1 Shows quality of thinking in writing
 2.2 Shows quality of thinking in speaking

3. Research skills
 3.1 Collects and organizes data intelligently
 3.2 Extracts and records information accurately

4. Interpersonal skills
 4.1 Attends to the ideas of others
 4.2 Helps facilitate group discussion

C. ATTITUDES

5. Personal perspectives
 5.1 Has a positive outlook
 5.2 Has a tolerance for ambiguity
 5.3 Sees problems/issues from a world perspective

6. Beliefs and values
 6.1 Shows that beliefs inform behavior

7. Self-evaluation
 7.1 Is open to self-evaluation
 7.2 Is skillful in self-evaluation

and analytical ways, the opportunity for student self-awareness and growth is enhanced. Moreover, such an assessment partnership can work productively in building student strengths and addressing weaknesses.

Teacher Form of the Profiles (Form A)

The Teacher Form of the *Profiles* is presented in its entirety below. It begins with directions to the teacher.

 Directions: Evaluating students' classroom behavior is a difficult task.

It is difficult for the teacher, who is occupied with many teaching responsibilities, to concentrate on the kinds of behaviors students are exhibiting, and to remember such behavioral patterns for a large number of classes. It is difficult, too, to insure that behavioral ratings are fair and legitimate representations of student behaviors. Yet, with thoughtful scrutiny, the assessment of student behaviors will provide teachers with helpful information in identifying those areas in which much growth is still needed to insure that all students attain those learning goals considered important in educational thinking.

In order to use the *Profiles* effectively, the following procedures are recommended:

1. Ratings should reflect teacher observations of student behavior from an "overall" perspective. Every student has a bad day and ratings should mirror the totality of a student's behavior rather than a single event.
2. Teachers may want to check their perceptions of a student's behavior with other teachers who also have that student in their class. To what extent is this behavior typical of that particular student in that particular class? To what extent is the behavior pervasive throughout the student's functioning in school?
3. Students themselves should be involved in rating their own behaviors, determining to the best of their ability how they see themselves functioning in relation to these desired learning outcomes.
4. Both teacher and student should meet to discuss their ratings. This can provide a rich opportunity for both self-assessment and articulating specific plans for that student's further growth.

An Individual Assessment Grid has been developed to facilitate marking for individual students (see Figure 9.2). Each student's work is represented on his or her own sheet. The grid allows for an overview of each student's ratings for one marking period, and when several are combined, they provide an "across the semester" profile of the student's performance.

On the following pages, the profiles are presented with 20 pairs of statements, each containing two views of a particular kind of behavior—a positive view, labeled "a" and a negative view, labeled "b."

If the teacher believes the positive characteristics in a profile are clearly evident in a student's behavior almost all the time, the student is given a rating of +3 for that profile on the positive side of the Assessment Grid. If the teacher believes the characteristics are frequently

Figure 9.2. Individual Student Assessment Grid

Marking Period _____   Student's Name _____

	-3	-2	-1	0	+1	+2	+3
1.1 Can see big idea							
1.2 Tolerates others' ideas							
1.3 Distinguishes opinion, assumption, fact							
1.4 Tolerates contrary data							
1.5 Can give examples to support ideas							
1.6 Interprets data intelligently							
1.7 Is original, inventive, creative							
1.8 Embraces thinking as a way of life							
2.1 Quality of thinking is seen in writing							
2.2 Quality of thinking is seen in speaking							
3.1 Collects and organizes data intelligently							
3.2 Extracts, records information accurately							
4.1 Attends to ideas of others							
4.2 Helps facilitate group discussion							
5.1 Has a positive outlook							
5.2 Tolerates ambiguity							
5.3 Sees larger perspective of problems, issues							
6.1 Beliefs inform behavior							
7.1 Is open to self-evaluation							
7.2 Is skillful in self-evaluation							

evident in the student's behavior, the student is given a rating of +2. If the teacher believes the characteristics are evident some of the time, the student is given a rating of +1. However, if the teacher believes that the negative characteristics are clearly evident in the student's behavior almost all the time, the student is rated –3 on the negative side of the grid. If the characteristics are frequently evident, the student is rated –2. If the characteristics are evident some of the time, the student is rated –1. If the teacher has had no opportunity to observe a student's behavior on a particular function, or if a student does not perform that function, the student is rated 0.

Ratings on individual profiles that fall consistently into the –3 range would reveal classroom behavior that is considered to be negative and counterproductive to intelligent classroom functioning. Students who consistently obtain negative ratings would be more likely to be "in trouble" with respect to having attained desirable standards. Teachers who rate students in these ways would know that much, much work is needed in helping these students to grow. They would also be able to identify those areas, in particular, in which work is needed. Ratings at the –2 and –1 levels indicate those areas in which students need considerable help to reach the desired standards. Ratings at the +1 and +2 levels indicate student strengths in those areas and where some help is needed to reach the desired standards. Ratings at the +3 level indicate that a student's functioning is at the highest level, in the teacher's estimation, and that the student is an exemplar of that particular standard.

A. INTELLECTUAL DEVELOPMENT

1. Quality of thinking

1.1 Sees the big idea
a. These students are able to see the "larger picture" in the examination of topics or issues. Their arguments are centered in the big ideas, and they are able to appreciate the complexities of these big ideas. In presenting arguments or points of view, these students "go after" the issues of substance and are unafraid to deal with what is important.

b. These students get bogged down in details. They seem to miss the big picture and concentrate instead on what is superficial or trivial. In dealing with issues or topics, they miss the important meaning and dwell on trivial details. They are unable to find differences between ideas of consequence and details.

1.2 Shows tolerance for the ideas and opinions of others

a. These students are open to and respectful of the ideas of others. While others' ideas may not agree with theirs, they are able to listen respectfully, see the other point of view, and consider that viewpoint rationally and thoughtfully. In addressing others with different ideas, these students are thoughtful, respectful, and rational in their responses.

b. These students are closed-minded about ideas that are different from theirs. They seem to believe that their ideas, alone, are the "right" ones. They are disrespectful in listening to others' views and their response to others is more emotional than rational in defense of what they believe.

1.3 Differentiates between opinion and fact; between assumption and fact

a. These students are critically aware of the difference between opinions and facts and between assumptions and facts. They use qualifying words like "perhaps" or "it seems to be" when there is reason to be cautious in offering opinions or stating assumptions. In their arguments, they indicate when they are sure (facts) and when they need to exercise caution (opinions, assumptions) in their reasoning.

b. These students use opinions and assumptions interchangeably with facts. It's not clear whether they are aware that facts suggest certainty and that assumptions or opinions require caution in arguments, or whether they are not sure that there is a difference between fact and opinion. As a consequence, their arguments lack factual support and are rooted instead in personal belief and in speculation that extends far beyond the data.

1.4 Shows tolerance for contrary data

a. These students, while holding strong beliefs of their own, are nevertheless open to the consideration of ideas/data that are discrepant with their own. When these students examine discrepant ideas, they do so thoughtfully and rationally, checking carefully to determine how the discrepant data may "fit" into their own belief systems.

b. These students are unable to see any idea different from their own as having any validity. They are dogmatic about their own views, and closed-minded in the rejection of discrepant data. Once the "answer" has been found, why bother looking at other points of view?

1.5 Gives examples to support ideas

a. These students are able to provide relevant examples to support a point of view. There is a clear relationship between the point of view and the examples that support it.

b. These students are unable to provide examples in defense of their arguments. They may be unable to think of examples or their examples may be inappropriate to support the argument. They are unable to make an intelligent connection between an argument and the examples that strengthen it.

1.6 Makes intelligent interpretations of data

a. These students are able to read, view, or observe data and draw intelligent and rational meanings from that data. The interpretations they make are based in the data, and they are cautious about drawing conclusions from data where there is insufficient evidence. The meanings they derive from the data are consequential and reflect what is important.

b. These students jump to conclusions without adequate data to back them up. Conclusions are drawn before the data are all in; or there are not enough data to warrant those conclusions. These students may also distort the data to back up their ideas. The result is a mismatch between what they believe and say and what the data allow.

1.7 Is original, inventive, creative in work

a. These students are able to go beyond the ordinary, to create new schemes, new forms, new products. They are original and inventive and what comes from them is fresh, new, and imaginative. These students are risk takers in their creative attempts, and they push the limits of what is standard, in generating what is new.

b. These students feel safer and more secure in following well-established routines. They are "low risk takers" and respond in more mechanical, formula-like ways. They resist new ideas, new ways of doing things, new situations. Change, in any form, is a threat, and they are safest when following established routines.

1.8 Embraces thinking as a way of life

a. These students value thinking as a means of solving problems and as a way to inform decision making. They *want* to think for themselves, they *want* to think their own ideas, and they value the power that thinking brings to their own lives. These students are independent and self-initiating, and value thinking as a tool to enrich their lives.

b. These students reject thinking for themselves. They *want* to be told what to do, and they believe that it's the teacher's responsibility to do the thinking and the student's job to follow orders. Their behavior is characterized by dependency on others, and they need help a lot of the time to deal with the higher order cognitive demands of the class.

B. SKILLS

2. Communication of ideas

2.1 Shows quality of thinking in writing

a. These students are able to show evidence of quality of thought in their written work. Their written ideas are presented clearly and are rooted in fact, observations, details, images, quotations, statistics—all sorts of forms of information. They are able to give examples that clarify what they mean. Written material is well organized, sentences are constructed as units of thought, and the mechanics of form (spelling, punctuation, capitalization, and other conventions) are in evidence. They are able to communicate ideas in a way that is interesting to the reader.

b. These students are unable to express their thoughts intelligently in their writing. This inability may come from *a priori* conditions of muddled thinking, i.e., they haven't thought through the ideas clearly, and are, therefore, unable to express them clearly. There may be an inability to translate mental thoughts to paper, to organize ideas coherently, logically; to express ideas in ways that are clearly understood. There may be evidence that the ideas are "off the cuff"—lacking connection to a meaningful data base. The written material may be incomprehensible for several of these reasons. Whatever the reason, these students' written work is incomprehensible and incoherent.

2.2 Shows quality of thinking in speaking

a. These students show evidence of quality of thought in the oral communication of their ideas. When they make oral presentations in class, their language is clear and what they say is based in data. They are able to give legitimate examples from valid sources to support their points of view. When they speak, it is easy to understand what they say, to follow their reasoning. The way they communicate their ideas is interesting, even compelling to the listener. When they argue a point of view, they make sense.

b. These students' oral presentations are hard to follow. This may be a result of their not having thought through their ideas before speaking; it may be because they are unable to articulate clearly the ideas they hold. Their ideas may be "off the cuff"—illogical and not represented by any valid data base. They may be unable to give legitimate examples to support their ideas. Whatever the causes, these students' oral presentations come across as incomprehensible, incoherent, irrational.

3. Research skills

3.1 Collects and organizes data intelligently

a. These students are able to locate sources to gather the data they need. They gather data from many sources and they use many sources in informing their arguments. In their oral or written reports, the data are organized in a way that makes sense, and the key issues are dealt with logically. They are able to see both sides of an issue; their analyses are literate, intelligent, and their conclusions are based on the data.

b. These students may use only one resource to gather data. They may be unable to find the sources, even though these are readily available in the school library. In their reports, they may present only one side of an issue; their data may be scanty; they may miss the key meanings; the arguments may be "circular"—that is, they keep on repeating the same thing; the reports may be lacking in critical analysis. Conclusions are merely repetitions of the original statement. These students seem unable to gather data thoughtfully, to make intelligent analyses of data, or to draw conclusions based on data in their research.

3.2 Extracts and records information accurately

a. These students are able to extract the big ideas from a variety of sources like books, lectures, films, graphs and tables, statistics. Their ability to extract demonstrates their intelligent discrimination of what is important and what is of minor consequence. In examining data sources, they are able to get to the heart of the issues of consequence and record them accurately.

b. These students are unable to discriminate between what is important and what is unimportant in a body of data. They are unable to extract the key meanings and consequently they dwell on detail. In taking notes, they write everything down because they are unable to tell the difference between what is important and what is not. They seem to lack the ability to get to the heart of the issues.

4. Interpersonal skills

4.1 Attends to the ideas of others

a. These students are able to attend to the ideas of other students. What's more, their responses to these students' statements reveal that they have heard and understood the important meanings in what has been said. Not only do they listen carefully, but they are able to perceive the meanings of the statements being made.

b. These students do not seem to listen. Instead of attending to what is being said, their minds may be occupied with formulating their own responses. Their responses do not attend to others' ideas; they are primarily concerned that *their* ideas be heard. They do not really enter a dialogue, but use the interpersonal forum as a way of getting their own ideas out.

4.2 Helps to facilitate group discussion

a. These students are "active listeners"—ready and willing to hear the ideas of others. They are supportive of others in the group and show respect for all ideas, whether or not they are in agreement with their own. These students are good "group members." They are nondogmatic in presenting their ideas and their flexibility encourages a sharing of different viewpoints.

b. These students impede the group process. They may be dogmatic about their own ideas. They may show disrespect for the ideas of others. They may want to "hog" the "air time" for themselves. Their presence in a group not only does not add to effective group discussion, but their behavior discourages such productive group work.

C. ATTITUDES

5. Personal perspectives

5.1 Has a positive outlook

a. These students tend to look at problems as challenges. They have a positive spirit, a sense of "can do" about what is possible. They are enthusiastic about learning, about school, about opportunities. These students consistently challenge themselves and, even when unsuccessful, they are undaunted.

b. These students are consistently pessimistic about themselves and about their work in class. Their outlook is permeated by defeatism. They may nag and complain a lot, and they seem unable or unwilling to take any kind of action that will change the pathway of their negativism. Their "can't do" spirits are pervasive and seem to affect everything they do in class.

5.2 Has a tolerance for ambiguity

a. These students have a high tolerance for uncertainty. They are able to suspend judgments, to wait until the data are in before making up their minds. They are able to see the complexities in complex situations, and the complexities do not defeat them. They have a vast appreciation for the "gray areas" and are able to see far beyond the two-valued orientations of "black and white" positions.

b. These students are very uncomfortable with uncertainty. They need closure. They are impatient with looking at complexity. They want resolution. They like things open and shut; true or false; good or bad; right or wrong, and they tend to see the world through these polar opposites. They use labels as convenient ways to group people, places, and things, since labeling brings closure and avoids the requirement of thoughtful examination. Only when these students have achieved closure can they relax. Their tolerance for uncertainty is very low.

5.3 Sees problems/issues from a world perspective

a. These students tend to see situations, problems, and issues from a "world perspective." They are able to see far beyond themselves, their school, their community, their city, to the larger picture. They understand about interdependence, about how world conditions transcend geographical boundaries. They appreciate that all peoples, all conditions, all world events are interconnected in important ways.

b. These students are ethnocentric in their perspectives about people, events, and conditions in the world. "If it's not happening here, man, why should *we* worry?" suggests their inability to see world conditions in an interconnected way. Famine in Africa, cholera in Peru, homeless Kurds and Bangladesh—none of these world events seem to have relevance for their immediate or future lives. Their world and world view are narrowly circumscribed by the geographical boundaries of their own community.

6. Beliefs and values

6.1 Shows that beliefs inform behavior

a. These students have thought a lot about their beliefs. They have talked about what is important to them. They know what they stand for. Their beliefs seem to have been chosen after some reflection, and there is a clear relationship between their beliefs and actions. If they express a strong belief, you can see that belief in the consistency with which they act on it.

b. These students are unclear about what it is they believe. They seem not to have thought much about their beliefs, and if asked about what is important to them, they are unable to tell, or may think it is a silly question. As a consequence, they may act out of whim, or caprice, rather than out of examined values, and their behavior is apt to be inconsistent, irrational, inappropriate to the situation.

7. Self-evaluation

7.1 Is open to self-evaluation

a. These students see self-evaluation as a chance to learn more about themselves, and as an opportunity to become "lifelong learners." They are open to self-examination and are nondefensive in discerning where they need help. They welcome the opportunity to participate in a self-evaluative process. Their nondefensiveness allows them to see their performance more objectively and makes them open to continued growth.

b. These students believe evaluation is the teacher's job. "That's what teachers get paid for, isn't it?" They do not want to look critically at the self. It's too hard and too uncomfortable, and they do not see a relationship between self-evaluation and personal growth. Evaluation, for them, is always an external process.

7.2 Is skillful in self-evaluation

a. These students are able to look at their own performance in class with an eye of "critical self-awareness." They understand what is required in self-evaluation, and give thoughtful, nondefensive consideration to their performance. They are able to be self-critical and introspective in their assessments of self, and they do this without being falsely modest or defensively arrogant.

b. These students are unable to see themselves critically. They are very highly defensive in self-examination and may distort the data to support their biased perceptions of self or "blame" others for their shortcomings. Their defensiveness prevents them from seeing themselves as they really are.

Student Form of the Profiles (Form B)

The teachers who developed the *Profiles of Student Behavior* also saw the engagement of students in self-assessment as an important and valuable aspect of furthering student learning. They then undertook to develop a self-assessment instrument adapted from the Teacher Form of the *Profiles*. The Student Form (Form B), reprinted in its entirety, begins with directions to the students.

Directions: In this self-evaluation exercise, you will find 20 *Profiles of Student Behavior*. Each profile has a pair of statements labeled "a" and "b," showing different views of how people learn and how they think. Your job is to decide for each profile how your behavior "matches" what is written in view a or view b. How do you see your behavior "fit" with the description in each of the profile views? Is your behavior more like that described in view a? Is it more like that described in view b? You are the one to make that decision. As you think about each of the views in these profiles, try to decide how your behavior "matches" that view, *in general*, rather than how your behavior "matches" on a single day.

Read each pair of behavioral descriptions. Think about how the descriptions "match" your behavior. Then, try to make a determination of that "match" by choosing the number that indicates the best match. You are to choose only one number for each of the profile pairs. Here's how the numbers are determined for each profile:

> Circle number 1, if you believe your behavior matches the description in View a almost all of the time.
> Circle number 2, if you believe your behavior matches the description in View a most of the time.
> Circle number 3, if you believe your behavior matches the description in View a some of the time.
> Circle number 4, if you see yourself falling right in the middle, between these two views.
> Circle number 5, if you believe your behavior matches the description in View b some of the time.
> Circle number 6, if you believe your behavior matches the description in View b most of the time.
> Circle number 7, if you believe your behavior matches the description in View b almost all of the time.

A. INTELLECTUAL DEVELOPMENT

1. Quality of thinking

1.1 Sees the big idea
a. When you read about or listen to a topic, you are able to understand the important ideas. When you present arguments or points of view, you are clear about what the important issues are.

b. When you deal with topics or issues you get so bogged down with the details that you miss the important ideas.

How does your behavior "match" either of these two views? Circle the number that makes the best match.

| 1 | 2 | 3 | 4 | 5 | 6 | 7 |

Use the space below to add any more thoughts you have about this profile. Provide examples from your work in the course to support your view, and indicate the reporting period in which your rating is made.

1.2 Shows tolerance for the ideas and opinions of others

a. You are open to what other people think. You respect their views even if they disagree with yours. You listen closely to other people's point of view and respond to their ideas in a thoughtful and respectful way.

b. You don't like ideas that are different from yours. You believe your ideas are the "right ones" and you find it difficult to listen to others' views. You get angry when others don't see things your way.

How does your behavior "match" either of these two views? Circle the number that makes the best match.

1   2   3   4   5   6   7

Use the space below to add any more thoughts you have about this profile. Provide examples from your work in the course to support your view, and indicate the reporting period in which your rating is made.

1.3 Knows the difference between facts, opinions, and assumptions

a. You understand the difference between facts, assumptions and opinions. When you present information to support your arguments, you are able to present your facts knowledgeably and your assumptions and opinions with caution. You let people know that you are stating your opinions when you do so.

b. You don't make much effort to show the difference between your opinions and facts when you are presenting your arguments. You don't see the need to make it clear that you are presenting your own opinions. Your opinions and the assumptions you make are as good as facts to you.

How does your behavior "match"either of these two views? Circle the number that makes the best match.

1   2   3   4   5   6   7

Use the space below to add any more thoughts you have about this profile. Provide examples from your work in the course to support your view, and indicate the reporting period in which your rating is made.

1.4 Shows tolerance for contrary data

a. Even though you may believe something very strongly, you are usually able to consider different points of view. When you are faced with information that is different from what you believe, you examine it thoughtfully and carefully to see how it fits in with your thinking.

b. Once you believe something to be true, you do not find it necessary to consider any other point of view. You don't see the need to continue thinking about an issue once you have figured out what you believe to be the right answer.

How does your behavior "match" either of these two views? Circle the number that makes the best match.

 1   2   3   4   5   6   7

Use the space below to add any more thoughts you have about this profile. Provide examples from your work in the course to support your view, and indicate the reporting period in which your rating is made.

1.5 Gives examples to support ideas

a. When you are asked to provide examples to support your arguments, you are able to do so without difficulty. What's more, the examples you choose are clearly related to what you are saying.

b. You are unable to find examples to support your arguments. You believe that your arguments don't need to be defended with examples.

How does your behavior "match" either of these two views? Circle the number that makes the best match.

 1   2   3   4   5   6   7

Use the space below to add any more thoughts you have about this profile. Provide examples from your work in the course to support your view, and indicate the reporting period in which your rating is made.

1.6 Makes intelligent interpretations of data

a. You are able to understand what you have heard, or observed, and you are able to communicate that understanding to others. What's more, you are cautious about drawing conclusions about what you have heard or seen when there is insufficient evidence.

b. You jump to conclusions without having adequate data to back them up and may twist information to support your ideas.

How does your behavior "match" either of these two views? Circle the number that makes the best match.

 1   2   3   4   5   6   7

Use the space below to add any more thoughts you have about this profile. Provide examples from your work in the course to support your view, and indicate the reporting period in which your rating is made.

1.7 Is original, inventive, creative in work

a. You are able to go beyond what is ordinary and create new ideas and products. You are original and inventive and your work is fresh, new, and imaginative. You are able to take risks and push yourself to the limits of creativity.

b. You feel more comfortable sticking with ways of doing things that are routine and have worked for you in the past. The idea of change makes you feel uncomfortable.

How does your behavior "match" either of these two views? Circle the number that makes the best match.

   1   2   3   4   5   6   7

Use the space below to add any more thoughts you have about this profile. Provide examples from your work in the course to support your view, and indicate the reporting period in which your rating is made.

1.8 Embraces thinking as a way of life

a. You value thinking as a way of solving problems and as a way of making decisions. You want to think for yourself and you want to think your own ideas. You are independent and view thinking as a tool to enrich your life.

b. You would rather have someone tell you what to do and believe than have to do the thinking for yourself. You believe it is the teacher's job to do the thinking and the student's job to follow orders.

How does your behavior "match" either of these two views? Circle the number that makes the best match.

   1   2   3   4   5   6   7

Use the space below to add any more thoughts you have about this profile. Provide examples from your work in the course to support your view, and indicate the reporting period in which your rating is made.

B. Skills

2. Communication of ideas

2.1 Shows quality of thinking in writing

a. Your written ideas are presented clearly and are based on many different sources of information, including facts, observations, details, and statistics. You are able to provide examples that clarify what you mean. Your writing is well organized. You use well-constructed sentences and give thought to spelling, punctuation, and capitalization. You are able to communicate ideas in a way that is interesting to the reader.

b. You are unable to express your thoughts in writing. This happens either because you are unable to organize ideas in your head, or because when you do get them organized, you are unable to transfer the information to the written page.

How does your behavior "match" either of these two views? Circle the number that makes the best match.

   1   2   3   4   5   6   7

Use the space below to add any more thoughts you have about this profile. Provide examples from your work in the course to support your view, and indicate the reporting period in which your rating is made.

2.2 *Shows quality of thinking in speaking*

a. When you make an oral presentation, your language is clear and you support your ideas with data. Your ideas are interesting, and it is easy for others to understand what you are saying. When you argue your point of view, you make sense.

b. You have difficulty with oral presentations. You are unable to articulate your ideas so they make sense to the listener. They come out as unconnected thoughts and are often not adequately supported with data.

How does your behavior "match" either of these two views? Circle the number that makes the best match.

1   2   3   4   5   6   7

Use the space below to add any more thoughts you have about this profile. Provide examples from your work in the course to support your view, and indicate the reporting period in which your rating is made.

3. Research skills

3.1 *Collects and organizes data intelligently*

a. You are able to locate information and gather data from many sources. When you use the information you have collected in your oral or written work, it is organized in a way that makes sense and focuses on the important issues. You use the information you collect to examine all sides of an issue and draw your conclusions based on this balanced examination.

b. When you prepare for a report or speech, you rely heavily on one source of information. Often, when you search for background material at the library, you come up empty-handed. Your reports usually take one side of an issue and sometimes you miss the important points altogether.

How does your behavior "match" either of these two views? Circle the number that makes the best match.

1   2   3   4   5   6   7

Use the space below to add any more thoughts you have about this profile. Provide examples from your work in the course to support your view, and indicate the reporting period in which your rating is made.

3.2 *Extracts and records information accurately*

a. When you research a topic, you use a variety of sources and you are able to gather the information that zeroes in on the important issues.

You don't have much difficulty knowing what is important, and what may be left out. You are able to record the information you have gathered in a way that makes sense.

b. When you do research for a project, you collect large volumes of information. You are unable to separate what is important from what is unimportant. You end up working with large amounts of material and your report meanders and lacks focus.

How does your behavior "match" either of these two views? Circle the number that makes the best match.

1   2   3   4   5   6   7

Use the space below to add any more thoughts you have about this profile. Provide examples from your work in the course to support your view, and indicate the reporting period in which your rating is made.

4. Interpersonal skills

4.1 Attends to the ideas of others

a. In group discussions, you are able to listen carefully to the ideas of other students and hear what they are saying. The way you respond to other students lets them know that you have heard them and understood what they have said.

b. When someone is speaking, you are so busy trying to figure out what you are going to say, that you are unable to listen to the speaker. Your reply does not relate to what the speaker said. When you get your turn, you just want to present your own ideas. It's more important for you to get your own ideas out than to hear the ideas of others.

How does your behavior "match" either of these two views? Circle the number that makes the best match.

1   2   3   4   5   6   7

Use the space below to add any more thoughts you have about this profile. Provide examples from your work in the course to support your view, and indicate the reporting period in which your rating is made.

4.2 Helps facilitate group discussion

a. When working in a group, you listen carefully to the ideas of other students even if the ideas expressed do not agree with your own. It's easy for you to be respectful of the ideas of others, and to show that respect in your group discussions. You take an active part in making sure that the group discussion is productive, and that is more important to you than getting out your own ideas.

b. Working in a group is difficult for you. You become frustrated with ideas that are different from yours. It is very important that you get your own ideas out. You usually take up most of the talk time in the group, and you don't really care about squeezing out other members.

How does your behavior "match" either of these two views? Circle the number that makes the best match.

    1   2   3   4   5   6   7

Use the space below to add any more thoughts you have about this profile. Provide examples from your work in the course to support your view, and indicate the reporting period in which your rating is made.

C. ATTITUDES

5. Personal perspectives

5.1 Has a positive outlook

a. You see problems as challenges. When faced with a problem, you feel good about your ability to solve it. You like to challenge yourself and even when you are not successful in solving a problem, you are able to keep your confidence as a "problem solver."

b. When you are faced with a new problem, you just assume that you can't do it. Instead of putting your energy into solving a problem, you are more likely to complain about your situation. You don't see how problems can be solved, and taking action on a problem is not what you would choose to do.

How does your behavior "match" either of these two views? Circle the number that makes the best match.

    1   2   3   4   5   6   7

Use the space below to add any more thoughts you have about this profile. Provide examples from your work in the course to support your view, and indicate the reporting period in which your rating is made.

5.2 Has a tolerance for ambiguity

a. When you are faced with conflicting information, you are patient, and you don't have to make a decision until better information is available. When you face a situation that appears to be neither right nor wrong, that does not make you uncomfortable. You are comfortable even when the "answers" have not been found.

b. You are very uncomfortable with situations that have no "right" or "wrong" answers. You need to see answers found. You see things as either true or false; good or bad; right or wrong. This helps you to know what is what! You have a great deal of difficulty in leaving things open and it really drives you crazy when the issues are not resolved.

How does your behavior "match" either of these two views? Circle the number that makes the best match.

1   2   3   4   5   6   7

Use the space below to add any more thoughts you have about this profile. Provide examples from your work in the course to support your view, and indicate the reporting period in which your rating is made.

5.3 Sees problems/issues from a world perspective

a. When you examine an issue, you are able to see how it affects other people in your school, community, or city. You realize how your school and your community are related to the whole world, and you appreciate all people as part of a world community.

b. You see events in terms of how they affect you personally. World events like famine, war, and homelessness are someone else's problems.

How does your behavior "match" either of these two views? Circle the number that makes the best match.

1   2   3   4   5   6   7

Use the space below to add any more thoughts you have about this profile. Provide examples from your work in the course to support your view, and indicate the reporting period in which your rating is made.

6. Beliefs and values

6.1 Shows that beliefs inform behavior

a. You think about what you believe and you really are clear about what is important to you. There is a clear connection between what you believe and how you act. Your actions over time are a clear reflection of your values.

b. You are unclear about what you believe and if asked about what is important to you, you don't really know, because you haven't thought this out. How you act does not seem connected to what you believe.

How does your behavior "match" either of these two views? Circle the number that makes the best match.

1   2   3   4   5   6   7

Use the space below to add any more thoughts you have about this profile. Provide examples from your work in the course to support your view, and indicate the reporting period in which your rating is made.

7. Self-evaluation

7.1 Is open to self-evaluation

a. You welcome the chance to evaluate your own work. You see self-evaluation as a chance to learn more about yourself, as an opportunity to examine your strengths and weaknesses, and determine where more work is needed. You are not afraid to be honest in owning up to where you are having trouble. This ability to look at yourself honestly allows you to be more open to learning.

b. You consider evaluation as the teacher's job. You think that's what teachers get paid for. You find it uncomfortable and difficult to examine something you have done. You learn more when someone else does the evaluation for you.

How does your behavior "match" either of these two views? Circle the number that makes the best match.

1   2   3   4   5   6   7

Use the space below to add any more thoughts you have about this profile. Provide examples from your work in the course to support your view, and indicate the reporting period in which your rating is made.

7.2 Is skillful in self-evaluation

a. You are able to look at your own work critically. You are thoughtful when you examine your work, and you can see your strengths and weaknesses realistically. You can recognize where you need help, and you are able to ask for that help as part of the process of learning.

b. You are unable to look at your work critically. Looking at yourself critically leaves you open to criticism that you like to avoid. Instead of owning up to your own learning needs, you are likely to blame others, or distort the facts, rather than acknowledge your shortcomings.

How does your behavior "match" either of these two views? Circle the number that makes the best match.

1   2   3   4   5   6   7

Use the space below to add any more thoughts you have about this profile. Provide examples from your work in the course to support your view, and indicate the reporting period in which your rating is made.

CONCLUSION

The *Profiles of Student Behaviors* provide an example of how a group of teachers developed explicit standards against which students in case method classrooms could be evaluated. Teachers who are looking to the development of similar standards for their own classes may wish to use these *Profiles* as a point of departure. If the standards in these *Profiles* are what teachers consider significant in their own students' learning, they are welcome to use all parts of the *Profiles* for their own classroom purposes. Once standards have been determined, tools for measuring students' abilities to attain the standards need to be identified. The next chapter provides scores of examples of assessment tools.

10 | Evaluation in the Case Method Classroom: Materials and Strategies

Teachers who are considering case method teaching want to ensure that their instructional program is effective. Are students learning to process data more intelligently? Are students becoming more informed? Are they developing habits of thinking? Teachers will want to know for themselves, for students, for parents, for administrators, not only that students *are* learning, but also what they are learning and how well it has been learned. The evaluation materials and strategies included in this chapter are examples of what can be used to make these determinations. The methods go beyond what is measured in single, correct-answer tests that examine only what students know and are able to recall in the pressure of an exam setting. They allow for gathering information about how students think and how they apply what they know in a wide range of problem-solving situations. Reflecting Gardner's (1983) theory of multiple intelligences, the methods call for students to reveal their skills in intrapersonal, interpersonal, artistic, spatial, and kinesthetic ways, as well as in traditional linguistic and logical-mathematical forms.

These assessment materials and strategies do not need to replace altogether examinations that assess students' ability to know and recall. They do, however, provide teachers with a greater array of options that give fuller, more complete pictures of what students have learned. Information gathered from these assessments allows teachers to be more effective in helping individual learners; in communicating with parents about student learning, if that is an aspect of the evaluative process; and in determining students' marks and grades. There are many advantages to these assessment methods.

1. They provide teachers with information about the extent and nature of students' understanding of complex concepts.

2. They allow for increased student choice, giving students more control over evaluative options and allowing them greater opportunity to reveal their strengths.
3. They call for students' careful preparation, intelligent gathering of resources, and application of concepts over an extended period of study.
4. They allow students to rework their materials, so that they may rethink and refine their work, to their best efforts.
5. They give greater opportunities for students to perform successfully. Success, rather than failure, is emphasized.
6. They give teachers more information about students' efforts over time.
7. They allow teachers to gather diagnostic information about each student's performance strengths and weaknesses, so that individual help may be offered.
8. They emphasize self-evaluation as an important means of promoting students' critical awareness of selves-as-learners, and thus contribute to their ongoing independence as learners.

These are, of course, qualitative assessment materials and strategies. There are no unequivocally "correct" answers that can be marked "right" or "wrong." These methods of assessment require teachers to exercise professional judgment about the quality of a student's performance. Can teachers use such discretion in making assessments? Do teachers have the necessary skills to evaluate students' work on qualitative performance tasks?

The materials and strategies are framed in the belief that a teacher's informed, professional judgment about a student's work, made in the context of fuller knowledge about that student, is an enormously valuable assessment device that yields rich, diagnostic data about student learning. To aid teachers in making these assessments, criteria for judging the quality of a student's work have been included in each of the performance arenas. These criteria should enable more informed assessments, as well as help to increase their reliability.

The evaluation materials and strategies presented in this chapter fall into three categories, each "testing" students' abilities to apply what they know in different types of performance arenas. These include class participation, generative activities, and analysis activities, and are discussed in the first three sections of the chapter.

A subsequent section is concerned with student self-assessment. How do students see themselves in these performance categories? To what extent are they able to discern their performance strengths and weaknesses? How willing are they to undertake the rigors of critical self-scrutiny as learners? Examples of materials and strategies that promote students' self-assessment are included here.

Finally, a discussion of record keeping and grading—how teachers keep track of all students' work and how they may convert all the qualitative data into the quantitative sum of a final grade—concludes the chapter.

CLASS PARTICIPATION

Class participation is one of the most important features of case method teaching, and the quality of that participation either makes or breaks what happens in a case method classroom. Class participation also offers the opportunity to observe the how and what of student thinking—how students process data, what reasoning skills are applied in the interpretation of data—through the statements they make. It also allows teachers to note how students are growing in their use of these reflective skills. That is why class participation should be an explicit component in the overall evaluation of students' work.

With respect to assessing the quality of students' participation in study groups, it is recommended that this be done through self-evaluation procedures. There are important reasons for this. First, it puts the burden of making quality contributions onto the student. These are, after all, the students' study groups, and it's a good idea that students take responsibility for what goes on. Second, since these are nonsupervised sessions, it would be inadvisable to couch them in a "big brother is watching you" framework. Self-evaluation forms, in which students evaluate their participation, in monthly, or bimonthly reports, would focus on those standards that make for quality contributions. (See the section on self-evaluation later in this chapter.)

Teachers who use cases will want to evaluate students' contributions in the whole-class discussion. Since what students say is a reflection of how they think, students' statements offer opportunities to assess how well they use reasoning in the analysis of problem situations. This is more difficult to do when the class is large and many students speak, but it is important that strategies be found to assess the quality of students' comments.

Finding ways to record students' statements seems to be requisite to making thoughtful evaluations of how they use thinking in analyzing problems. It is difficult to evaluate without such a record—difficult to remember, let alone make responsible judgments. Taking a few minutes to jot some notes after each class is particularly helpful. These notes need not be verbatim scripts of the class session. They could be a short-hand form of who contributed and the nature of the particular contribution. If available, a teaching assistant may record that information. Tape recording a class session is also a good strategy for post-class reflection on the quality of student contributions.

In evaluating students' contributions, teachers will want to note evidence of thoughtfulness and intelligent analysis in what they are saying. Do students show depth of understanding of the issues? Are students' statements related to the topic being discussed? Do students' statements reveal a grasp of the nature of the dilemma? Are leaps to judgment made before all the data have been considered? Criteria for assessing the quality of students' thinking are found in the *Profiles of Student Behaviors*, particularly Profiles 1.1, 1.3, 1.5, 1.6, and 2.2 (refer to Chapter 9, "Teacher Form of the Profiles"). Quality participation will be seen in students' statements that reflect the data in the case; in their ability to give examples to support their ideas; in statements that are intelligible; in statements that are representative of the content in the case; in understandings about the deeper meanings of the issues; in their ability to differentiate between assumption and fact. Teachers will also be looking for evidence of lack of intelligent analysis in statements that go way beyond the data; in impulsive judgments that draw conclusions based on insufficient data; in opinion that is presented as truth; in inflexibility and closed-mindedness; in lack of consistency between means and ends. Other behaviors in and around students' statements are also telling; for example: Are students able to take the risks of presenting new ideas? Do they show that they are listening to others' ideas? Do they have respect for thinking as an analytical tool?

There will doubtless be other characteristics that teachers will want to include, as they look for quality of thinking in student statements. But these will, at least, point in the direction of assessing students' contributions to the whole-class debriefing.

GENERATIVE ACTIVITIES

The emphasis in case method teaching on building habits of thinking requires consistency in using evaluation materials that assess students' competence as thinkers. That is why evaluation tasks must go beyond testing only what students know. They must provide data on how well students are able to apply learned principles and concepts to the solution of problems.

The assessment tasks included in this section have been labeled *generative* because they require students to apply what they have learned in new and creative ways. These tasks offer opportunities for students to demonstrate competence in doing projects, field studies, and oral and written presentations. Generative tasks are readily applicable to virtually every subject area and instructional level, and an extensive list of suggestions is offered below to show what may be included to assess students' competence in this performance arena.

Projects

Project work includes formal assignments given to individual or small groups of students on a topic related to an area of study. Projects include activities that may require students to research, create, and analyze data that coincide with the specific objectives of the assignment. The following criteria may be used in assessing students' ability in project work:

- Is the student's project on task?
- Is there evidence of research of relevant facts and information reflected in the project?
- Is there evidence of meaningful analysis of the information gathered?
- Are the project layout and organization compatible with the purpose of the assignment?
- Does the project presentation reflect creativity, originality, and innovation on the part of the student?
- Is there evidence of sound grammatical structure in any written presentation?

Examples of possible project activities include

1. Slide-sound shows—creating and organizing audiovisual presentations that examine specific themes/ideas related to subject matter
2. Interviews—gathering information from personal accounts, anecdotes, oral histories, recollections, as a means of furthering understanding of events, eras, issues
3. Company studies—in-depth economic analyzing of companies, tracing historical development, present situations, and future plans
4. Cases—constructing narratives that highlight complex issues in problem situations
5. Plays or stories—demonstrating understanding of an event or system by writing a playscript or story about it

6. Artwork, sculpture, models, inventions, cartoons—creating artistic and communicative depictions of major ideas or themes through the use of visual media
7. Books, newspapers, magazines, journals—creating literary accounts of specific events through narratives, biographies, newspaper and magazine articles, brochures
8. Computer projects—developing artwork, designs, plans, caricatures, newspaper accounts, and information packages on computers
9. Film, video—creating audiovisual representations characterizing a particular event, issue, or theme of significance
10. Music—creating and/or interpreting music and lyrics that reflect the values and the political and social climate of a period
11. Scientific experiments—designing and carrying out credible, reliable, controlled experiments that involve practice with formulating hypotheses, predicting, data collection, data recording, and interpretation, and drawing conclusions

Student Presentations

Student presentations give students in all subject areas an opportunity to express their ideas and feelings in other than written form. These presentations may be undertaken by single students or groups of students. They may take the form of debates, mock trials, dramatic readings, fashion shows, exhibits, musical performances. The following criteria may be used for assessing students' presentations:

- Are the presentations well organized, easy to follow and understand?
- Does the presentation reflect a fresh, new, imaginative and interesting perspective on the topic?
- Does the presentation reflect use of legitimate examples to support the viewpoint of the presenter?
- Does the presentation indicate that the students have developed their own ideas with respect to the data they have gathered?

Examples of possible student presentations include

1. Oral presentations—preparing individual or group presentations that reflect students' research, comprehension, and analysis of particular topics of study
2. Theater—presenting plays, poetry readings, readings, monologues of literary works; creating original plays

3. Simulations and debates—preparing analysis, interpretation, and presentation of important legal and social issues
4. Fashion shows and festivals—using clothing, food, music, and visual props to portray trends and changes in social values of specific periods

Field Study

Field study requires the active involvement of students in applying the general principles of classroom learning to real-life situations. Students may be directly involved in survey work and projects, participating in "walkabouts," cultural exchanges, field trips, as well as actual work and volunteer experience. The following criteria may be used to assess students' abilities in field studies:

- Do students' assignments identify a specific problem or hypothesis?
- Do students' assignments reflect evidence of systematic data collection?
- Do students' assignments show meaningful interpretation of data?
- Do students' assignments draw relevant conclusions or identify significant relationships that are related to the topic?
- Do students' assignments show evidence of sound grammatical structure in any written presentations?

Examples of possible field study activities include

1. Community service—working in social service agencies such as soup kitchens, recycling stations, fish enhancement projects, preservation of heritage buildings, after-school programs for homeless children, children's hospital, homes for the elderly
2. Work experience and volunteer work—participating in jobs in the community to gain firsthand work experience
3. Surveys—collecting and analyzing data related to issues of community, civic, or national concern
4. Cultural exchanges—participating with students from culturally diverse regions
5. Field trips—making direct investigations in the field
6. Community study—examining various components of a working community in order to understand the social, political, and economic forces at work
7. Walkabouts—extending the capacities of students in real, rather than simulated, experiences; based on the Australian

aborigines' rite of passage into adulthood, students choose one of five types of challenge that are themselves important learning experiences.

Adventure: challenges to students' daring, endurance and skill in an unfamiliar environment

Creativity: challenges to explore, cultivate and express imagination in some aesthetically pleasing form

Service: challenges to identify a human need for assistance and provide it; to express caring without expectation of reward

Practical skill: challenges to explore some useful activity, to learn the knowledge and skills necessary to work in that field, and to produce something of value

Logical inquiry: challenges to explore one's curiosity, to formulate questions or problems of personal importance, and to pursue answers or solutions systematically, and where appropriate, by investigation (Gibbons, 1976)

Written Presentations

Formal assignments may be given to individual students on a topic related to the curriculum. These assignments may require out of class research, interviews, and gathering of empirical data to provide a basis for students' own analysis and understanding. The following criteria are used in assessing students' abilities in written presentations:

- Does the work reflect quality of thought in the analysis of the topic?
- Does the interpretation of data and the research support the thesis?
- Are the significant ideas of the assignment substantiated with fact?
- Is the work well organized and coherent?
- Does the work reflect sound grammatical structure?

Examples of some possible written presentation activities include

1. Research reports—writing papers that examine a particular point of view or idea
2. Scrapbooks and manuals—collecting thematic materials to illustrate and examine particular topics or areas of inquiry
3. Annotated bibliographies—preparing bibliographic citations and accompanying summaries
4. Editorials, letters to the editor—writing critical commentaries that express the writer's point of view

5. Journals, diaries—composing diaries or journals that might have been kept by a person living through a particular experience
6. Biographies, scenarios—writing personal histories of famous persons outlining their rise to prominence and the accomplishments for which they are well known
7. Critiques—preparing analyses and evaluations of certain events, ideas, writings, films, plays, programs, to demonstrate ability to do critical commentary

Teachers will survey this list of suggestions and notice, at once, that none of these generative activities is beyond what they regularly use in their classrooms. What is new, perhaps, is that these activities are being called into use as primary evaluative measures. And what is being suggested further, is that evaluation based on such performance indicators may offer teachers more comprehensive and reliable pictures of the quality and quantity of students' learning than does performance on formal tests.

Teachers who have used these tasks to evaluate students have indicated the importance of allowing students' choices with respect to what they do. In that way, students can choose the medium and the means that give them the best chance for success, as well as the area of inquiry that stimulates their interest. When teachers have given students a list of choices, they have also discovered that students will add to the list, thereby extending what is possible. Teachers who worry that students will seek the "least possible work effort" may be surprised to find that students' initiatives are often considerably more challenging than what is on the list.

ANALYSIS ACTIVITIES

The ability to make intelligent written analyses of data is an aspect of critical thinking that is closely tied to case study teaching. In this section of evaluation activities, students' analytic skills are put to the test in the higher order cognitive functions of comparing, applying principles, evaluating and judging, interpreting, summarizing, classifying, decision making, creating and inventing, and designing investigations.

Analysis activities, like generative activities, are also applicable to a variety of subject areas and instructional levels. What follows are many different examples of the kinds of assessment tasks that fall into this performance arena.

Making Comparisons

Skill in making intelligent comparisons is shown in students' ability to identify similarities and differences that are significant. The analysis of similarities and differences may be examined in virtually any subject area. Criteria for assessing students' ability to compare include

- Is the student able to zero in on those similarities and differences that are significant? (Or is the comparison bogged down in trivialities?)
- Is the student's comparison of what is significantly similar and different extensive? (Or is the comparison limited to one, two, or three points?)

The following examples indicate the type of activity that may be included in this category:

1. What are some significant differences in immigration policies in 1896 and 1990? What are some important similarities?
2. What are some significant differences between plant photosynthesis and human respiration? What are some important similarities?
3. In what important ways is news gathered from newspapers similar to news gathered from TV news broadcasts? What are some differences?
4. What are some significant differences between operant conditioning and Rogerian therapy? What are some similarities?
5. What are some similarities in Dewey's and Thorndike's approaches to the education of children? What are some differences?

Applying Principles

In this category of analysis, students who have learned certain principles, rules, generalizations, or laws are asked to demonstrate how these are applicable to new and different situations. Intelligent analysis calls for the ability to discern relevant principles; to know which principles are applicable; to know how they are to be applied; to disregard irrelevant data. Criteria for assessing students' ability to apply principles include

- Is the student able to recognize those principles or rules that apply in a given situation? (Or do the principles elude him or her?)

- Is there logic in the way the student has connected one situation to another? (Or is there no connection between the situations?)
- Do the principles for Situation A fit for Situation B? (Or are the principles for Situation A inappropriate for Situation B?)
- Is the logic of the connection clear? (Or is the student unable to discern the relationship?)

The following examples indicate the type of task that may be included in this category:

1. What principles are considered important in the gathering and reporting of the news? How are these principles upheld and/or violated in your comparisons of news reports of the same events?
2. What implicit/explicit principles dictated the treatment of women in the 1920s? How are these implicit/explicit principles seen in the treatment of women today?
3. What principles of law guide the justice system in your state (province)? In what ways are these principles seen in application in (current court case)?
4. What principles of physics apply in bridge building? How are these principles applied in the construction of a bridge that transverses the space between two towers?

Evaluating and Judging

In this group of tasks, students are required to generate thoughtful, intelligent criteria that are then used to make determinations of worth. In these activities, the generation of criteria is relevant, as is the students' ability to relate judgments of worth to these criteria. Criteria for assessing students' ability to evaluate and judge include

- Are students able to specify the criteria they are using to make the judgments? (Or are the criteria irrelevant to the judgment?)
- Are the criteria reasonable? sound? appropriate to the item being evaluated? (Or are the criteria illogical, inappropriate?)
- Is the relationship between the criteria and the judgment adequately shown? (Or is the judgment made "off the cuff"?)

The following examples indicate the type of task that may be included in this category:

1. Generate criteria for assessing quality medical care for premature, or elderly, patients. Then make critical assessments of medical care provided in a particular case.
2. Generate criteria for a humane immigration policy toward refugees from other countries. Then make critical assessments of immigration procedures used in a particular case.
3. Generate criteria to assess "good art." Then make critical assessments of a particular work of art.
4. Generate criteria for determining the quality of poetry. Then use the criteria to make a judgment about selected poems.
5. Generate criteria to determine optimal athletic functioning in a particular sport. Then make an evaluation of human performance in that sport.

Interpreting

In this category of activities, students are called upon to read (view, listen to) information presented in a particular context and to discern what is relevant in that information. The information may appear in different forms—in commentary, in documentary, as "evidence," in drama or stories, in newspaper or journal articles, in passages from texts. These analysis exercises call for making intelligent meanings from a body of information. Do the students understand the important meanings in this body of information? Are they able to comprehend the big ideas? Are they able to "read into" the data discerning the deeper meanings that are not explicitly spelled out? Criteria for assessing students' ability to interpret data include

- Do the students comprehend the big ideas? (Or have they missed the meanings?)
- Are the students' analyses focused on the important meanings? (Or are they focused on trivialities?)
- Are the students able to articulate what is important in the data in an intelligible, articulate manner? (Or is the presentation incomprehensible?)
- Are the students able to dig more deeply into the content, to discern what is implicit, to make inferences? (Or does the interpretation deal only with surface issues?)
- Are the students' interpretations of the deeper meanings expressed with caution, as a way of suggesting uncertainty about what is speculative? (Or are the students certain when they should be cautious?)

The following examples indicate the types of activities that would be included in this category:

1. Examine the War Measures Act. What did this law allow the Canadian government to do in 1914? How did this law allow the Canadian government to respond to the events of World War I? How did the War Measures Act influence events in Canada during the period 1914–1918?
2. As you read Tuchman's article, "How We Entered World War I," how do you interpret the events that led to the beginning of hostilities between the nations? What do you see as the "points of no return"? What data support your view? In your view, what steps might have been taken to avoid this conflict that left 37,000,000 soldiers and civilians dead? What data support your ideas?
3. Based on your viewing of the film *Broadcast News*, what do you see as the important messages? What data from the film and from your supplementary reading support the film's position?
4. What is your interpretation of Bernoulli's Law? How does this interpretation inform your understanding of the way aircraft are built?
5. What is your interpretation of the term *medical ethics*? What data are you using in making that interpretation? What, in your view, is medically ethical behavior? On what data are you basing your interpretation?

Summarizing

The skill of summarizing calls for students to distill, and synthesize, from a larger body of data, what they discern to be the key ideas. Criteria for assessing students' skill in summarizing include

- Do the students' summaries reflect the key ideas? (Or have the students included what is largely irrelevant?)
- Are the summaries succinct? (Or have they included everything?)
- Are the summaries articulate, intelligible? (Or are they incomprehensible?)
- Are the summaries faithful and accurate representations of the key issues? (Or have they missed or distorted the important meanings?)

The following examples indicate the types of activities that may be included in this category:

1. What do you see as the media's role in informing the public about events in the news? Write a short data-based statement that summarizes that role.
2. View the film *My Left Foot* and write a short (100 words or less) summary that could be included in a film anthology.
3. Write a proposal for a new law that is protective of the rights of children in elementary school. Make your proposal succinct, clear, and based in data.
4. Write a summary of how the body's immune system works. Make sure your summary is based in fact.

Classifying

Classifying calls for the ability to discern attribute-alike qualities in a group of items and to arrange or sort them, for some particular purpose. Good classifying goes beyond the simple act of placing items in groups. In more sophisticated classifications of data, new meanings are able to be discerned and new perspectives revealed. Criteria for assessing students' abilities to classify include

- Do the categories include attribute-alike items? (Or are the attributes of the items unconnected?)
- Does the classification serve some larger purpose? (Or is it largely a trivial or meaningless system?)
- Does the classification enable us to find new meanings in the data? (Or does the irrelevance of the system prevent such awareness?)
- Does the classification go beyond the obvious in searching out new relationships? (Or does the classification stay close to the obvious in pointing out what is already well known?)

The following are examples of the types of activities that may be included in this classification:

1. Make a list of adjectives that would, in your opinion, be descriptive of women. Make a list of adjectives that would, in your opinion, be descriptive of men. Classify all the adjectives on your list.
2. Make a list of all the laws passed by Congress this year. Classify the laws.
3. Make a list of all the physical disabilities you can think of. Then classify the items on the list.
4. Make a list of all the World War II terms you can think of. Then classify all the items on your list.

5. Make a list of all the people you call "friends." Then, classify the people on your list. Using your classification as data, write a short summary of the kinds of people you choose to be your friends.

Decision Making

Decision making calls for the ability to make choices, based on articulated values that guide them. Decision-making abilities are seen in situations where we are confronted with moral and/or ethical dilemmas. How we choose, and what values guide those choices, is an indication of informed choice. Some criteria that are useful in assessing students' abilities to make informed decisions include

- Are there articulated values that lie behind the choice? (Or is the decision an impulsive one, based on immediate, personal need?)
- Are the values humanly sound? (Or are they based on personal selfishness?)
- Is the decision an informed choice, based on the best available data? (Or is it based on personal opinion?)
- Has the decision been carefully thought out? (Or does it seem to be a "knee jerk" response, where action is more important than thoughtful consideration of consequences?)

The following are examples of the types of activities that may be included in this category:

1. In designing future immigration laws, how would you decide what groups, if any, should be given preference? How would you decide which groups should be given least preference? How did you determine this? What values guide your choices?
2. You have an opportunity to influence a major governmental decision with respect to the homeless in the cities. What kind of recommendations do you make? What data support your decisions? What values do you hold that influence your choice?
3. What works of art are worth dying for? In the film *The Train*, many lives are lost to save great works of art. Is this a waste of life? What do you think? What values do you hold that support your choice?
4. The loggers are up in arms. Restrictions on old-growth logging have put their jobs in jeopardy. They want to be able to cut timber and feed their families. Environmentalists are opposed to cutting old-growth forests. Once the trees have been cut, this

natural resource will be completely depleted. Where do you stand? You have an opportunity to make your voice heard. What do you advise? What data support your view? What values do you hold that support your decision?

5. Ernest is a physically challenged boy who requires considerable personal attention. You have a choice about accepting him into your fourth-grade class. What would you decide? What do you see as some disadvantages/advantages in your decision? What personal values guide your position?

Creating and Inventing

Creating calls for students' ability to form new ideas, new structures, new designs, new ways that depart substantially from what is currently known. While creating new ideas and new ways liberates students from relying on supporting data and calls for generating the new, the inventive, the fanciful, the application of analysis skills is seen in how the new ideas or new forms are related to what it is they intend to do. Criteria that are useful in assessing students' abilities to create and invent include

- Are the students able to take cognitive risks in their creations? (Or do the students stay close to what are known and acceptable forms?)
- Do the students' new plans (inventions) show the ability to generate what is truly new, fresh, imaginative? (Or does the students' work lack freshness, inventiveness, originality? Does "slapdash" substitute for originality?)
- Are the students' creations appropriate to the demands of the task? (Or do they go too far beyond the limits of what is appropriate, becoming "silly"?)

In making determinations between "very imaginative and inventive" and "too fanciful to be appropriate," teachers will be wrestling with their own personal criteria for creativity. While criteria for "what is creative" rely more heavily on a teacher's personal judgment, it is helpful to keep two points in mind: First, "very imaginative" may seem to some to have gone beyond the bounds of what is appropriate; take care lest the most creative ideas are not being rejected by some narrower view of what is acceptable. Second, "too fanciful to be appropriate" may seem to some to be "highly creative"; take care lest "slapdash" or "silly" becomes acceptable as creative.

The following examples indicate the types of activities that may be included in this category:

1. Create a plan that would end hunger in this country.
2. Design a poster that would inspire teenagers to embrace more socially responsible values.
3. Imagine that it is the year 2010 and the requirement of genetic testing of a fetus was made into law. Write about the social implications of such a law.
4. Imagine a world in which a 3-day work week was made into law. Write or draw about the social, cultural, and economic implications of such a law.
5. Design a car that will operate without the use of fossil fuels. Draw your design and include representations for all the mechanical features.
6. Design the "perfect" classroom. Include the physical as well as the educational features.

Designing Investigations

Skill in designing investigations subsumes several other analytical skills that are implicitly contained in this area. Students must be able to frame problems in a way that enables thoughtful investigation. They must be able to collect and organize data, to analyze assumptions critically, to generate appropriate hypotheses. Beyond that, designing investigations requires that students have awareness of how to evaluate the effectiveness of what they have done. These skills may not necessarily be explicitly articulated; but evidence of knowledge is seen in the way the design of the investigation is formulated and in the way the design has allowed for the problem to be thoughtfully investigated. Criteria for assessing students' ability to design investigations include

*   Are the students able to frame the problem in a way that allows for thoughtful investigation? (Or is the framing of the problem unclear or off the mark with respect to what is important?)
*   Are the students' proposed plans for the investigation logical? thoughtful? (Or is the plan unrelated to the problem?)
*   Are the students' proposals designed to gather data that will yield information about the problem? (Or are the data gathering procedures unlikely to provide information that will illuminate the problem?)
*   Is the proposed plan viable? (Or is the plan based on unwarranted and unexamined assumptions that will make it unworkable?)
*   Does the plan have a built-in method of determining its effectiveness as a solution? (Or has evaluation not been considered?)

• Is there a clear relationship between the plan and what is being examined? (Or, is the plan unconnected to the problem?)

The following are examples of the types of activities that may be included in this category:

1. Design an investigation that would give information about the kinds of TV commercials that promote consumerism in young children.

2. Design an investigation that would provide information about how students in secondary school spend their money. When the data have been gathered, organize them so that they allow for an overview of student consumerism. Make sure your plan articulates what you consider to be the problem, in a way that allows for the construction of your investigation. Articulate the ways in which you would gather data that are reliable.

3. Design an investigation that would provide information on the numbers of Native peoples in prison in Canada, in relation to other ethnic groups. When the data have been gathered, organize them so that they tell us more about the percentages of people of different ethnic group who spend time in prison.

4. Design an investigation that would provide information about people with physical handicaps. Make sure your investigation begins with an identification of what you see as the problem to be investigated. When your data have been gathered, organize them so that they shed light on the problem you have investigated. Based on the data, suggest some plans for the remediation of the problems you have uncovered.

5. Design an investigation that provides information about the functions of air traffic controllers in relation to airline safety.

The examples of activities that call for students to make intelligent analyses of data will seem familiar to teachers who have habitually included higher order cognitive tasks in their curriculum. These activities are being proposed, however, as primary assessment tasks—indicators of how students function in their ability to apply knowledge to the intelligent analysis of data.

Student performance in class participation, and on generative and analytical tasks, ought to provide a substantive body of data on how well they have learned to apply knowledge from course material to problem situations. Student performance on these assessment tasks are likely to provide a wealth of information from which teachers may make reliable and valid judgments about student growth.

STUDENT SELF-EVALUATION

> Perhaps the most fundamental condition of creativity is that the source or locus of evaluative judgment is internal. The value of his product is, for the creative person, established not by the praise or criticism of others, but by himself. Have I created something satisfying to me? Does it express a part of me—my feeling or my thought, my pain or my ecstasy? These are the only questions which really matter to the creative person, or to any person when he is being creative. (Rogers, 1961, p. 354)

One of the more profound changes being advocated for students in classrooms of the 1990s is the shift of locus of control over student evaluation from being totally and irrevocably in the teacher's domain, into that of the students. This is not just a frivolous idea; it is borne out of studies of how exclusive teacher evaluation works against the very kinds of growth toward maturity and creativity that schools seek to inspire. This is not to say that teachers give over all evaluation to students, removing themselves totally from the process. It is rather a tilt in the direction of partnership, in which teachers evaluate students, and students evaluate themselves, and the results are examined and compared in a collaborative effort at helping students to take the next steps in their learning.

There are important reasons for students to engage in this process and learn how to do it well. First, it frees them from dependence on the teacher to know that what they have done is "good." Students who graduate from programs in which evaluation is done exclusively by teachers, never have occasion to learn to make these judgments for themselves, leaving them with an important facet of their education absent. Second, students who do learn to engage in such a process are better able to take on independent learning projects as adults and to guide themselves in the process of successful performance. There comes a point in one's life when one must be one's own teacher; this will not occur if the resources to make critical and intelligent assessments of one's own work have been neglected.

Teachers who are suspicious of student involvement in self-assessment ask if students' evaluations can be trusted. Of course, there will always be students who use such opportunities to inflate their successes and diminish their weaknesses. This, however, can and should be treated diagnostically, rather than by invoking guilt for such indiscretions. These are, of course, anomalies in student self-assessment, as teachers who use these methods will tell you. For the most part, students do learn to assess their work thoughtfully, honestly, and with considerable intro-spection on how they have performed their tasks. And when students can engage intelligently in this process, it is to their, and the teachers', benefit.

The Student Form of the *Profiles of Student Behavior* has been pre-sented in Chapter 9. This is one means by which students examine them-selves in relation to standards of classroom performance. Portfolios are another means that are increasingly used by teachers in compiling lon-gitudinal data of a student's entry behaviors, what she or he has ac-complished in terms of quality and quantity, and where he or she has gotten to at the end of the class. (For more information about using port-folios, see Broadfoot, 1986; Davies, Cameron, Politano, & Gregory, 1992; Graves & Sunstein, 1992; Hargreaves, 1988–89; Wiggins, 1993.)

In developing individual portfolios, the student is usually the one who makes the choices about what is to be included: to reflect his or her very best work, so that what has been done is seen to the student's best advantage. At the end of the semester, or at the conclusion of marking periods, the portfolio is presented in a conference with the teacher (and perhaps parent), at which time, in a collaborative arrange-ment, student and teacher examine the quality of the student's work and reach an agreement about standards of performance.

Student self-reports are used in both secondary and postsecondary classes, in which students are asked to make self-assessments in rela-tion to specific course criteria. One such self-report form is presented in Figure 10.1 as an example of how this may be done. Modifications would, of course, be made in keeping with a teacher's evaluative crite-ria for a specific course.

THE SUM OF THE PARTS:
KEEPING RECORDS AND GRADING

Teachers who look for "pure" and unequivocal systems of marking and grading students will not likely be those who would consider case method teaching in the first place. Those who would add students' scores, and divide by the number of tests, to get an "average" that is then converted into a letter or number grade, will not take easily to what is being proposed below. How do teachers "add up" what students have done in case method classrooms? What does student performance "add up" to? If marking and grading are tough tasks for teachers in the best of circumstances, how may teachers translate what happens in a case method class to the demands for grades that exist in almost any tradi-

Figure 10.1. Student Self-Evaluation Report

Name _____ Date _____

This self-evaluation report provides you with the opportunity to reflect upon and assess your fulfillment of the requirements of the course.

I. FULFILLMENT OF COURSE REQUIREMENTS
Please reflect on the extent to which you have fulfilled the course requirements. You may choose to rate yourself using the scale, or you may choose to comment, or both. Give yourself a rating of:

      1 if you believe the statement is true to a very great extent
      2 if you believe the statement is generally true
      3 if you believe the statement is minimally true

A. Attendance and participation
1. My attendance in class was perfect (no missed classes for whatever reason) and I was there on time.
2. I was a very active participant in the study groups and my contributions consistently contributed to the thinking of others in the group.
3. I was an active participant in whole-class discussions and I was able to use these discussions to examine my own thinking about the issues.
4. I completed all required readings.
5. I was responsible in setting and meeting deadlines for the completion of my work. All projects and assignments were complete and submitted on time.

B. Understanding
1. I have grown to understand the issues studied in this course. I am able to determine what are the significant factors in these issues and see their significance beyond the classroom.
2. My work in study groups and in the whole-class discussion demonstrates a genuine value for the thoughts and ideas of others.
3. I appreciate the value of self-evaluation. I am able to analyze critically my strengths and weaknesses. I think self-evaluation is an important factor in my personal growth.

II. SELF-ASSESSMENT AND GRADING
1. Using all completed work, your portfolio, teacher's feedback, and your own evaluative responses on this report, indicate what you consider to be a final grade that reflects your work in this course.

III. OPEN QUESTION
Add any comments you'd like to make that have not been addressed in your responses above.

tional instructional context? And how is this done so that the principles of fairness, validity, and morality are upheld?

There are no easy answers to the dilemmas that come from the search for better ways to mark students. Yet, many have struggled with the questions, and have come to some form of compromise. No teacher enjoys giving grades; some would even prefer to do away with the ranking of students. Yet, as long as systems still demand them, grades need to be given, and rationales for the rankings need to be fair and valid.

While examples are presented below, it is important to note that they are offered as prototypes. Most teachers will devise their own systems, based on their own criteria and weightings of what they consider important in assessing student performance. However the system is constructed, certain operating principles should apply.

1. Course requirements should be made clear at the very beginning of the semester. What is expected of the students, for example, in class participation? How many written papers are to be required? How many generative tasks? How many analytical tasks? What role will self-evaluation play in the total process? Teachers will have to make these determinations first, deciding on what will be required and what options students have with respect to redoing their work to bring it "up to grade."

2. Grading procedures should also be made explicit to students at the very beginning of the course. In most courses, satisfaction of course requirements and quality of work are primary factors in determining grades. Ways of determining quality should also be made clear. These explanations are often made in a course outline.

3. The weights, or values, of different tasks should be made clear. For example, to what extent will class participation count toward the final grade? To what extent will other performance tasks count? Will there be formal tests? If so, how will these be weighted?

4. Teachers will need to create some means of keeping records of student performance. Where authentic forms of assessment are replacing formal tests, much more student work will be counted toward the final grade, and written documentation will need to be recorded that notes both the extent to which a student has satisfied the requirement and the quality of the work. While keeping records may be time-consuming, their value is well worth the effort, both in assessing overall student growth and for the profile they reveal for use in calculating the student's final grade.

Making requirements, procedures, and weights clear at the outset of a course and having them contained in a written document, such as a course outline, takes much of the ambiguity out of the process. Keeping good records allows for a comprehensive picture of student growth and provides valuable data in making final grade determinations.

Making Requirements Explicit

A formal course outline, distributed to students at the beginning of class, establishes a contract between teacher and students. The requirements written into the outline give direction to students and make the teacher's expectations clear. In a course outline, the teacher is saying: Here's what this course is about; here is the pathway down which we will be traveling in our studies; here are my expectations for you; this is what you must do in order to earn a passing grade. A course outline that contains such specific information is likely to alleviate problems later on with respect to how grades are determined. No student will be able to say, "I didn't know that I had to do that!" The outline becomes the contract of responsibilities by which students are bound.

Often, course outlines begin with course goals: This is what this course is about, and these are the conceptual understandings that the course aims for. As well as being a healthy exercise for teachers, statements of goals provide students with clear direction to the learning journey that the course is offering. Goal statements are different in spirit and in design from "behavioral objectives," which are more restrictive and therefore less appropriate for case method classes.

Outlines also contain descriptions of course requirements and criteria for evaluation. Requirements include reference to how each performance task is to be weighted toward the final grade, make the teacher's expectations in this difficult area clear, and tend to alleviate student anxiety about what "counts." Having articulated all of this in the written contract, the teacher is constrained to be more consistent, fair, and accurate in issuing grades.

The outline for a college course for sophomores that uses case method—Social Issues in Education—is offered in Figure 10.2 as an example.

Using Recording Systems to Help in Determining Grades

To facilitate record keeping, teachers may wish to use something like the Student Record Form (see Figure 10.3) devised by Fukui (in Adam et al.,1991). In this system, each student's work is recorded on his or her own document, in which the teacher notes what has been handed

Figure 10.2. Example of Course Outline

COURSE GOALS
1. To promote awareness of educational practice as a decision-making process
2. To examine how educational decisions are influenced by complex and interrelated social, political, cultural, and economic factors
3. To promote intelligent meaning making of the complex processes of decision making in educational practice
4. To promote a healthy tolerance for the uncertainties in professional decision making
5. To develop an understanding of how one's own beliefs and values bear on the professional choices one makes

COURSE REQUIREMENTS AND CRITERIA FOR EVALUATION
1. Attendance and participation
Students are required to attend both the tutorial sessions and the large class sessions regularly, be on time, and participate actively in small and large group discussions. Thoughtful, responsible participation in class discussion constitutes the primary criterion in evaluation and counts for about 60% of the mark.
2. Readings
Students are required to read the required text, plus all articles distributed in class. At least two other readings should be selected from books listed in each of the topical sections in the outline. Evidence of having read constitutes an important criterion of evaluation.
3. Written work
Students are required to write a case that describes an educational dilemma relative to one of the topical areas in the course. The case should demonstrate the student's awareness of and appreciation for the complex factors that influence decision making in an educational context. Students who wish to choose an alternative to writing a case may do so in consultation with the instructor. The fulfillment of this requirement constitutes an important criterion of evaluation, about 30% of the mark.
4. End of semester self-evaluation profile
Students are required to complete a self-evaluation profile that demonstrates growth in the learning outcomes listed in the goal statements of this outline. Evidence of thoughtfulness and self-awareness in completing this self-evaluation profile is an important criterion of evaluation, about 10% of the mark.

EVALUATION
Students are evaluated on the basis of fulfillment of course requirements. The following criteria are used in determining final grades:
• the degree to which the student has satisfied the four course requirements based on the instructor's assessment
• the quality of the student's work in each of the four areas, based on the instructor's assessment
  A grade of A indicates the student's completion of all course requirements with demonstrated excellence in quality of performance.
  A grade of B indicates the student's completion of all course requirements with demonstrated good quality in performance.
  A grade of C or below indicates lack of completion of all requirements and/or less than demonstrated good quality in performance.

Figure 10.3. Student Record Form

Student's Name _____

	Comments	Mark	Mark Total	Accumulated Total
1. Written assignments				
2. Student presentations				
3. Projects				
4. Field study				

in, comments on the work, and indicates the point value assigned to each piece of work. A cursory glance at the record reveals, at any given time during the course, the status of the student's performance and how well he or she is doing.

Fukui's system highlights four major areas in which students are evaluated.

1. Written assignments (including analyses, essays, book reviews, critiques)
2. Student presentations (including oral and audiovisual presentations)
3. Projects (including collages, models, computer designs)
4. Field studies (including surveys, photographic essays, interviews)

Teachers make final grade determinations based on student work in any of these four categories, but they may wish to include formalized tests, quizzes, and homework assignments as well.

In using Fukui's system, teachers are offered the following guidelines:

1. Each reporting period has a fixed and equivalent accumulated point total. This total is determined by the teacher, and grades are issued in relation to the extent to which the student has accumulated sufficient points.

2.   In addition to written assignments, students complete at least one project, one presentation, and one field study during each semester, or two in each category during a full school year.

3.   These major assignments can be applied to any reporting period point total.

4.   The topics and requirements for each assignment are developed in consultation between teacher and student.

5.   The point value assigned to individual student projects, presentations, and field studies is determined by the teacher, but should be based on criteria that include, at least, the complexity of the work and the student's effort in completing the assignment.

6.   Final grades are determined based on work from a combination of these performance areas, but teachers may include traditional tests, quizzes, and homework assignments as they choose.

7.   For each reporting period, students will have an accumulated point total made up from the different areas. For example, Term I: J. Smith 174/220 points; S. Johnson 200/220 points.

8.   Students cannot exceed the accumulated point total set by the teacher for each term, but they may choose to do extra assignments, or redo assignments, as long as appropriate point modifications are reflected in the total.

Fukui explains that his method of record keeping and marking gives teachers more flexibility in marking and evaluating students' assignments. Teachers will find they are not always marking full class sets of assignments since students have the option to choose different assignments and different deadlines for submitting them during the semester. This, in itself, may help to reduce the pressure placed on teachers to be constantly marking, and should also improve the quality of evaluative feedback on student assignments and projects. Successfully implemented, these strategies should benefit both teachers and students, so that all become "winners" in education.

Record systems do not have to be complicated. A "softer" system than Fukui's uses a single looseleaf page for each student, on which teachers record, after each class, the nature and extent of class participation, performance tasks submitted, and the fulfillment of other course requirements, with teacher's comments about each (see Figure 10.4). This ongoing commentary may also include a quantitative ranking. For example, the teacher may wish to use, for each performance task recorded, a five-point scale that would reflect the extent to which that task has met specified criteria, with 1 equaling high levels of performance; 2, good; 3, average; 4, below average; 5, poor. Standard grades

Figure 10.4. Teacher's Record of Student Performance

Student's Name _____

1. Attendance:

2. Participation in whole-class discussion:

3. Demonstration of having completed the required readings:

4. Generative tasks:

5. Analytical tasks:

6. Self-evaluation profile:

such as A, B, C, etc., may also be used in lieu of numerical ratings. What is important in keeping student records is to include the teacher's qualitative assessment of how each performance (written task, oral presentation, class contribution, etc.) satisfied the articulated criteria for excellence.

Whichever methods are used, teachers are urged to make the criteria for marking and grading clear to students at the beginning of the class and to provide students with opportunities to redo and resubmit tasks for reconsideration. If the end result of evaluation is the continued promotion of student learning, opportunities to redo assignments would be a normal class occurrence.

CONCLUSION

In a perfect world, students would not have to compete with each other for high marks. They would come to school ready and eager to learn, and learning, rather than marks and grades, would be elevated to a position of importance. In an imperfect world, students do compete for grades, and often a grade is inextricably linked with a student's self-worth. In a very imperfect world, students are rewarded with "toys and perks" commensurate with their parents' satisfaction with the mark they receive. All of this baggage around marks and grades makes a difficult task that much more difficult.

The two chapters on evaluation have presented materials, drawn from the work of case method teachers, that may be helpful in alleviating some of the stress and some of the ambiguity around evaluating students' learning. These are presented as examples of what other teachers might consider developing for their own use. Good evaluation practices, like good case teaching, depend, to a large extent, on a teacher's willingness to try, to experiment, and to change procedures, based on his or her own assessment of what is good and what works.

There is just one final evaluative question to be addressed before bringing this book to its conclusion, and that is, "How will I know it is working?" It is not enough that students enjoy these classes. Teachers who embark on case method teaching should have some reliable means of assessing whether what they are doing is to the benefit of student learning.

One important indicator of whether case method teaching is working is found in the more productive functioning of study groups. Is there evidence of student growth in the way they address issues on their own? Do students listen to each other's ideas respectfully? Is there increased tolerance for each other's ideas? Do students work productively with each other in examining issues; for instance, asking for examples, asking that assumptions be identified, asking that supporting data be provided? Are students more willing to suspend judgment? Has their tolerance for ambiguity grown? Such criteria are also used in examining what is happening in the whole-class forum of debriefing.

The *Profiles of Student Behavior*, presented in Chapter 9, provide another means of making assessments. Are students becoming more thoughtful in their everyday classroom behaviors? Is there observable evidence of more intelligent behaviors and better decisions? Are problem-solving skills improving? Are attitudes toward the subject and toward school improving? Is there a healthier respect for data? Is the classroom a place where students are eager to learn? Is there increased respect for each other? Whatever the class—whether physics, or law, or business, or government; whether in secondary school, or in college, or in a professional school—students who are growing in these directions will give explicit evidence that what is being done in their classrooms is to their benefit.

Teachers may want to consider more rigorous and systematic data gathering on the effectiveness of what they are doing as case method teachers. Designing and carrying out classroom research is one way to provide hard data that point to the effectiveness of case methods. Of course, using one's classroom as a laboratory to gather relevant data on student learning is a healthy and desirable process no matter what teaching strategies are being used.

Finally, asking students to evaluate their course experiences is a procedure that is advocated no matter what kind of teaching is going on. Provided the responses are allowed to be anonymous, so that marks and grades do not influence student feedback, students' responses to questions about what they have learned and what they perceive to be the quality of what they have learned, will give teachers considerable insight into the learning process as seen from the students' perspectives. This process is helped when students' feedback is cued into specific questions. That is, if the teacher is clear about what questions to ask, this will help students to focus their feedback on the relevant issues. It is less likely to be productive if students are asked to evaluate the course without any guidelines. Data from student feedback forms should be taken seriously when patterns emerge that point to how students feel they have benefited from being in a case method classroom.

An eleventh-grade boy knocks on the classroom door. Steve Fukui has stayed after school to mark some student papers. The boy is not one of Steve's students. Steve looks up and asks, "Yes? Can I help you?"

"My name is Sean Warnecke," he says. "I was wondering if I could talk to you. I tried to get into your Socials 11 class, you know—the one you are doing with cases? But I was told it was full. I had to take Mr. _____'s class instead. I was wondering, you know, if I could borrow some of the cases you are studying in your class, just to read, for my own interest. I've got to do something to get myself interested in social studies this term, and I figure that if I could just read those cases, I'd learn a lot more. Would you be willing to lend them to me?"

There are many anecdotes that come from teachers who work with cases. This is just one of them; but they tell important stories about the quality of life in classrooms, as lived by teachers and by students. For those of you who are embarking on a case method teaching journey, it is my sincerest wish that your own stories be as satisfying.

Appendixes

References

Index

About the Author

A | Welcome Aboard!

Notes to the Teacher

This case draws on the theme of racial prejudice, and does so in the context of the Jews in Germany during World War II. The case centers on a single event—the departure in 1939 of 936 Jews from Hamburg, on the ship St. Louis, for Havana, with paid-for Cuban "landing certificates" that would allow them to enter Cuba legally. Many of the Jews who were embarking for Cuba as a safe haven had already had members of their families taken away to concentration camps, and their immigration to a country outside Germany meant, for all, the difference between life and death.

Because of anti-Jewish sentiment in Cuba, and because of behind-the-scenes corruption in the granting of the Jewish "landing certificates," the Cuban officials chose not to honor them and invalidated them as the ship was on its way to Havana. Only 30 of the refugees were allowed to land. When Captain Schroeder radioed this news back to Germany, he received explicit instructions for the ship, which sailed under the German flag, to return home at once. This, he knew, meant certain death for the refugees. In an heroic effort, he attempted to contact other countries, pleading for permission to allow his passengers to enter. Both the United States and Canada refused permission. Without recourse, Captain Schroeder set sail for Germany on June 5.

In what was truly a last minute rescue, the captain learned that Great Britain, the Netherlands, Belgium, and France had each agreed to take a share of the passengers. The passengers drew lots to determine which families were to go where. Two hundred and eighty-seven went to England; 214 went to Belgium; 224 went to France, and 181 went to the Netherlands. Of these, most who went to Belgium, France, and the Netherlands later became victims of the "Final Solution."

The big ideas on which this case is built are

1. Racial hatred was responsible for the murder of six million men, women, and children in Germany during the Nazi regime.
2. Denoting a particular group as "undesirable" or "less" allows us to treat them in less than human ways.
3. Racial hatred makes it possible for people to behave in ways that they would otherwise consider irrational, inhuman, aberrant, and evil.

They came when I was asleep, dreaming of better days. The pounding at the door woke me abruptly. As I lay there with the covers over my face, with only the slits of my eyes showing, I tried to see in the half light. I heard my father go to the door and then the sounds of voices, in German, so cold they brought chills to my marrow. They commanded my father to go with them and they took him away into the night, with only the clothes he had on when he answered the door. I heard my mother's cry, a long painful wail, like an animal whose limb had been torn off. I crept out of my bed and saw my mother weeping, her hand pressed against the door that had closed behind my father's departure.

I was eleven when the SS came to take my father. It was April 1— April Fool's Day. Only fools would have chosen to remain in Germany so long, you say? Foolish Jews who thought that any day things would get better; who thought that this nightmare couldn't really be happening. Every day there were more signs of brutality against the Jews and we were constantly singled out for the most vicious attacks and humiliations. It became impossible even to walk down the street without the fear that you would be spat upon, hit by a rock or even worse, taken away never to be seen again. Yet, some of us, in our very civilized and respectable city of Augsburg, in the heart of civilized Germany, still felt we were Germans. We were citizens of a great country, with a great literary, cultural, and artistic heritage. This was the birthplace of genius —of Beethoven, of Nietzsche. How could such civilized people be doing this to us?

In the cold gray dawn of that early April morning, my mother sat us down at the kitchen table. Her ashen face told of her terror and we three children listened in stunned silence. My sister Ilse, who was only five, hardly made much sense of my mother's words, but even she could tell that this was bad. My other sister, Lotte, was nine, and she and I were old enough to know there was real horror in this nightmare. My father had been taken by the SS—Hitler's special force of military elite, the guardians of pure blood, who were trained to strike without fear or compassion. Dressed in sleek black uniforms, with the fearful double zigzag insignia, they were the very essence of cold, calculated evil. Their special job was to preserve the pure Aryan blood of the true German people. Jews were considered "undesirables." They had to be eliminated to keep the race pure. The SS removal of my father was a part of a larger plan to exterminate Jews and other "undesirables" in Germany and then, eventually, in all the other countries that were to be occupied by Hitler's advancing armies. We had no way of knowing where my father was being held and no one, despite my mother's tearful pleas, would tell her. Visit after visit to City Hall and to the Central Police Station left her in helpless frustration. Nobody knew anything, or would say they did. All we did know was that other men from our block had also been taken, like my father, in the night. All sons who were 18 and older were taken with their fathers. But so far, no women and children. This news was small comfort to us.

I stopped going to school and so did my sister Lotte. Our winter coats hung in the hallway, their yellow stars sewn on the sleeves to identify us as Jews, silently mocking us as we brushed by. We stayed in the apartment, quiet and solemn, as if already mourning for a dead father. It was my mother who was a beehive of activity. She left the house early every day and returned only at dinnertime. Her usual carefully cooked meals dwindled into cold suppers. We ate sausage and bread and were glad of it. At least Jews were not yet prohibited from spending their Deutschmarks at the market. We ate always in silence. If Ilse asked about our father, my mother would cry. Lotte and I knew better than to ask, although our hearts yearned to know. My good, kind, gentle, patient father—the neighborhood doctor, who gladly and willingly treated every patient with the utmost kindness and consideration—it was unbearable to think we might never see him again.

At eleven years, I was luckier and unluckier than my sisters. I was luckier to be able to have a fuller understanding of what was going on. I was unluckier, because I had a fuller understanding of the unspeakable terror in our situation. Through our local Jewish community group, my mother had finally found out where my father had been taken. He was in a concentration camp, Dachau, that had been set up in Germany—one of many—to hold Jews and other undesirables who were thought to be a threat to the purity of the Aryan race. In these still early years of Hitler's plan—the "Final Solution," in which six million European Jews were to be systematically and methodically murdered—it was still possible, if you had the money, to purchase a prisoner's freedom. That is, *if* you had the money. And *if* you were prepared to leave Germany immediately afterward.

My mother—how did she manage it alone?—gathered from our

apartment everything of value—silver candlesticks, her gold earrings and bracelet, my father's gold watch—whatever she could turn into cash—and took these to the pawnshop. One day she left with a large bagful of Deutschmarks and when she came home, her bag was empty. In two days, my father, haggard and thin, appeared at our door, in the very same clothes he had worn on the evening that he was taken. In those six weeks in the camp, he had become a very old man. We four gathered around him, clutching him to us, and wept silent tears of thanks.

We had less than 48 hours to pack and leave home. My mother and father were now both in a frantic race with the clock. Passports and visas to purchase, tickets to be bought. Belongings—treasures that had been with our family for generations—had to be abandoned. We could take only what we could carry. And outside of a narrow margin of just enough money to cover our immediate expenses, we were not allowed to take any of our family's savings. No money was allowed to leave Germany. My parents purchased five first-class tickets for passage on the German ship, the St. Louis, which was scheduled to depart from Hamburg for Cuba on May 13, 1939. They also purchased landing certificates from a Cuban government official, for $160 each, that would permit us to land, legally, as immigrants in Cuba. Cuba seemed far enough away to be untouched by the madness and the reign of terror that had been unleashed against the Jews. It seemed like an excellent plan.

We traveled from Augsburg to Hamburg by train, always watching behind us, never knowing when a tap on the shoulder would mean my father would be taken again. When we began the climb up the gangplank of that beautiful ship, I felt that we would all be able to breathe again. Never in my life had I felt such terror as in those last two days. At the top of the gangway, Captain Schroeder stood in his smart blue uniform, with his cap with the gold braid on the visor. He looked at our family of refugees, smiled, and said with sincere warmth, "Welcome aboard!" I let out a long sigh. Safe at last.

To my child's eye, the voyage across the Atlantic was a trip in fantasyland. Because my parents were not permitted to take any money out of Germany, they had used their savings to purchase the most expensive tickets for the trip. We traveled first class and I could not believe the luxury. Our cabins looked like scenes from a lavish movie production. The food was unbelievable. I had ice cream for dessert every day. Ice cream! Up to that time I had not eaten ice cream more than twice in my entire life! The ship even had a swimming pool on our deck. If the past six weeks had been a hell, this now was surely heaven.

Heaven lasted two weeks, and then the nightmare returned. When the St. Louis reached Havana on May 27, the 936 passengers were not permitted to disembark. The Cuban government officials, supported by vocal anti-Jewish Cuban citizens, took decisive action against the influx of new Jewish refugees. They invalidated their Cuban landing certificates. In a governmental wave of the hand, what had been purchased legally and legitimately in Germany by 936 trusting German Jews was now declared invalid. After several days of negotiating, twenty-two of the 936 passengers were found to have "valid" visas and they alone were permitted entry to Havana.

Captain Schroeder dropped anchor in Havana harbor, not knowing where to turn. When he radioed back to Germany to tell of this turn of events, he received an unequivocal command: RETURN AT ONCE TO GERMANY! To obey this command meant, Schroeder knew, certain death for all the passengers. For several endless days he disobeyed the orders, while radioing desperately to the United States and Canada. Would these governments allow the ship to land the refugees who were fleeing for their lives? Neither the United States nor the Canadians could be persuaded to allow the refugees to land. To add to the turmoil, the Cuban government insisted that the St. Louis leave Havana Harbor.

I watched from the railing as the ship left the harbor, Havana growing smaller on the horizon, until it was completely lost. I watched, too, as Captain Schroeder steered the ship in circles, in the area off Florida, while he was desperately trying to find a safe haven for his passengers. On June 6, it no longer mattered that there was ice cream for dessert every night, or that we could swim every afternoon in the pool. Captain Schroeder had no other choice. He had to return with his ship to Europe. When we learned the news, no one spoke, but several of the passengers began to weep. Then I heard one man say, "This is the end of us for sure. " I let a thought that had been hovering in the back of my mind for many months now spring to the surface. What was "undesirable" about being Jewish? Why were Jews being brutally treated in Germany, their lives in constant danger, their rights as citizens taken away? Why were we subject to constant humiliation and degrading treatment? Why now, would Cuba and those great countries, Canada and the United States, reject us and forbid us to enter where we could be safe?

Captain Schroeder never gave up his efforts to help us find a safe port. On the way back to Europe, we learned that Great Britain, Belgium, France, and the Netherlands had agreed to take us in. We were to be split into four, approximately equal groups, and where we were to end up would be decided by lot. My father was the one to pick for our family. I didn't know which country I should pray for. I guess it wasn't going to matter where we went. We'd be safe as long as it wasn't Germany.

Study Questions

1. As you see it, what are the significant issues in this case? Talk together and make a list of those issues that you see as the most important ones.

2. From what you can tell from the information in this case, what was life like in the town of Augsburg, in 1939, for the boy who is the narrator of the case? Talk together and see if you can draw a verbal picture of his life. Try to put as many details in the picture as you can.

3. What do you suppose it might be like—can you conceive of it?—to live in a country where government officials are not only allowed, but commanded, to come to your home and take a member of your family away, without being charged with any crime? What, in your view, made these actions possible in Germany in 1939? As far as you know, where does this happen today?

4. The case makes a point of Jews being "undesirable" and of Germans being fearful that the pure blood of the Aryan race would be contaminated. How does this work? What are your ideas about this?

5. How, do you suppose, was it possible for Captain Schroeder to be different from other Germans in his actions to protect the Jews on the ship? How do you explain the difference?

6. How, in your view, was it possible for those great nations, Canada and the United States, to deny permission for the refugees to land? How do you explain it?

7. This case is an example of racial hatred in its most extreme form. Can you give examples, from your own experience, in which racial hatred has touched you, or someone you know? If you feel comfortable in doing so, talk about that experience and about its effects on all the parties concerned.

SUPPLEMENTARY RESOURCE MATERIALS

Books

Abella, Irving, & Troper, Harold. 1983. *None Is Too Many*. Toronto: Lester & Orpen Dennys.

A powerful, compelling, and thoroughly documented account of the denial of permission to European Jews, looking for escape from Nazi-occupied Europe, to emigrate to Canada. The story is summed up in the words of an anonymous Canadian official who was asked how many Jews would be allowed into Canada after the war: "None is too many," he said.

Epstein, Helen. 1980. *Children of the Holocaust.* New York: Bantam.

The author, a daughter of Holocaust survivors, relates tales of other children of survivors, who, while raised in freedom and security, nevertheless suffer the impact of their parents' concentration camp ordeals.

Frank, Anne. 1967. *The Diary of Anne Frank.* New York: Doubleday.

Well-known autobiographical story of Anne Frank's days in hiding in an attic in Amsterdam, during the Nazi occupation of Holland.

ten Boom, Corrie. 1984. *The Hiding Place.* New York: Bantam.

Author ten Boom recounts a story similar to that of Anne Frank, of how she and her family and others were hidden by a Dutch family during the Nazi occupation of the Netherlands, and of their capture and the murder of all but ten Boom by the Nazis.

Uris, Leon. 1961. *Mila 18.* Garden City: Doubleday.

Uris's novel, based on fact, about the last days of the Warsaw Ghetto and the annihilation of the Jews who lived there.

Schwarz-Bart, Andre. 1961. *The Last of the Just.* New York: Bantam.

An unnerving and vivid novel, based on the author's life, of the capture, resistance, and annihilation of the Jews in France during World War II.

Hersey, John. 1988. *The Wall.* New York: Random House.

Hersey's strong and vivid tale of life in the Warsaw Ghetto during the Nazi invasion of Poland.

Frankl, Victor. 1963. *Man's Search for Meaning.* New York: Pocketbooks.

Frankl writes from his own experiences as a three-year inmate of Auschwitz.

Lanzman, Claude. 1985. *Shoah.* New York: Pantheon.

An oral history of the Holocaust, describing in detail the inhuman bureaucratic machinery of the Final Solution (see film list).

Keneally, Thomas. 1982. *Schindler's List.* New York: Simon & Schuster.

The (true) account of Oskar Schindler, a German industrialist who risked his life to save many Jews in Germany at a time when all were being rounded up for extermination in the camps.

Thomas, Gordon, & Morgan, Max. 1974. *The Voyage of the Damned.* New York: Stein and Day.

True account of the families who sailed on the St. Louis in their aborted attempt to leave Germany for Cuba.

Szwajger, Adina Blady. 1991. *I Remember Nothing More.* New York: Pantheon.

Dr. Szwajger, now in her seventies, uncovers memories of her years as a doctor in the Warsaw Ghetto. A harrowing personal account of the events in the Warsaw Children's Hospital during the Nazi occupation.

Dwork, Deborah. 1990. *Children With a Star.* New Haven: Yale University Press.

Eloquent and moving stories of Jewish children in Nazi Europe.
Langer, Lawrence L. 1991. *Holocaust Testimonies.* New Haven: Yale University Press.

A compilation of personal recollections of Holocaust survivors, revealing conflicts between levels of memory, between the urge to tell and the conviction that no one will understand.
Bettelheim, Bruno. 1970. *The Informed Heart.* London: Paladin.

Bettelheim's personal account of his experiences in the Dachau and Buchenwald concentration camps.
Chartock, Rosellee, & Spencer, Jack. (Eds.). 1970. *The Holocaust Years: Society on Trial.* New York: Bantam.

A collection of essays that examine events of the rise of Nazism and the reign of terror against the Jews.
Speer, Albert. 1970. *Inside the Third Reich: A Personal Memoir.* New York: Macmillan.

Speer's memoir, written during his imprisonment for "crimes against humanity," tells in detail of his life and work as one of Hitler's close associates and builders of the war machine in Nazi Germany.

Films

Shoah (1985, 9 hrs.). A documentary film in two parts, each lasting about 4-1/2 hours (!), chronicling the memories of those who lived through the Holocaust, both victims and oppressors. Done with interviews. "Lanzman's persistent interview approach hammers away at details in order to intensify our cumulative response, and we begin to see exactly how the unthinkable became a reality." A unique and eloquent film. Shattering and heartbreaking.

Playing for Time (1980, TVM, 150 min.). With Vanessa Redgrave and Jane Alexander. Outstanding drama about the true story of Fania Fenelon, who survived Auschwitz by performing in a bizarre orchestra "playing for time" while other inmates are marched to their death. The teleplay was written by Arthur Miller.

Sophie's Choice (1982, 157 min.). Feature film with Meryl Streep and Kevin Kline. The film centers around a Polish woman's attempt to live after surviving a nightmarish existence in a concentration camp during World War II. A sophisticated and mature film.

Garden of the Finzi-Continis (1971, 95 min.). Feature film directed by Vittorio De Sica. Beautiful and slowly unfolding story about an aristocratic and wealthy Italian-Jewish family during World War II who conveniently ignore the spectre of the concentration camps until it's too late. A sad, haunting film.

Au Revoir, Les Infants (1988, 103 min.). Directed by Louis Malle, this feature film is based on his own childhood experiences in a boys' Catholic school in France, in which the principal hid and sheltered escaping Jewish boys during the Nazi occupation of France. In French, with English titles.

Dark Lullabies (National Film Board of Canada, 81 min.). The daughter of concentration camp survivors undertakes a quest to understand how the Holocaust could have happened and why, through interviews with survivors and their children in Montreal, Israel, and Germany. A documentary, the film is provocative, offering no easy answers.

Two Men (CBC 97 min.). Alex Koves, a survivor of Auschwitz, is a Hungarian immigrant who now has a comfortable new life in Canada. Years later, in Toronto, he sees Michael Barna, the man he believes is responsible for his family's extermination. Barna is an upstanding citizen, a successful businessman, a good husband. What should Alex do to see that Barna is made to answer for his crimes?

Wallenberg: A Hero's Story (1985, TVM, 200 min.). Made for TV film with Richard Chamberlain portraying Raul Wallenberg, the idealistic Swedish diplomat who outsmarted Eichmann and rescued more than 100,000 Hungarian Jews. Wallenberg was taken prisoner by the Russians at the end of the war and was never seen again.

Judgment at Nuremberg (1961, 178 min.). Feature film with a star studded cast including Spencer Tracy, Burt Lancaster, Richard Widmark, Marlene Dietrich, Judy Garland, Montgomery Clift, Maximilian Schell, and directed by Stanley Kramer. Chilling and memorable film revolving around U.S. trials of Nazi war criminals in the aftermath of World War II.

Inside the Third Reich (1982, 250 min.). Made for TV movie with John Gielgud, Trevor Howard, Derek Jacobi, and others. An adaptation of Speer's autobiography in typical TV overblown fashion. Worth a view because of the depiction of the historical events, and especially for Jacobi's standout performance as Hitler.

Schindler's List (1993, 3 hr.). Steven Spielberg's realistic account of Thomas Keneally's book documenting how a single man, Oskar Schindler, saved 1,100 Polish Jews from the gas chambers. Among historical films of the Holocaust, this is considered a masterpiece in its power to affect viewers.

B | The Case of the Yahagi Maru

with Tom O'Shea

Notes to the Teacher

Measurement plays an important role in transportation. In this case, of transportation of crude oil across the Arctic Sea, measurement plays the key role. The Case of the Yahagi Maru examines the uncertainty of measurement, in the context of the different kinds of measurement tools and techniques used in modern-day navigation.

The big ideas embedded in this case are

1. Measurement is a process that is carried out with a variety of measuring tools.
2. Navigating a ship safely is dependent on accuracy of measurement. Modern navigation makes use of sophisticated measuring instruments that allow for plotting the ship's position.
3. There are other procedures, beside sophisticated measuring instruments, for plotting a ship's position.
4. One hundred percent accuracy in measurement is rarely possible. Measurement error may occur as a consequence of several conditions, including human fallibility, instrument breakdown, instrument malfunction, instrumental imprecision.

"My God!" he yelled. "We're sinking!" The captain searched the panel of dials frantically, as if he could find the one that had betrayed him, the one that had caused this terrible accident. The alarms throughout the ship reached screaming intensity, as men scrambled to reach the lifeboats. In the background of the turmoil, the calls, "Abandon ship! Abandon ship!" repeated, like staccato drumbeats, marking time in the chaos.

Captain Tanaka, his face a gray mask, listened to the sounds of his ship breaking up on the iceberg, its jagged knives of ice cutting through the ship' s jugular, spilling its cargo of oil and men into the icy seas. The disaster was incomprehensible. How did it happen? How could this fine, modern supertanker, with its cargo of 500,000 tonnes of crude oil, its state of the art equipment and technology—how could this ship have been defeated by an iceberg?

The first mate, Shiguru Watanabe, gently put his arm around the captain's shoulders. "Captain," he said in a kind but urgent voice, "you must get off the ship. We are sinking fast and the men are holding the last lifeboat for you. There is no more time. Please, Captain Tanaka. Come with me now." Watanabe led the captain from the bridge out into the dark, cold night. As they lowered the last lifeboat into the sea, the men watched the tanker break apart, as if it were made of rotten cotton, and sink slowly into that deep, black sea. The water around them was already thick with crude oil. Captain Tanaka, a gray blanket around his shoulders, sat with his face in his hands, unable to watch his ship go to its watery grave. A small, thin sailor, looking around him at the terrible scene of destruction, kept saying, "My God. My God."

Two hours later, a cold, frightened and defeated group of sailors and officers of the Yahagi Maru were airlifted, by helicopter, to the rescue ship that had heard its distress calls and been sent to pick up the men. Safely aboard the rescue ship, Captain Tanaka was summoned to the commanding officer's cabin.

"How did this happen, Captain? How do you explain the collision of the Yahagi Maru with an iceberg? How did your navigator let the ship come so close?" Commander Imanishi's voice was gruff and angry at what he already believed to be the captain's negligence.

Tanaka, his eyes on his shoes, was unable to look the commander in the eye. He was not the ship's navigator, but he, nonetheless, was responsible. Somehow, although he couldn't explain how, the ship's navigator had made a miscalculation in plotting the coordinates of the tanker and the iceberg. Where the error was, how it had been made, he did not know. He only knew that his career in the merchant navy was over and that he was disgraced. He knew too that 500,000 tonnes of crude oil, let loose into that fragile ocean, was an environmental disaster of gigantic proportions.

Four months later, an inquiry was held in the civil court to determine the extent of loss and culpability. The chief witness was the ship's navigator, Akiro Sato, who was responsible for plotting the course of the ship and guiding it safely through the glacial seascape. As Sato gave his evidence, the pieces of the puzzle began to be revealed.

MR. SATO'S TESTIMONY

INVESTIGATOR: Now, if you would be so kind, Mr. Sato, would you please take us through the events that led up to the collision of the Yahagi Maru with the iceberg.

SATO: I will try. Over the past four months, I have had much time to think about the sinking. Immediately following our rescue, I noted as best as I could the times that the events occurred, to try to make sense of how the tragedy came about. If I could, please, may I refer to my notes?

INVESTIGATOR: Of course. Now, tell this court, Mr. Sato. How did this happen?

SATO: I remember very well the beauty of the night. I had spent a few moments on deck, just before beginning my shift at midnight. The sky was clear and there was no moon. The stars almost leaped from the sky, they were so bright. Orion and his dog hunted near the horizon and the Great Bear circled overhead.

INVESTIGATOR: Can we just come to the facts of the sinking, please?

SATO: But you shall see that this moment was important later on, sir. At the beginning of my shift, all was normal. We were proceeding on course, 17 degrees, for that leg of the trip, at our usual cruising speed of about 15 knots. Of course, there was some tension on the bridge because we knew that at that latitude, and time of the year, there was some danger from icebergs in the shipping lanes. But we had seen none since the voyage began.

INVESTIGATOR: But you certainly did that night.

SATO: Yes. At 2:02 a.m., the instruments picked up an iceberg located about 19 nautical miles away, and about 3 degrees off the port bow. Had we continued our course, we would have passed about a mile from the iceberg. Since that is too close for safety, the decision was made to alter our course 20 degrees to starboard. This put us on a new course of 37 degrees. We noted our exact location at the time we changed course. Our navigation system allows us to identify our latitude and longitude to the nearest second of angular measure. That means we can locate ourselves on a navigational chart within a square 100 feet on a side. Our new course would allow us to clear the iceberg by a comfortable seven miles.

INVESTIGATOR: But you didn't clear it.

SATO: No. At 2:23 a.m., we experienced a failure of a number of instruments. We immediately put our technicians to work to diagnose the fault and start repairs. About ten minutes later, they returned to say that they were unable to make the repairs, but the problem seemed to be confined only to the radar and satellite communication systems. This was problem enough for us, because it meant we no longer were able to track the iceberg on radar and we were not able to make use of our satellite navigation system to locate our own position.

INVESTIGATOR: But your compass was still operational and that allowed you to maintain your course?

SATO: Yes, sir. To some extent. But in that area of the ocean, there are a number of magnetic anomalies that affect compass readings. That's why satellite navigation systems have been so valuable.

INVESTIGATOR: So you had some misgivings about relying on the compass to navigate.

SATO: Well, not at first, sir. But as we continued, the ship seemed to veer slightly to port. It was very subtle. Then, I remembered how clear the sky had been and stepped outside to check the positions of the stars. I noted that the ship was moving very slowly, but surely, toward the north. I returned to the bridge and we stabilized the ship's direction by visual observation of Polaris.

INVESTIGATOR: You are referring to the North Star?

SATO: Yes, sir. Shortly after, I decided to use my sextant to take a reading on Polaris, so we could check on our position, at least regarding latitude. There's a direct connection between the angular height of Polaris in the sky and your latitude, or north–south location, on the earth. With the sextant, I was able to determine our latitude to the nearest minute of arc, or about one nautical mile. Just as I completed my observation, a light fog started to obscure the sky.

INVESTIGATOR: But were you able to use your observation to adjust your course?

SATO: First, I plotted our location as best I could, given the possible change of the ship's direction and the one-mile limit on the precision of the sextant observation. That gave me a region on the map within which I could reasonably expect the ship to be located. Let me call this the "region of probability." When I plotted the ship's location based on the changed course of 37 degrees, at 15 knots for the time that had elapsed, the location was inside the "region of probability" but very close to the boundary.

INVESTIGATOR: And were you concerned?

SATO: Not so much concerned, as uncomfortable. At 3:00 a.m., I informed the captain of the reading, and he ordered the ship to be slowed to 10 knots, just as a precaution. A couple of minutes later,

I returned to the deck to take a second reading on Polaris, for con-
firmation, but the fog had become more dense and it was not possible to see the stars.

INVESTIGATOR: So at this point you assumed you were close enough to
the course you had set to miss the iceberg?

SATO: That is what we assumed. I continued to monitor the fog outside
and finally got a break at 3:30 a.m. The fog cleared momentarily,
not enough to see objects on the surface of the sea, but enough to
take a quick star shot.

INVESTIGATOR: Now just a moment. You say this occurred at 3:30 a.m.?
You first sighted the iceberg 19 miles away at 2:02 a.m.? Almost
an hour and a half had passed while you were making between 10
and 15 knots? Were you not concerned that you might now be dan-
gerously close to the iceberg?

SATO: Some concern had been expressed by the officers on the bridge,
but there was some pressure to enter port on time the next day
because of extra docking costs that would be incurred on late ar-
rival. For my own part, all I could do was give the best advice I could
about the progress of the ship.

INVESTIGATOR: And what happened as a result of the observation at 3:30
a.m.?

SATO: Well, I knew that we had traveled 30 minutes at 10 knots, for a
total distance of 5 miles during that time. I used our assumed location at 3:00 a.m. as center and drew an arc of radius 5 miles. I knew
we were located somewhere along this arc. Then, I used the information on latitude from the star shot to draw east–west lines one
mile apart and I knew we were located somewhere between these
two lines. When I saw the results, I noted with alarm that there
were now two regions of probability for our location. One of them
corresponded to our assumed track, but the other put us on a collision course with the iceberg. I realized that the collision course
was possible if the ship had continued to drift after we lost sight of
the stars. I knew then that we could be in serious trouble. At 3:35
a.m., I informed the captain.

INVESTIGATOR: And what action did the captain take then?

SATO: He decided the best course of action was to halt the ship until repairs could be made, or the fog lifted to allow visual navigation.
He ordered an emergency stop.

INVESTIGATOR: But the ship didn't stop.

SATO: With a vessel the size of this one, you need over a mile to bring it
from cruising speed to a full stop. Even at a speed of 10 knots, you
need almost a mile. The captain ordered a change of course, 30

degrees to starboard. Then he called the crew on deck to assist in sighting the iceberg.

INVESTIGATOR: And what happened?

SATO: We suddenly saw the iceberg just off the port bow and less than 200 meters away. The captain ordered hard to starboard and the ship seemed to have cleared the danger. Then we heard a terrible screeching sound, as the side of the keel scraped along a hidden shelf of the iceberg. The port side cargo tanks ruptured and the ship began to list to starboard.

INVESTIGATOR: And then?

SATO: The captain gave the order to abandon ship. (A long silence). And we did.

INVESTIGATOR: Thank you, Mr. Sato. You may step down now.

The courtroom hushed, as Sato stepped down from the witness box. He was unable to hide his feelings, and tears came rolling down his cheeks as he heard the whispers behind him. Who was to blame for this tragic disaster?

Study Questions

1. In your observation, how would you describe the chain of events that led to the sinking of the Yahagi Maru?

2. As you see it, what role did mathematics play in this case?

3. In your view, to what extent were the following variables important to the calculations of the navigator:
   a. the speed at which the ship was traveling
   b. the ship's course
   c. the condition of the sea
   d. the sighting of the North Star
   e. the radar system
   f. the captain's horoscope for that date
   g. the time of night
   h. the pressure to get the ship to port on time
   i. the compass
   j. the time at which each of the events was recorded
   k. the fog
   l. the satellite navigation system

4. Which of the variables, in your view, were the most critical?

5. What hypotheses can you come up with that might explain how the ship drifted in a way that resulted in the collision with the iceberg?

6. How, in your view, did measurement play a role in the disas-

ter? How do you account for the uncertainty associated with measurement? What, in your view, contributes to measurement error?

7. How, in your view, might a diagram help in understanding the testimony of the navigator?

8. In this case, two systems are used to locate positions. In your view, what are the strengths and limitations of each?

9. How might it be possible to find your way around the Pacific Ocean without the use of instruments or navigational satellite systems? What ideas can you come up with? What data support each idea?

10. From the evidence given by the navigator, how would you decide who is to blame in this disaster?

C | The Unbearable Ugliness of Subaru

Notes to the Teacher

This case examines the mathematical concept of probability theory. A high school student wrestles with the problem of which car to buy as she examines variables of cost, economics of operation, interest rates, value for the money, and potential for trouble-free mechanical functioning. These variables are also juxtaposed with and confounded by the nature of personal preference on the part of the buyer.

In this case, probability theory allows for making a mathematically based decision about a car's potential for mechanical breakdown. Other mathematical functions in the case include the calculation of interest, of cost of operation, and of the relationship of value to cost.

The big ideas on which this case is grounded include

1. It is possible to use mathematics to inform a decision about a purchase.
2. Probability theory allows us to predict the outcomes of certain events.
3. Collected data are used to calculate probability. The more data you have, the more reliable your prediction.
4. In determining probability, it is important to identify underlying assumptions.
5. Reason and logic in mathematical calculations sometimes give way in the presence of emotional attachments.

"I can't believe it! I just can't believe it!" Bonnie put the telephone down and turned to her mother. "Grandma just told me that she is giving me $3,000 for my sixteenth birthday so that I can buy my own car! Oh, mom. This is so wonderful, I can hardly stand it!"

Mrs. Clark put the pencil down on top of the sheaf of papers she had been working on and looked at her daughter's face. Was there a more important moment in the life of a sixteen-year-old than the promise of her own car? Vivian Clark thought back to when she had gotten her first car—not until she was earning a good salary as a junior partner in the law firm of Evans, Thornhill and Pattel. But the excitement of it—she could remember that as if it were yesterday. It was that excitement that she saw in Bonnie's face, and her eyes were illuminated by it.

"I must call Miko." Bonnie sprinted to her room, where she could telephone from her private extension. Even though her mom was pretty cool, as moms go, there were some things a girl wanted to share only with her best friend.

Snuggled against the large, decorative pillows on her bed, Bonnie talked softly but rapidly into Miko's ear, telling her the news.

"So what will you get?" Miko asked. The options were vast, but the amount of money Bonnie had would mean that she would have to choose carefully.

"Well," said Bonnie, as if she had been planning for this moment all of her life, "this is how I figure it, Mik-Mik. With the $3,000 from my grandma and the $1,500 I have from my own savings, I have a shot at probably a good used Honda Prelude, or maybe even a Toyota Celica. I know what I don't want. I couldn't stand to drive a Subaru. I think they are incredibly ugly cars. Of course, if I had $20,000 instead of $4,500, I'd buy a cute little BMW. But we're talking about poverty level purchases, here, Mik-Mik. What do you think?"

Miko had been Bonnie's best friend since they were in Grade 5 together. They were in the same classes, studied together, and even dated together. Bonnie depended on Miko for her thoughtfulness, her intelligence, her clear-headed logic. For Miko, Bonnie was the extroverted partner of the duo—creative, talented, and social. They made a compatible pair.

To this question, as to others that Bonnie had put to her over the last 6 years, Miko responded logically. "Oh, you know what I think, Bonnie. I think you should get the best car for the money. One that is not going to break down on you every 12 miles. One that you can depend on. But I know you, Bonnie. You'll probably go for the flashiest big red sucker on the lot. You are a fool for glamour, Bonnie."

Bonnie chuckled at Miko's dead-on appraisal of her judgment. She knew that Miko's advice was logical, sound, rational. She also knew that Miko was right in pinpointing Bonnie's fatal flaw. Bonnie was a sucker for glamour. Could she just this once restrain herself and pick a car she could depend on? Or would she once again go for the flash, rather than the real value?

"Yeh, Miko. I know, I know. But I've got to do this thing my way. I promise you that I'll try not to go completely crazy. Will you come car shopping with me this Saturday, then?"

"Yeh, you bet. But I'll be jealous as anything and I might have to drool on my shoes. See you later and for Pete's sake, don't buy anything between now and then!"

As Bonnie put the phone down, she nestled back into the embrace of the large, down pillows and closed her eyes. Her brain sent messages of red Corvettes, red Mercedes sports coupes, and red Porsches, to dance on the inside of her eyelids as if they were movie screens and her mind the projector. In the next scene, she projected herself first into the red Corvette, then into the red Mercedes, then into the red Porsche. All the images felt good.

That Saturday morning, Mrs. Clark drove the girls down to the Richmond Auto Mart. Vivian Clark had gotten a tip from one of her law firm colleagues about a salesman who was quite savvy and who could be trusted to negotiate a good deal. Without that tip, Vivian might have counseled Bonnie to find her car through a private sale. She had always had a dim view of used car salesmen. Weren't they all supposed to be the worst kind of sleaze buckets? "Not Benny Chan," Bill Bracken told her. "You can depend on him. He won't take advantage of you."

Bonnie and Miko stood at the edge of the huge used car lot and let their eyes take in the small army of vehicles that stood at smart attention, hoods and chrome polished, like soldiers on dress parade. "Oh, Miko. Look at that nifty BMW," Bonnie groaned, as Miko's elbow dug into her ribs.

"Bonnie, get serious. You don't have all day here and if you are going to make any headway, you'll have to lower your sights. With the kind of money you have to spend, you'd have to get a BMW that was 40 years old. And I don't think they made them that long ago."

Benny Chan came out onto the lot and offered his hand first to Mrs. Clark, and then to the girls. "Now, who is buying the car?" asked Benny.

"It's my daughter," said Vivian Clark, at the very same moment that Bonnie said, "It's me."

"Okay, then. What kind of car are you looking for, Bonnie, and how much money do you want to spend?"

"Well, I was thinking about either a Honda Prelude or a Toyota Celica. Something sporty, you know. I've got $4,500."

Benny Chan looked thoughtful. "Let me give you the skinny on this, Bonnie. For $4,500 you will be looking at a 'Lude or Celica that will be at least 8 years old. If, however, you were interested in a Civic or Tercel, maybe 5 years old. Now, I've got a very good Subaru that would fall almost in your price range. It's only 2 years old and I could give you a real deal on it. It is also in excellent condition; has had only one driver; and has only 70,000 km. It was a distress sale, and that car is a steal for $6,995."

Bonnie looked at Miko and then, almost pleadingly, at her mother. "I don't want a Subaru. They are ugly and I wouldn't be seen dead in one. The Subaru looks like it was designed by a sophomore in an auto mechanics shop. No class. Absolutely not. No way. No."

Benny Chan laughed. "I can see you've already made up your mind and I'm not going to try to persuade you otherwise. People have different attachments to different kinds of cars, and what you like, is what you like. I want to respect that. But before you punch me out for trying, let me tell you that in spite of what you think it looks like, the record on Subaru is that it is a relatively trouble-free car. It is dependable. On a model that is only 2 years old, you will probably have at least 3 to 4, maybe 5, years of trouble-free driving. Good gas mileage and economical upkeep. You can't ask for a better deal."

Bonnie looked at her mother again. "It's no use, Mr. Chan. I'm not going to buy a Subaru and we're just wasting time here. Can we see what else you've got?"

Chan glanced at Vivian Clark, caught her eye, and shrugged his shoulders. "Okay, Bonnie, I get your message loud and clear. Let's look at some 'Ludes."

"Don't the Hondas also have a good performance record?" piped in Miko, trying to help.

"Yeh, sure they do. But when you are looking at an 8-year-old car, you are going to have to expect some trouble. A car's parts have only a certain lifetime—like an electric light bulb. Of course, when you take good care of a car, the life of the parts is increased. But eventually, like a light bulb that burns out, car parts wear out and have to be replaced."

"I still want to see the Prelude," pouted Bonnie, unwilling to be deterred.

"Well, let me show you what I have and then you can see for yourself." He guided them down a row of cars whose shiny exteriors and good looks belied any potential mechanical flaws.

"Here's an '84 Honda Prelude. It's had a single owner and has never been in an accident. That's important to know, you know. But it's got 400,000 km and that's a lot of kilometers. Interior pretty clean. It runs well. But you have got to remember that it's 8 years old. By car standards, that is an old car. But the price is right for you, $3,995. With provincial tax and GST, that will be just in your price range."

Chan pointed to a Toyota Celica, three cars down the line. "That Celica is 2 years older, a clean car, runs well. This is going for $2,900, plus taxes. While you'll have money to spare, you will most certainly have to think about mechanical upkeep on a car that is over 10 years old."

"Mr. Chan, what about a newer model Prelude?" asked Vivian Clark. "Perhaps you can quote us some prices and then tell us what it would cost to finance the difference between what Bonnie has to pay and the price of the car. Maybe it's a better idea to pay interest on a loan on a newer model than to pay for repairs in an older model?"

"That's good thinking, Mrs. Clark. What do you say, Bonnie?"

By this time, Bonnie's eyes had taken a glazed look. The differences in models, in car age, in price, in potential mechanical breakdowns, in interest on loans, were beginning to wear out her brain. She was tired of figuring out what was the best deal for the money. She felt stressed and wanted to make a decision and get it over with. Reluctantly, she turned to Benny Chan, sighed, and said, "Okay, Mr. Chan. Let's see what you've got."

The three women followed the salesman to another line of cars, where Benny pointed to a good-looking, silver Honda Prelude. "This is an '87—only five years old, and still a lot of trouble-free miles ahead of it. It is in excellent mechanical condition, and has a very clean interior, with an AM/FM radio and tape deck, and only 200,000 km. The sticker price is $8,000, but I'll tell you what. If you like this car, and are willing to finance the rest with us, I'll absorb the provincial tax and the GST myself. This would be a real deal." He punched some numbers into his pocket calculator and looked at the totals. "If you give me $4,500 cash, you would be looking at 35 monthly payments of $137.50. That's with our standard interest loan at 12-1/2%."

Bonnie's mind was beginning to feel numb and she thought she needed to get away fast and clear her head. She looked at her mom and Miko, and they both saw her anxiety. "Mr. Chan, you have been very helpful," said Bonnie, as she extended her hand to him. "I've got to go home now, have a cup of tea, and think this through carefully. But I'll come back tomorrow morning, test drive the cars that I'm really interested in, and let you know what I decide." Her voice trailed a "thank you" as she turned and walked quickly from the confusing array of four-wheeled alternatives that gleamed in the noonday sun.

In the Clarks' kitchen, the three women sat down to re-examine Bonnie's choices. Miko, ever rational, armed herself with a pencil and a pad, and said, "Look, I'll help by calculating what the costs are for each, as well as the probability for each of a trouble-free driving year. Maybe having the numbers right in front of us will help you to choose."

With Miko's help and mathematical expertise, they began by listing the important variables that would be considered in Bonnie's decision.

Age of Car:
Initial Cost:
Upkeep, including:
  Gas mileage:
  Probability that repairs will be needed in first year:
  Interest on loan:

"If we are able to fill in these blanks for each of the cars Mr. Chan showed you, then you should have a good idea of the value of the car in relation to its cost," Miko announced with some authority.

Mrs. Clark smiled and looked at Miko and Bonnie. "There's just one more thing, Miko, that you must enter into your calculations, and that is the variable of desire. This is hard to put a number on, but clearly it is influencing Bonnie's decision about the Subaru, which may easily be the best value for the money option."

Bonnie sighed and looked into her teacup, as if she would find the right answer in the tea leaves. "Oh, Mik-Mik," she said softly. "Let's see if we can figure this out."

Study Questions

1. What do you see as the role of mathematics in helping Bonnie and Miko make a good decision about purchasing a used car?

2. Using what you know of probability theory, what do you see as the likelihood of a repair-free year on the purchase of the '84 Honda Prelude, with 400,000 km? How would test driving the car help in your calculations? What assumptions are being made?

3. Based on probability theory, what do you see as the likelihood of a repair-free year on the purchase of the '82 Celica? How would test driving the car help in your calculations? What assumptions are being made'?

4. How do you calculate the difference in costs between what Bonnie might have to pay on 3 years' interest, at 12-1/2%, on a $3,500 loan, for the newer car (Prelude, '87) and the mechanical breakdown potential, over 3 years, of the less expensive and older car ('82 Celica)?

5. How might you calculate the cost of operation for 1 year of the '82 Toyota Celica? The '84 Honda Prelude? The '87 Prelude? The '90 Subaru? What variables would be included in the calculation?

6. In making a decision about the purchase of a car, to what extent should the variable of personal preference take precedence over mathematical calculations? In making your car choice, would you go with the numbers or with your heart? How would you defend that position?

7. Ruling out the Subaru, which car do you see as the best value for the money? What calculations have you made that support that choice?

8. Which car should Bonnie buy? How would you advise her? What data support your choice?

Notes to the Teacher

Voting, the key act in a democratic society, is the right and the responsibility of each eligible adult. It has been said that the strength of a democracy is dependent to a large extent on an informed electorate. The assumption is made that as people exercise their franchise wisely and thoughtfully, based on knowledge and data, their choices become informed choices. How does the electorate make choices? What factors influence people's decisions when making the choice about whom to vote for?

This case presents a microcosm of decision making in a leadership convention, where delegates are assembled to elect the new head of British Columbia's Social Credit party. This person would, upon election, assume the post of Premier of the province. While the context of the case is based on real events, the names of delegates and their ways of making their choice are entirely fictional.

While focusing on a specific type of election, the issue of making a choice is easily translated to other electoral contexts.

The case draws its narrative from the following big ideas

1. The franchise is the right and responsibility of each eligible adult in a democratic society.
2. Voting, in a democratic society, occurs at various levels and in various contexts of the electoral process.
3. The strength of a democracy is largely dependent on an informed electorate.
4. How voters make decisions about whom to vote for is dependent on a variety of factors, not all of them "rational."
5. Voters are vulnerable to a variety of pressures from different

sources, and different groups use different means to "win" the voter's confidence and support.

The smell of freshly brewed coffee filtered down the thickly carpeted corridor, and Earl and Donna followed the scent to the large oak-paneled doorway.

"Mmmm, they've got the coffee ready in this area," Donna said, as she followed her nose into the room. "Let's see what Grace McCarthy is offering on her breakfast buffet."

The two delegates to the party's leadership convention made a trail to the food-laden table. "I see they've got fresh croissant," said Earl, pointing to the buttery-warm, crescent-shaped flaky pastries piled a foot high in a basket large enough to hold a pair of 3-month-old twins.

"Look there," said Donna, indicating baskets of assorted muffins. "There's cranberry-orange, banana-nut, and apple spice. My mouth is watering, Earl. Let's do this one."

"Come on, Donna. You know what we decided. We were not going to make a hasty decision about this before we saw what all the candidates were offering. Grace McCarthy may have won the battle of the muffins, but we don't know what else we may find. So put a zipper on your salivary glands and let's get over to the next area before we make a commitment." Reluctantly, Donna followed Earl out of the room as she cast one last, longing look over her shoulder at the breakfast buffet. What could the other candidates offer that would match this?

The corridor of the Vancouver Trade and Convention Centre was, by now, filling up with delegates. The first full day of the Social Credit leadership convention was just getting up steam as 1,900 Socred delegates assembled for the critical task of choosing their party's new leader. Even though Rita Johnston had occupied the premier's chair since the resignation of Bill Vander Zalm, and even though Johnston had the clear support of a group of party "loyals," the leadership election was still a crapshoot. It was very much an open contest as to whom the party delegates would choose as the Social Credit leader. The newly elected leader would assume the role of Premier of the province until at least the next provincial election. Three candidates were actively campaigning for the leadership position: Grace McCarthy, who was pulling considerable support from a strong following; Norm Jacobsen, a dark horse, who everyone agreed "had the least negatives and is everyone's second choice"; and Rita Johnston, who was hoping to remain in the chair she had been temporarily filling—this time, by due process. Now, in this leadership convention, the party's delegates would indicate their preference for the best person. The candidates, and their high profile campaign managers, were making one last-ditch attempt to win delegates' votes in appealing to their most basic interests: their stomachs. Would such an obvious ploy as the battle of the breakfasts make any difference to how a delegate would vote?

Earl and Donna elbowed their way over to Rita Johnston's camp. Talk about temptation! Donna's mouth began to water when she saw the table. Rashers of bacon and sausage warming in a large, oval chafing dish, English muffins, and a thick, creamy Bernaise sauce. Make your own Eggs Benedict! Danish pastries, freshly baked cinnamon buns with an aroma that could melt a pirate's heart, a glass bowl heaped to the cusp with fresh fruit salad. It was enough to make a hungry delegate weep. But that wasn't all. A small group of musicians were playing Dixieland jazz. Donna's eyes met Earl's. This has got to be it, they said. Earl nodded.

Johnston's breakfast buffet and foot-stomping musical show had won their hearts. They didn't even bother to go over to Norm Jacobsen's area; he couldn't possibly top this.

Donna and Earl picked up their plates. Two English muffins and three rashers of bacon, slathered in rich, creamy Bernaise sauce; sausages on the side; a cinnamon bun and a bear claw; and just enough room for a large spoonful of fresh fruit salad. The two delegates found two empty chairs at a nearby table. Was it their long, hungry tour of the breakfast buffets, or the quality of the food itself that made each forkful taste so good? Plates cleaned, both went back for seconds.

Rita Johnston was a candidate who was clearly savvy about putting together the "right stuff" for a breakfast buffet. Isn't it possible that she might be the one to be savvy enough to lead the Social Credit party?

Three cups of coffee later, Earl and Donna thought it was about time to get serious about how they would cast their votes. McCarthy's breakfast buffet was attractive, they admitted. Those croissant and the assorted muffins—they clearly deserved high points. If the candidates were going to vie for the votes of the delegates by appealing to their stomachs, then why not make the choice based on the quality of the breakfast buffet? Earl and Donna both conceded that Jacobsen was not even in the running. The real choice was between McCarthy and Johnston. They were both good candidates, so why *not* let the breakfast buffet be the deciding factor?

Study Questions

1. What, in your view, are the important issues in this case? Make a list of those issues that you believe to be the "critical" issues.

2. Based on your own experiences and knowledge, discuss your ideas about how voters choose the "best" candidate. What examples, from your own experience, can you give about how voting choices are made?

3. In your view, is it possible that voters can be influenced by a dazzling breakfast? What, in your view, are some other ways in which voters' choices are influenced?

4. In your view, what are some "good" ways of making a choice about whom to vote for in an important election? Give some reasons why you consider those to be "good" ways.

5. How might voters learn to deal more critically with the variety of ways in which candidates try to win their votes? What strategies can you suggest that would promote this more critical behavior?

6. When you are uncertain about the "best" candidate, is it better not to vote, or to vote for the person with the "best breakfast"? Where do you stand on this issue? What are the implications of each of these positions?

7. In your opinion, what is the relationship between the way people vote and the governments we have? What examples can you give that support your views?

8. Think of a time when you had to decide on the "best" candidate. How did you make that choice? In retrospect, how might your choice have been "more informed"?

SUPPLEMENTARY RESOURCE MATERIALS

Books and Articles

Camp, Dalton. 1970. *Gentlemen, Players and Politicians*. London: Penguin.
Camp's chronicles of Canadian politics and politicians, written from his own experiences in the political process. (Canadian content)

Films

The Candidate (1972, 109 min.). Robert Redford plays an idealist, who is persuaded to run for the Senate. His campaign is based on absolute integrity, and since he's bound to lose, he can afford to be utterly truthful. The film chronicles the election campaign, the way Redford is swept up in the political process, and his confusion about what to do next when he actually wins. (U.S. content)

The Best Man (1964, 102 min.). Gore Vidal's play, translated to screen, depicts several presidential candidates who will stop at nothing to win the party's nomination. The screenplay is sharp, and unsparing, and shows the inside manipulations and maneuverings of the important players in the behind-the-scenes political process. (U.S. content)

State of the Union (1948, 124 min.). Spencer Tracy and Katharine Hepburn in a film classic of a presidential candidate who is conflicted between his own integrity and his need for the backing of those with the big bucks. The film centers on the conflicts between the candidate's integrity and his need for financial support for his campaign from backers with vested interests. (U.S. content)

The Last Hurrah (1958, 121 min.). Spencer Tracy gives a compelling performance in a film about dirty politics in Boston. (U.S. content)

All the Kings Men (1949, 109 min.). Broderick Crawford, in a brilliant adaptation of Robert Penn Warren's Pulitzer Prize winning novel about the rise and fall of a Huey Long-type senator, in a southern U.S. state. This is one of the classic films that show the inner workings of the political process from the vantage point of those in and around the candidate's center. (U.S. content)

E | Where Have All the Salmon Gone?

Notes to the Teacher

This case deals with current issues confronting commercial fishing—the decline in fish stocks due to overfishing and contamination, and the consequences of limited supplies on the industry and on the economy.

On the west coast, salmon, once abundant, are now in decline. On the east coast, off Nova Scotia and Newfoundland, cod is in very diminished supply. In areas such as the Gulf of Mexico and Chesapeake Bay, oysters and shrimps have been made inedible due to contamination of the waters by toxic waste dumping.

People who were dependent on commercial fishing for jobs and earnings, are now faced with the economic realities of an industry in decline.

Unemployment, bankruptcies of large packing houses, and cost of fish are all economic consequences.

This case deals with one family, dependent on fishing for their living, facing the crisis that depletion of fish stocks has brought.

The big ideas underlying this case are

1. Fish stocks (particularly salmon and cod), once abundant, are now in serious decline.
2. Overfishing, high tech equipment resulting in high yield, and contamination have contributed to the decline of this resource.
3. The decline of fish stock has serious economic consequences for those involved in the industry, with inevitable spillover to the rest of the population.

"Selling the boat?" Chad Wiggins let out a howl like the cry of an animal in pain. "Dad, you can't mean it. I can't believe you mean it."

Cy Wiggins turned away, unable to face his son, feeling as if his life was being crushed like so many oyster shells. Chad looked at his father's back, shoulders bent, a man in defeat and heard the words, small and soft, coming from a voice he barely knew. "I'm sorry son, but there just aren't enough fish anymore to make the money we need to feed this family and pay all our expenses. Commercial fishing is dead in the water." Nobody laughed at the pun. Chad kicked the screen door open and burst down the steps into the backyard, leaving his father alone with the stone in his heart.

Chad Wiggins began fishing with his father on his twelfth birthday. He'd been waiting for that day for a long time, waiting for the time he would be old enough to help, old enough not to be a nuisance and in the way. His father used to tell him, "When you are 12. That's when I'll take you. That's when it will be safe. Not before then. It can be dangerous out there. You have to be old enough to be able to look after yourself. This is not a party, you know. This is hard work and I'm responsible for the boat and for all the men on board, and for our livelihood."

It wasn't until the summer that he went out with his father for the first time that Chad knew what his father had meant. The Rip Tide, Cy Wiggins's 24-meter boat, cost him $350,000 new. It had nine berths, two bathrooms with showers, a spacious, well-lit galley, and a wheel house that contained about $75,000 in electronic equipment, a state-of-the-art drum seiner. The Rip Tide carried a crew of six—men that had all worked with Cy Wiggins for many years. At age 12, Chad would learn to crew. By the time he was 15, his father said that he had learned enough to merit a share of the catch. Even though the work was hard, and at times even dangerous, even though his hands felt like leather and his face was toughened by the sun and wind, Chad could not even think of another way of life. He loved the Rip Tide, the crew, the business of bringing the fish back to port. His father was his hero and all Chad ever wanted for his own future was to finish school and work with his father on the Rip Tide, until he was able to get a boat of his own.

That was 5 years ago—a time when salmon were still plentiful. Commercial fishing off the west coast of Canada was not a year-round job. Because of weather conditions, government restrictions on fishing, and seasonal fish runs, fishing was, at best, a 6-month occupation, with the rest of the year spent in maintaining and upgrading the boat and equipment, and, if the catch was less than good, filling in with other, temporary jobs. When the salmon season was good, Cy Wiggins and his crew might pull in a catch of about 100,000 kilograms (about 250,000 pounds) of fish, worth about $100,000, in a single trip. In a good season, each crew member might earn as much as $35,000—his share of the catch. In a good season, Cy Wiggins would be able to make a net profit of about $50,000—that is, after paying fuel bills, insurance, licensing fees, maintenance on the boat, and provincial and federal taxes, which added up to about $90,000. Running a boat was not cheap! The work was hard and sometimes dangerous, the expenses and boat maintenance costs high, but Cy would not have traded places with any man in any other job in the country. Fishing was in his blood.

At first, Cy would not believe the reports in the newspapers that told of the decline in fish stocks. He thought that these were false alarms, ignited by radical environmentalists who cared more about fish than they did for the "little guy who has to make a buck." Almost overnight, the reports about fish-starved fisheries on the Atlantic and Pacific coasts broke out in the press like a bad case of measles. The cod fisheries in the Northern Atlantic, off the coast of Nova Scotia and Newfoundland, were going bankrupt. The cod had been fished out, they said, and season after season of poor catches and high expenses had left commercial fishing reeling from plant closures and layoffs.

In the Gulf of Mexico, the newspapers reported that those fishermen whose livelihoods had been tied to the seafood-rich bays and estuaries of the Texas coast were also in jeopardy. They had, for several years, to contend with the United States government-set limits on their daily catch—a step intended to prevent overfishing. But now, shrimpers were faced with contamination of their catch from petrochemical plants that had state permits to dump their toxic waste material into the gulf. Cy Wiggins could no longer believe that the fish-starved ocean was an environmental ruse. He could see from his own work, season after season of small catches and declining profits, that there had to be some truth to this appalling news. Last week he and his crew had been lucky. But there had been 47 other boats in the area that hadn't done as well and he knew that at least 18 of them hadn't caught a single fish.

Cy knew that he would have, somehow, to break the news to his family. He knew what it would mean to Chad, whose only dream was to follow in his father's footsteps. He had planned to retire, one day, and leave his boat and the business to Chad. Chad had never even considered another occupation. What would he do? One evening he tried to explain the situation to his son.

"We've got to think of the future, Chad," he said, unable to look his son in the eye, feeling, unexplainedly, as if it was somehow all his fault.

"What do you mean, dad. I don't understand."

"Well, it's this way, son. I've talked to Jim Lavaca, the chairman of our organization, and he says if we're smart, we've got to start thinking about making some plans to find other sources of income. Certain salmon species have definitely gone down and the coho and spring have been fished out, until there's almost nothing left. Pink and sockeye are still okay, but we don't know how long they will be holding. There's herring, of course, and they are still abundant, but there's less of a demand for them, and the prices are not very good."

"So what are you saying, dad?" Chad would not let himself comprehend the issues.

"Son, it all boils down to this. Too many boats out there, and not enough fish. Each season it's going to get harder and harder to make a buck. And our expenses will kill us."

"This is crazy, dad. Just crazy." Chad felt his voice rising, going out of control. "How can there be no more fish? Where have all the fish gone? There have got to be jillions of fish out there. We're just not finding them. But they're out there. They've got to be out there." Chad's voice exploded with emotion and his fist thumped the table, making it bounce back in response.

"I know, son. I know. At first, I thought that, too. I thought that there was an unending supply of fish in the ocean and that all we had to do was go out and catch them. Well, it turns out that that was just wishful thinking. Too many boats and high tech equipment have badly overfished the stocks. On top of that, toxic waste dumping into the oceans have further reduced stock by contamination. It's true, son. The fish are disappearing. If I want to feed this family, I'm going to have to consider other options."

No matter how Cy Wiggins tried to impress his son with the seriousness of the situation, Chad seemed to push the idea away from him. He just did not want to believe that such a thing could actually happen. Maybe next season his father would see that he, and all the other alarmists, had been dead wrong.

This season, however, in 12 weeks, they had barely fished in enough to make ends meet. To make matters worse, the Deep Bay Packing Company, to which Wiggins sold his catch, went into receivership and was unable to pay him for the fish. It was at that point that Cy Wiggins decided to pack in commercial fishing and look for employment opportunities elsewhere. But who would hire a 50-year-old man who only knew one trade: commercial fishing? To what other job would his skills be applicable? He felt defeated and saw his life washing away, like a bad undertow.

Cy Wiggins knew that Chad would take the news hard. But he had hoped that the boy would at least try to understand and to see the situation from his point of view. Selling the boat would give them a bit of a stake—a few dollars in the bank after all the bills were paid. He looked out to the garden, where Chad sat, with his back to the house and his head down, and wondered how he had failed his son. How was it possible that fish, in such abundance, could now be in such short supply? How could we have let this happen?

Study Questions

1. What do you see as the important issues in this case? Talk together in your group, and decide on the significant issues raised in this case. Then, list them in the order that you consider to be important.

2. Based on the data in this case, how would you describe the life of a commercial fisherman? What do you see as the ways in which money is earned in this occupation? What kinds of expenses work to reduce gross profit?

3. The data in this case indicate that expenses for a commercial fisherman are high. How do you explain this? What, in your view, accounts for the expenses connected with this business?

4. What is your understanding of how fish are caught? What is your understanding of the different ways in which different kinds of fish are caught?

5. How, in your view, has "high tech" equipment on boats contributed to the decline of fish stocks? What examples can you give of how this works?

6. How is it possible that fish, once abundant, are now in short supply? What, in your view, have been the contributing factors? What data support your ideas?

7. To what extent is it possible to turn this situation around? What actions might be taken to turn this situation around? What do you see as the economic implications of the actions you are proposing?

8. Cy Wiggins feels responsible for the way his son's future has been compromised. Where do you stand on the issue of responsibility for the decline of fish?

9. What should Cy do now? What suggestions would you make to him about plans for the rest of his life? What suggestions would you make to Chad?

RELATED ACTIVITIES

National Film Board of Canada Documentary Films

10 Days—48 Hours. Shows the tedium of life on a modern fishing boat, including the processing plant, fishing boats, and men who work on them.

Changing Tides. Explores the economic, social, and political issues surrounding fish farming.

Fish By-Catch. Describes waste in shrimp trawling.

Fishermen. Shows choices that face Canada's east coast fishermen.

Incident at Restigouche. Describes conflict between province of Quebec and Micmac Indians over salmon fishing rights.

One out of Three Is a Fishboat. Documents the dangers to lives and property of those at sea, with reference to lack of adequate safety precautions, bad habits, and poor seamanship.

Pacific Highliners. Describes life on the salmon fishing boats on the British Columbia coast.

F | Old Age Ain't for Sissies

Notes to the Teacher

The process of aging brings inevitable biological changes in all living things. This case examines the deterioration in biological functioning that occurs in the family dog, and examines this decline in relation to human aging.

The big ideas that propel this case are

1. Aging is a normal process in which deterioration of biological functioning is a natural occurrence.
2. Skin, hair, muscular deterioration, loss of teeth, failing eyesight and hearing, chronic disease are all conditions associated with aging.
3. The process of aging occurs in all living things.
4. The process of aging is variable in the human condition; the process of biological deterioration can be retarded.

She lay there, not moving, her dark eyes filled with pain. Each time I went over to touch her, she'd whimper and look at me as if to say, "Help me. Please help me." I couldn't bear it. I knew my dog was dying and I knew that the best decision our family could make was to have her put down. Yet, I kept hoping that by some miracle, by some impossible magic kiss, my dog would revive and live to run and play another day. Why did dogs and people have to grow old and die?

Keela came into our family before I was born, so she was really our family's first child. She was the runt of a litter of four huskies, the only one left when Mom and Dad went to answer the ad, THREE-MONTH-

OLD HUSKY PUPS FOR SALE. Dad told Mom that runts were not good investments. She would likely be a sickly dog and not have a very long life. But Keela, with those soulful dark eyes that looked as if black rings had been painted around them, put her cold, wet nose into Mom's ear and it was all over. Mom never listened to another word dad said about health and longevity. They made out a check for $250 and gave it to the breeder, and Mom took Keela in her arms and bundled her into the car. It was like trying to wrap up magic jumping beans. Somehow, Keela knew that she was going home.

Dogs have different growth cycles from people. By the time Keela was a year old, she was already full grown, although in many ways still a puppy. She was not a big dog, like a shepherd, or a collie, but she was not small either, like those tiny breeds that are the size of cats. I guess she was just about the right size for a dog. When I was little, she easily outsized me, but when I got to be around 10 or so, she just about came up to my knees. Of course, when she stood on her hind legs, she could still put her front paws on my shoulders and lick my face. Even when I was 10.

They say that every year in the life of a dog is equivalent to 7 years in the life of a human. So when I was born, Keela was already 21 human years old—old enough to be like my big sister. From my earliest memories, Keela was always there. I can't even think of what our family would be like without her.

Before my brother Mikey was born, Keela was my friend and constant companion. Even before I could walk, when my mom put me outside in my stroller, she would tell Keela, "Okay, Kees. Now you mind Timmy. I'll be out in a few minutes, but you watch and see that he doesn't get into mischief."

Keela would look at my mom seriously, as if she understood every word my mom was saying. Then, when my mom went inside to finish her work, Keela would sniff the grass around the stroller, and circle it two times, just to make sure the territory was safe. Then, she'd put her paws up on the stroller and lick the pretzel crumbs off my face and I'd laugh and pull her ears. I never minded waiting for my mom when Keela was taking care of me.

By the time I was 6, Keela was way ahead of me in people years. Nine dog years didn't seem *that* old, but 63 people years sounded ancient. Wherever I walked in the neighborhood, she was at my side—especially when I was going down to the Dari Queen. Chocolate was her favorite flavor and she would sit there, watching me hopefully, just in case some ice cream would drip through my fingers and find its way to the sidewalk. When I was learning to ride my two-wheeler, she would sit on the grass and watch me. If I stumbled or got discouraged, she would come over and lick my face, as if to say, "It's okay, Timmy. I know you can do it. Try again." When I finally did learn to ride, she'd run along with me, barking at birds. For 63 people years, she certainly had a lot of spunk.

I remember how she was when my obnoxious brother, Mikey, was born. Even though Mikey had to be the worst kid that fate ever delivered to a nice family, Keela was still generous with her affection to him. Mikey didn't understand about dogs. He'd pull Keela's tail or her ears or try to climb on her back for a pony ride. Keela didn't ever seem to mind. I guess she just accepted Mikey because he was part of our family. I'll tell you, though, Keela was much nicer to Mikey than I was. If truth be told, I couldn't stand Mikey and couldn't wait for him to grow up and get some sense!

By the time I was in Grade 2, it was clear that Keela was more my dog than anyone's. I don't know how that happened, but it just seemed to work out that way. I was the one who fed her every morning. I took her to the park to play frisbee and took her to soccer practice, so she could watch my game. And, of course, it was my bed that she slept on every night. That is, unless my mom came in and saw her, and scolded her off. But even then, she'd only jump off and sit on the rug until my mom left the room. As soon as she did, Keela was up again. In the morning, that sleek gray and black fur coat was the first thing I saw when I opened my eyes.

It's funny that when you are living close to people, you hardly notice their growing. For example, my grandma, who lives in Victoria, and who sees us only about twice a year, always says, "My, how you've grown!" when she sees Mikey and me. And my mother says, "They have?" as if she hasn't really noticed. Then Mom would stand us up against the kitchen wall, where she has been recording our heights ever since we could walk.

"You're right, Mom," she'd say. "Tim's come up almost a full inch since your last visit. And Mikey's up by, would you look at this? An inch and a half! My goodness!" I never noticed Mikey was getting taller and I know Mikey never noticed me, either. Maybe we needed Grandma to come and point it out.

"And look at Keela," Grandma would say.

"What's the matter?" my mom would ask.

"Oh, nothing. But I can see that some of her dark hair is beginning to turn gray and she's getting gray around the mouth, too. She's getting old, Phyllis. Old, like me."

It was funny that Grandma should say that, because when she did, and I took a good look, she was right. Keela was getting gray hair around her mouth. And Grandma had gray hair all over her head. But I never noticed that until Grandma came to visit.

I was in sixth grade when Keela got really sick for the first time. When I got up that morning, she was not in my bed, nor was she under the bed, or even in my room. I found her curled up in a corner in the kitchen, near the stove.

"What's the matter, Keela? What's the matter, girl?" I reached down and patted her head, and felt her shaking. I didn't want to go to school that day, but Mom said she would take Keela down to Dr. Wagner, the vet who specializes in dogs and cats. I worried all through school and couldn't concentrate on anything. When Mr. Fox called on me in social studies to answer a question about the important rivers in Quebec, he had to scold me for not paying attention. He didn't know that my dog was more important to me than the rivers in Quebec.

Mom was waiting for me at the bus stop. I think she knew I would be worried. She put her arm around my shoulder and we walked home together. If it was going to be bad news, I didn't want to hear it.

"She's going to be all right, Tim," she said with a trace of doubt in her voice. "You know, Keela's getting old and she's got something that older people and older dogs often get. It's called diabetes. That means that there's something wrong about the way her body is unable to metabolize carbohydrates—you know, sugars and starches."

"Is she going to die?" I faltered, unable to get the words out. My tongue felt thick, like a baseball glove.

"No, no," my mother squeezed my shoulder. "You don't die from diabetes, if you are careful about your diet. We just have to watch her diet carefully. No more sweets, no more table scraps. Just her dog food and, of course, she can have all the bones she wants."

I raced out of my mother's grip, up the path, and into the kitchen. Keela was still curled up by the stove, but at least she picked up her head when I came in.

"Keela. Keela." I put my head down into her neck and whispered in her ear. That was the first time I really seriously considered the fact that Keela was getting old and that one day I'd come home and she would no longer be there. But in the meanwhile, Dr. Wagner had put Keela on a diet and had given her a vitamin supplement to take along with her meals. I didn't know that dogs took vitamins, but if they were going to keep her healthy, I was all for it.

Even without my grandma's visits to remind us that we were all getting taller and growing older, I could see that Keela was not a young dog anymore. She couldn't run as fast and when she did play frisbee with me, she couldn't jump as high, or play as long as she used to do. I could also see signs of her paws getting a little crooked. When we took Keela to Dr. Wagner for her regular 6-month checkup, she noticed that Keela now had the beginnings of arthritis in her joints. This is a disease that occurs in older people and dogs, affecting joints in hips, knees, and fingers. When the joints become inflamed, there is considerable pain and loss of mobility. Keela was now 15 dog years and 105 people years old. She was an old dog. Dr. Wagner gave her a good report for her checkup and said that we could give her aspirin if she seemed to be in discomfort from her arthritis. When I asked the vet if we needed to take any special care about her exercise, Dr. Wagner said that Keela would be the best judge of what she could and could not do. "That is," Dr. Wagner said, "if she feels okay, she will run and play with you. If not, you will see that she won't. It's as simple as that. Let her tell you how she feels."

I nodded, fully understanding. Keela always had a way of telling me her feelings.

In the next 3 years, I moved from elementary school to Rudyard Kipling High, and got involved with a lot of extracurricular activities, so I was out of the house a lot. I continued to play soccer and was on the school team. I also went out for basketball, and even found time to play in the school band, although the trumpet and I were never going to reconcile our differences completely. I still looked after Keela's food and vitamins in the mornings, though. But Mom kept an eye on her during the days and evenings when I was out, with Mikey picking up the slack, to his credit. Even obnoxious little brothers grow up and finally get some sense.

It's funny how I felt when I looked at my dog, going downhill into old age. I can't really explain it, but I didn't want to look at her. I don't know if it was because she was not the dog I loved anymore, but just some old, decrepit thing who hung around the house and sat by the stove; or if it was because I really couldn't stand to see her that way. I avoided her as much as possible. We all knew that her days were numbered, but we didn't talk about it much.

Mom said that as long as she was not in a lot of pain, and as long as she still enjoyed her food, we would continue to look after her and love her. That sounded okay to me.

One day, when I was in the library studying for a physics exam, I noticed a book on aging, which I pulled from the shelf and thumbed through. When you grow old, the book instructed, there are several changes in the body and its functioning that are associated with the natural deterioration process that comes with age. Outward appearance, including skin wrinkling and hair loss; porous, weak, and fracture-prone bones; diminished mass in muscles; joint deterioration; teeth loss; loss of cardiovascular efficiency; deterioration of vision and hearing; loss of memory. I closed the book and put it back on the shelf, thinking, "Hell, old age surely ain't for sissies!" Some of these aging conditions were what was happening to my dog and I couldn't hide my eyes from it. This is what happened when people and dogs got old. It would happen to me. Ugh! But not for another hundred years or so. Understanding the process of aging did not help me to deal with it better. I still kept avoiding Keela. I thought she began to smell funny, too.

Then, Keela no longer got up. She just lay there, not moving. I went over to her and saw her dark eyes filled with pain. She did not understand what was happening to her and I couldn't explain it. I tried to tell her, with my eyes, that I was sorry I had not been a very good friend to her in her old-age years. I hoped she would understand that, but I was not sure she would.

Mom sat us down, Mikey and me, at the kitchen table. "This has to be a family decision," she said. "I won't make this decision on my own. We all have to agree. But I know it's a more humane act to put Keela to sleep now. It's cruel to let her suffer." Mikey shot up and kicked his chair over in a loud crash. "I don't care," he said. But you could see he cared very much.

"Is there no chance she'll get well?" I asked, looking to my mom to make a miracle.

"Sweetheart, she is 133 people years old. She has had a very good life. We've loved her and she's loved us. It's time to let her go."

The tears came fast and hot and fell down my face in a torrent of sorrow. Numbly, I nodded my head in agreement, in a barely perceptible movement.

Dr. Wagner came to the house and we all stroked Keela's fur as she gave her the shot that would put Keela out of her pain. When it was over, I ran out to the garden and put my arms around the cedar tree and wept.

That afternoon, Mikey, Mom, and I dug a hole under the cedar and buried our dog. Why couldn't she live 5, 10, 20 more years? Why did dogs and people have to get old and sick? It just wasn't fair.

Study Questions

1. What is your understanding of the aging process, as it affects dogs? People? How is it different for people and dogs? What are your ideas?

2. What, in your understanding, are the biological conditions associated with aging? How do you explain the process?

3. Wrinkled skin, graying hair, and loss of hair seem to be a normal part of aging, for animals and for people. What is your understanding of how this occurs in aging? How do you explain it?

4. Other conditions that are associated with aging include chronic disease, like diabetes and arthritis. What is your understanding of these diseases? How do you explain the vulnerability of the old to chronic diseases?

5. How, in your understanding, does pain enter into the process of biological deterioration? How does this work? What examples can you give to support your ideas?

6. Hearing loss, vision loss, and memory loss are also associated with the aging process. What is your understanding of how this occurs with age? How do you explain it?

7. If biological deterioration is a normal part of the aging process, how do you explain the variability of such deterioration among different individuals? What data can you give to support your ideas?

8. What, in your view, might contribute to the retardation of the aging process? What are your ideas on it? What data support your ideas?

9. Dr. Wagner prescribed a vitamin supplement for Keela in this case. What is your understanding of the role that vitamins play in maintaining good health? What data support your ideas?

10. Tim, in this case, has a hard time spending time with Keela, watching her be old. How do you explain the feelings younger people have about aging?

11. How do you explain our society's preoccupation with youthful appearance? What is your understanding of the various strategies that people use to try to "stay young" as long as possible? What is your understanding of how these strategies work physically? Psychologically?

RELATED ACTIVITIES

Books

Bumagin, Victoria, & Hirn, Kathryn F. 1979. *Aging Is a Family Affair*. New York: Crowell.
Canadian Conference on Aging. 1983. *Fact Book on Aging in Canada*. Ottawa.
Cosby, Bill. 1987. *Time Flies*. New York: Doubleday.
de Beauvoir, Simone. 1973. *Coming of Age*. New York: Warner Books.

Kotre, John, & Hall, Elizabeth. 1990. *Seasons of Life: Our Dramatic Journey from Birth to Death.* New York: Little, Brown.

Life's Career. 1978. *Aging: Cultural Variations on Growing Old.* Beverly Hills, CA: Sage.

Myerhoff, Barbara. 1978. *Number Our Days.* New York: Touchstone.

Quinn, M., & Tomita, S. 1986. *Elder Abuse and Neglect.* New York: Springer.

Roy, F. Hampton, & Russell, Charles. 1992. *The Encyclopedia of Aging and the Elderly.* NY: Facts on File.

National Film Board of Canada Documentary Films

Discussions in Bioethics; The Old Person's Friend. Examines the question, Should the old be allowed to die when they ask to be unhooked from life support systems?

Don't Take My Sunshine Away. Explores ways of care for the elderly, without undermining self-respect.

A House Divided. Four moving portraits shed light on the tragedy of caregiver stress and elder abuse.

Mr. Nobody. Legal and ethical dilemmas concerning the self-neglect of the elderly.

Growing Old. Examines the question, Should the aged be looked after, or encouraged to do for themselves?

Charles and Francois. Touching story of the friendship between a grandfather and his grandson. This is a film about aging and death.

Arthritis: A Dialogue with Pain. Examines the nature of the disease and its effects on people's lives.

Daisy: Story of a Facelift. Examines the values that prompt people to seek cosmetic surgery.

References

Adam, Maureen. 1992. *The Responses of Eleventh Graders to Use of Case Method of Instruction in Social Studies*. Unpublished Master's thesis, Faculty of Education, Simon Fraser University, Burnaby, BC.

Adam, Maureen, Chambers, Rich, Fukui, Steve, Gluska, Joe, & Wassermann, Selma. 1991. *Evaluation Materials for the Graduation Program*. Victoria, BC: Ministry of Education.

Barnett, Carne. 1991, April. *Case Methods: A Promising Vehicle for Expanding the Pedagogical Knowledge Base in Mathematics*. Paper presented at the American Educational Research Association, Chicago.

Berlak, Ann, & Berlak, Harold. 1981. *Dilemmas of Schooling*. London: Methuen.

Bickerton, Laura. 1993. *Case Method Teaching in Senior Biology: A Synthesis of Curriculum Content and Goals with Year 2000 Goals*. Unpublished Master of Science thesis, Faculty of Education, Simon Fraser University, Burnaby, BC.

Bickerton, Laura, Chambers, Rich, Dart, George, Fukui, Steve, Gluska, Joe, McNeill, Brenda, Odermatt, Paul, & Wassermann, Selma. 1991. *Cases for Teaching in the Secondary School*. Coquitlam, BC: Caseworks.

Bramer, Lawrence M. 1979. *The Helping Relationship*. Englewood, NJ: Prentice Hall.

Broadfoot, P. (Ed.). 1986. *Profiles and Records of Achievement: A Review of Issues and Practice*. New York: Holt, Rinehart & Winston.

Bromley, D. B. 1986. *The Case Study Method in Psychology and Related Disciplines*. New York: John Wiley.

Bruner, Jerome. 1966. *Toward a Theory of Instruction*. Cambridge: Belknap.

Bruner, Jerome. 1985. On Teaching Thinking: An Afterthought. In S. F. Chipman, J. W. Segan, & R. Glasser (Eds.), *Thinking and Learning Skills* (Vol. 2, pp. 597–608). Hillsdale, NJ: Lawrence Earlbaum Associates.

Carkhuff, Robert R., & Berenson, David H. 1983. *The Skilled Teacher*. Amherst, MA: Human Resources Development Press.

Carter, K., & Unklesby, R. 1989. Cases in Teaching and Law. *Journal of Curriculum Studies, 21,* 527–536.

Case Studies: The Cowichan Collection. 1993. Duncan, BC: School District #65 (Cowichan).

Chambers, Rich, & Fukui, Steve. 1991. The Case of Injustice in Our Time. In Laura Bickerton et al., *Cases for Teaching in the Secondary School* (pp. 53–58). Coquitlam, BC: Caseworks.

Christensen, C. Roland. 1991a. Every Student Teaches and Every Teacher Learns: The Reciprocal Gift of Discussion Teaching. In C. Roland Christensen, David Garvin, & Ann Sweet (Eds.). *Education for Judgment: The Artistry of Discussion Leadership*. Boston: Harvard Business School Press (pp. 99–119).

Christensen, C. Roland. 1991b. Taped interview. Boston: Harvard Business School Media Center.

Christensen, C. Roland, Garvin, David, & Sweet, Ann. 1991. *Education for Judgment: The Artistry of Discussion Leadership*. Boston: Harvard Business School Press.

Christensen, C. Roland, & Hansen, Abby. 1987. *Teaching and the Case Method*. Boston: Harvard Business School.

Cuban, Larry. 1993. *How Teachers Taught*. New York: Teachers College Press.

Dart, George. 1991. The Case of the Nazi Art Purges. In Laura Bickerton et al., *Cases for Teaching in the Secondary School* (pp. 109–115). Coquitlam, BC: Caseworks.

Davies, Anne, Cameron, Coren, Politano, Colleen, & Gregory, Kathleen. 1992. *Together Is Better*. Winnipeg: Peguis.

Dewey, John. 1938. *Experience in Education*. New York: Macmillan.

Dewey, John. 1964. The Child and the Curriculum. In *John Dewey on Education: Selected Writings* (pp. 339–358). Chicago: University of Chicago Press.

Eggert, Wally, & Wassermann, Selma. 1976. Profiles of Teaching Competency: A Way of Looking at Classroom Teaching Performance. *Canadian Journal of Education, 1*(1), 67–73.

Ewing, David W. 1990. *Inside the Harvard Business School*. New York: Random House.

Festinger, Leon. 1957. *A Theory of Cognitive Dissonance*. Stanford, CA: Stanford University Press.

Freire, Paulo. 1983. *Pedagogy of the Oppressed*. New York: Continuum.

Furth, Hans G. 1970. *Piaget for Teachers*. Englewood Cliffs, NJ: Prentice-Hall.

Gardner, Howard. 1983. *Frames of Mind: The Theory of Multiple Intelligences*. New York: Basic Books.

Gerlach, Ronald A., & Lamprecht, Lynne W. 1980. *Teaching About the Law*. Cincinnati: W. H. Anderson.

Gibbons, Maurice. 1976. *The New Secondary Education*. Bloomington, IN: Phi Delta Kappa.

Glasser, William. 1986. *Control Theory in the Classroom*. New York: HarperCollins.

Gluska, Joe. 1991. Let's Have a War! That's a Good Idea! In Laura Bickerton et al., *Cases for Teaching in the Secondary School* (pp. 33–38). Coquitlam, BC: Caseworks.

Goodenough, Daniel. 1991. Changing Ground: A Medical School Lecturer Turns to Discussion Teaching. In C. Roland Christensen, David Garvin, & Ann Sweet (Eds.), *Education for Judgment: The Artistry of Discussion Leadership* (pp. 83–98). Boston: Harvard Business School Press.

Goodman, D. M. 1982. Making Liberal Education Work in a Technological Culture. *Liberal Education, 68*(1), 63–68.

Graham, B. P., & Schwartz, S. H. 1983. Try the Case Approach in the Features Course. *Journalism Education, 38*(1), 45–48.

Graves, Donald, & Sunstein, B. (Eds.). 1992. *Portfolio Portraits*. Portsmouth, NH: Heinemann.

Greenwald, Bruce. 1991. Teaching Technical Material. In C. Roland Christensen, David Garvin, & Ann Sweet (Eds.), *Education for Judgment: The Artistry of Discussion Leadership* (pp. 193–214). Boston: Harvard Business School Press.

Greenwood, Gordon E., & Parkay, Forrest W. 1989. *Case Studies for Teacher Decision Making*. New York: Random House.

Hansen, Abby. 1987. Reflections of a Casewriter: Writing Teaching Cases. In C. Roland Christensen & Abby J. Hansen. *Teaching and the Case Method* (pp. 264–270). Boston: Harvard Business School Press.

Hansen, Abby, Renjilian-Burgy, Joy, & Christensen, C. Roland. 1987. I Felt As If My World Had Just Collapsed. In C. Roland Christensen & Abby Hansen (Eds.), *Teaching and the Case Method* (pp. 120–122). Boston: Harvard Business School Press.

Hargreaves, Andy. 1988-89. "The Maturation of Educational Measurement." *E + M Newsletter*. No. 45. Toronto: OISE Educational Evaluation Center.

Johnson, J., & Purvis, J. 1987. Case Studies: An Alternative Learning–Teaching Method in Nursing. *Journal of Nursing Education, 26*, 118–120.

Kleinfeld, Judith. 1989. *Teaching Cases in Cross Cultural Education*. Cross Cultural Education series. Fairbanks: University of Alaska, Center for Cross Cultural Studies.

Kleinfeld, Judith (in press). *Gender Tales*. New York: St. Martin's Press.

Kohn, Alfie. 1993, September. Choices for Children: Why and How to Let Students Decide. *Phi Delta Kappan, 75*(1), 8–20.

Kowalski, Theodore J., Weaver, Roy A., & Henson, Kenneth T. 1990. *Case Studies on Teaching*. New York: Longman.

Lawrence, Paul. 1953. The Preparation of Case Material. In Kenneth R. Andrews (Ed.), *The Case Method of Teaching Human Relations and Administration*. Cambridge, MA: Harvard University Press.

Lloyd-Jones, Esther (Ed.). 1956. *Case Studies in Human Relationships in Secondary School*. New York: Teachers College Press.

Lortie, Dan. 1975. *Schoolteacher*. Chicago: University of Chicago Press.

Lowe, I. 1975. Using Case Studies in the Teaching of Physical Principles. *Physics Education, 10*(7), 491–492.

Lowell, Mildred Hawksworth. 1968. *The Case Method in Teaching Library Management*. Metuchen, NJ: The Scarecrow Press.

McAninich, Amy Raths. 1993. *Teacher Thinking and the Case Method*. New York: Teachers College Press.

McCleary, W. J. 1985. A Case Approach for Teaching Academic Writing. *College Composition and Communication, 36*, 203–212.

Maltin, Leonard. 1993. *Movie and Video Guide*. New York: Signet.

Manley-Casimir, Michael, & Wassermann, Selma. 1989. The Teacher as Decision-Maker: Connecting Self with the Practice of Teaching. *Childhood Education, 65*(5), 288–293.

Merseth, Katherine. 1991. The Early History of Case-Based Instruction: Insights for Teacher Education Today. *Journal of Teacher Education, 42*(4), 243–248.

Nolan, A. W. 1927. *The Case Method in the Study of Teaching with Special Reference to Vocational Agriculture: A Case Book for Teachers of Agriculture*. Bloomington, IN: Public School Publishing Co.

O'Shea, Thomas, & Wassermann, Selma. 1992. The Case of the Yahagi Maru. Burnaby: Faculty of Education Case Clearinghouse, Simon Fraser University.

Pietrowski, M. V. 1982. Business as Usual: Using the Case Method to Teach ESL to Executives. *TESOL Quarterly, 16*, 229–238.

Posner, George J., Strike, Kenneth A., Hewson, Peter W., & Gertzog, William A. 1982. Accommodation of a Scientific Conception: Toward a Theory of Conceptual Change. *Science Education, 66*, 211–227.

Raths, Louis E., Wassermann, Selma, Jonas, Arthur, & Rothstein, Arnold. 1986. *Teaching for Thinking: Theory, Strategies, and Activities for the Classroom*. New York: Teachers College Press.

Rogers, Carl. 1961. *On Becoming a Person*. Boston: Houghton Mifflin.

Rokeach, Milton. 1960. *The Open and Closed Mind*. New York: Basic Books.

Rosmarin, Adena. 1985. Profile: The Art of Leading a Discussion. In Margaret Morganrouth-Gullette (Ed.), *On Teaching and Learning*. Cambridge, MA: Harvard–Danforth Center for Teaching and Learning.

Shulman, Judith. 1992. *Case Methods in Teacher Education*. New York: Teachers College Press.

Silverman, Rita, Welty, William M., & Lyon, Sally. 1992. *Case Studies for Teacher Problem Solving*. New York: McGraw-Hill.

Small, Robert C., & Strzepek, Joseph E. 1988. *A Casebook for English Teachers. Dilemmas and Decisions*. Belmont, CA: Wadsworth.

Snygg, Donald. 1966. A Cognitive Field Theory of Learning. In Walter B. Waetjen (Ed.), *Learning and Mental Health in the School*. Washington, DC: Association for Supervision and Curriculum Development.

Stakes, Robert, & Easley, Jack. 1978. *Case Studies in Science Education*. Urbana: University of Illinois, Center for Instructional Research and Curriculum Evaluation.

Sykes, Gary. 1989. Learning to Teach with Cases. *NCRTE Colloquy, 2*(2), 7–13.

Sykes, Gary, & Bird, Tom. 1989. Teacher Education and the Case Idea. In G. Grant (Ed.), *Review of Research in Education, 18*, 457–521. Washington, DC: American Educational Research Association.

Turow, Scott. 1977. *One-L*. New York: Warner Books.

Wassermann, Selma. 1990. *Serious Players in the Primary Classroom*. New York: Teachers College Press.

Wassermann, Selma. 1991a. The Case of Donald Marshall. In Laura Bickerton et al., *Cases for Teaching in the Secondary School* (pp. 91–97). Coquitlam, BC: Caseworks.

Wassermann, Selma. 1991b. Welcome Aboard! In Laura Bickerton et al., *Cases for Teaching in the Secondary School* (pp. 59–66). Coquitlam, BC: Caseworks.

Wassermann, Selma. 1992a. *Asking the Right Question: The Essence of Teaching*. Bloomington, IN: Phi Delta Kappa Fastback.

Wassermann, Selma. 1992b. The Cranberry-Orange Muffin Vote. Vancouver: Faculty of Education Case Clearinghouse, Simon Fraser University.

Wassermann, Selma. 1992c. The Unbearable Ugliness of Subaru. Vancouver: Faculty of Education Case Clearinghouse, Simon Fraser University.

Wassermann, Selma. 1993a. *Getting Down to Cases: Learning to Teach with Case Studies*. New York: Teachers College Press.

Wassermann, Selma. 1993b. Old Age Ain't for Sissies. Vancouver: Faculty of Education Case Clearinghouse, Simon Fraser University.

Wassermann, Selma. 1993c. To Care or Not to Care. Vancouver: Faculty of Education Case Clearinghouse, Simon Fraser University.

Wassermann, Selma. 1993d. Where Have All the Salmon Gone? Vancouver: Faculty of Education Case Clearinghouse, Simon Fraser University.

Wassermann, Selma, & Ivany, J. W. George. 1988. *Teaching Elementary Science: Who's Afraid of Spiders?* New York: HarperCollins.

Wheatley, J. 1986. The Use of Case Studies in the Science Classroom. *Journal of College Science Teaching, 15,* 428–431.

Wiggins, Grant. 1993. Assessment: Authenticity, Context and Validity. *Phi Delta Kappan, 75*(3), 200–214.

Winchell, Paul. 1954. *Ventriloquism for Fun and Profit.* Baltimore: Ottenheimer.

Zarr, M. 1989. Learning Criminal Law Through the Whole Case Method. *Journal of Legal Education, 34*(4), 697–701.

Index

About the Author

Selma Wassermann is a Professor in the Faculty of Education at Simon Fraser University, Vancouver, Canada. A recipient of the Excellence in Teaching Award at Simon Fraser University, she has published widely and is in much demand as a leader of teaching-for-thinking seminars and for case study teaching throughout the United States and Canada.